CW01202495

THE
VALE OF RHEIDOL
LIGHT RAILWAY

Looking down the Vale from above The Stag. The train is rounding the Cnwch-yr-arian and there is, as yet, no reservoir below.

AN ILLUSTRATED HISTORY OF

THE
VALE OF RHEIDOL
LIGHT RAILWAY

THE LITTLE LINE ALONG THE RHEIDOL

HANES DARLUNIADOL
RHEILFFORDD YSGAFN DYFFRYN RHEIDOL
YR LEIN FACH AR HYD Y RHEIDOL

BY

C. C. GREEN M.B.E.

WILD SWAN PUBLICATIONS LTD.

© Wild Swan Publications Ltd. and C. C. Green 1986
ISBN 0 906867 43 6

DEDICATION

To the kindly folk of Aberystwyth and the valley
without whose help this book could never
have been written.

CYFLWYNIAD

Cyflwyniad y gyfrol hon i bobl caredig Aberystwyth
a Chwm Rheidol gyda diolch am eu cymorth urdh
ei ysgrifennu.

All photographs taken by the author unless otherwise credited.

BIBLIOGRAPHY

The Locomotives of the GWR Part 10. Railway Correspondence and Travel Society.
Lead Mining in Wales. W. J. Lewis.
The Old Metal Mines of Mid Wales. David Bick.
The Mining District of North Cardiganshire and West Montgomeryshire. O. T. Jones.
Narrow Gauge Rails in Mid Wales. J. I. C. Boyd.
Rheidol Journey. C. C. Green.
The Vale of Rheidol. West Wales Naturalists' Trust.
The Vale of Rheidol Railway. Lewis Cozens.
The Vale of Rheidol Railway. W. J. K. Davies.

RECORDS

Cambrian Railways — Minutes of the Board and Officers' Reports.
Great Western Railway — Minutes of the Board, Finance Committee, Engineering Committee, Locomotive, Carriage & Stores Committee, Civil Engineer's Records and Signals Record.
Vale of Rheidol Light Railway — Minutes of Board and Finance & General Purposes Committee, Accountant's Journal and Ledger.
Board of Trade — Inspector's Reports and correspondence with Light Railways Commissioners.

Designed by Paul Karau
Typesetting, printing and binding by Butler & Tanner Ltd., Frome

Published by
WILD SWAN PUBLICATIONS LTD.
1-3 Hagbourne Road, Didcot, Oxon OX11 8DP

Edward VII **about to leave Aberystwyth c.1904.** *A. J. Lewis*

FOREWORD

Much of what is written here does not quite conform with the accepted histories of the line. When these were put together, access to minutes and other official records was a matter of influence or personal good fortune. Now we can study many of them by acquiring a reader's ticket at the magnificent Public Record Office at Kew. There are additional records now in many other places.

The author's first personal recollections at the age of four are vague but impressive, reinforced by some later visits. The great impetus towards detailed research was imparted when a relative started farming Troed-rhiw-las on the other side of the river opposite Nantyronen, in 1954, and thereafter we went every year.

Old gentlemen who had worked on the building of the line courteously gave of their memories which have since been confirmed by the arid minutes. Shopping expeditions started with scanning the valley from the caravan for the first sign of the Crosville bus, and ended with a laden journey home to Aberffrwd by train. Almost invariably the author was kindly invited onto the footplate by the old Western Region crews. This is the story as it really happened.

Plans, drawings and photographs still turn up to the author's great delight. More detail is still needed about the goods yard at Aberystwyth and about the mines, particularly the Cwmrheidol and the Erwtomau. Photographs of the headgear at Rhiwfron and of *Rheidol* on the Stone Quay would be especially nice, but a sight of any item not covered in this book would be most welcome. Fresh material can be included in a further work in which locomotives and stock will be surveyed in greater detail, with drawings and photographs. Buildings and other lineside features will also be covered, together with an account of the mines.

Fitter Alwyn Thomas checking the blower in 1958.

CONTENTS

Chapter One	INCORPORATION AND EXTENSION	1
Chapter Two	CONSTRUCTION	11
Chapter Three	ADMINISTRATIVE HISTORY	17
Chapter Four	PERMANENT WAY	33
Chapter Five	RUNNING THE LINE	45
Chapter Six	THE JOURNEY UP THE VALLEY	59
Chapter Seven	STATIONS, HALTS AND SIDINGS	
	(incorporating notes on signalling)	95
	Aberystwyth Original Terminus	99
	The Harbour Branch	105
	Aberystwyth Great Western Terminus	109
	The Manchester and Milford Siding	124
	The Cambrian Transfer Siding	124
	The Great Western Exchange Siding	126
	Llanbadarn Station	128
	Geufron Ballast Siding	130
	Glanrafon Halt	132
	Lascrug Ballast Siding	132
	Lovesgrove Station	133
	Capel Bangor Station	135
	Nantyronen Station	143
	Aberffrwd Station	145
	Meithrinfa Halt	152
	Rheidol Falls Halt	152
	The Erwtomau Mine	154
	Rhiwfron Siding and Halt	155
	Devil's Bridge Station	159
Chapter Eight	THE LOCOMOTIVES	
	Nos. 1 and 2 The Davies & Metcalfe 2—6—2 Tanks	177
	The Swindon-Built 2—6—2 Tanks	188
	No. 3 The Bagnall 2—4—0 Tank *Rheidol*	204
	Festiniog Railway No. 4 *Palmerston*	206
	Motive Power etc. which failed to arrive	207
Chapter Nine	ROLLING STOCK	
	The Original Carriages	209
	The Swindon-Built Carriages	211
	The Vans	219
	The Box Wagons	221
	Timber Trucks, Toast-Racks and Trolleys	224
Chapter Ten	A SAMPLING OF TIMETABLES	231
Chapter Eleven	SPECIAL EVENTS AND OCCASIONS	235
Chapter Twelve	UNDER LONDON MIDLAND REGION	237
Appendix	A Sampling of Tickets	261
Acknowledgements		264

This incomparable valley. Looking up Cwmrheidol from Gwaith-coch. The mine in the foreground is Caegynon.

CHAPTER ONE

INCORPORATION AND EXTENSION

Long Before the Railway

First there was the formation of this incomparable valley. Its Silurian rock was laid down as sediment below the surface of an ancient sea some 425 million years ago. During long periods of calm, mud accumulated on the sea floor. At intervals, stormy conditions or earthquakes occurred, producing thin layers of coarser material such as silt or sand. This ensured that the resulting rock would be brittle and flakey, characteristics which would have a considerable influence over the building of the railway in the yet long-distant future.

Eventually, after a great thickness of sediment had been built up, the lower layers were compressed by later deposits and were folded like an old hearth-rug getting ruckled up into waves. With the folding had come fracturing and faulting with the emplacement of lead veins, which then lay in readiness to influence the future of the valley. Very much later (during the past 50 or so million years) the upper layers of the then rock-hard sediment were eroded away (just before the onset of the Ice Age about 2 million years ago), leaving a landscape not greatly differing in general outline from that which we see today.

Then the main river of the district, which was later given the name Teifi, rose on Plynlimon and flowed south past the future sites of Ponterwyd and Devil's Bridge and Tregaron and that of the future Cardigan, and so to the sea. The Rheidol itself would have been very much smaller and probably rose somewhere by where Rhiwfron is today, or even further west.

During the Ice Age the area was covered on a number of occasions, though never very deeply because the district lay fairly near to the southern limit of the ice. Nevertheless, the wastage of successive ice sheets choked valleys with debris, and meltwater found new ways to the sea. As a result, some valleys ceased to be and others were deepened or diverted. One of these last was the Teifi which broke away to the west by Devil's Bridge to complete the course of the Rheidol as we know it – a valley of three distinctly different aspects.

From Aberystwyth upstream to Aberffrwd runs Dyffryn Rheidol, the true Vale of Rheidol with its wide, flattish and only gently-sloping floor deeply underlaid by river gravel. Beyond Aberffrwd the mountains close in to give Cwmrheidol, the steeply-sided valley above which the future railway must cling to narrow ledges. Above the right-angled turn by Devil's Bridge the headwaters descend in a steep gorge cut out of an older and wider valley, as can be seen from the terrace in front of the Hafod Arms Hotel.

The first to appreciate the beauty and magnificence of it all was the Duke of Newcastle; in 1832 he bought the Hafod Estate which extended to Devil's Bridge and, shortly afterwards, he had the old hotel pulled down and replaced by a Swiss-style building as a holiday resort for the gentry. Later, in 1854, George Borrow was to extol it in florid Victorian prose and its future as a tourist attraction and as the terminus of a very special railway was assured.

In the riverbed itself the forces of change are still at work, particularly along the Vale where river meanders are constantly changing and altering the banks. On the outside of each bend the flow is faster and the bank is cut away, the shingle brought down being dropped by the slower water on the inside of a bend, so that in effect the bend is slowly moved downstream. It is truly amazing how the course of the Rheidol today differs from that on the first revision of the O.S. maps which showed the railway. Farmers have won and farmers have lost while the Dyfed Council, who are the River Authority, have tried hard to engineer more advantageous courses for the river in many places during recent years; but always the Rheidol attacks the new work and is ever seeking to move each bend a little nearer to Aberystwyth each year.

Mining brought the first rails into the valley and, in the 1950s, one could drag out of the spoil-heaps specimens of cast-iron bridge rail and bar-headed flat-bottomed rail at any one of half-a-dozen sites. However, because such were used and re-used in different places as mining moved the place of discovery is not always related to their original use. The tramways themselves were a mixture, horse-drawn and man-pushed, and several were working during the early 1800s and some possibly even earlier.

Under Threat 1845 to 1871

There very nearly was no Vale of Rheidol Light Railway, no lein fach, no little line, whatsoever. Instead there might have been yet another example of an unviable, or at best barely viable, standard gauge branch over a route very similar to the one used by the 1'11½" gauge.

With the Victorian railway mania had come a great yearning for Wales to have its own north-east to south-west diagonally-routed railway linking the manufacturing area of Lancashire with a seaport in Pembrokeshire. Many ships and cargoes were lost against the rock-bound coasts of Western Wales and Anglesey, and lives and money would be saved by eliminating this risky sea passage by means of a safe direct railway.

There was little to be disputed geographically over the northern end of the route across Denbighshire and Montgomeryshire (now restored to their older names of Clwyd and Drefaldwyn which has become a part of Powys), and into the Upper Severn to Llanidloes. To the south the Teifi Valley was an easy natural choice and all the difficulties lay in the bits in between.

The key to several of the schemes considered was Devil's Bridge which had been a focal point for centuries for foot-travellers, horsemen and herders. The deep east-to-west trenches of the Myherin and of the Rheidol had dictated the building of a bridge, almost certainly of wood, even before the days of Giraldus Cambrensis, as an alternative to the long struggle down from Ystumtuen into the bottom of the Rheidol and up the face of Rhiwfron to regain the lost height leading to the easier going over the common lands of Rhos-y-gell. There were two other crossing places over the Rheidol, one south of Ponterwyd and the other at Parson's Bridge.

The first threat came in 1845 as a true forerunner of the Manchester & Milford Railway and the details of the route may have been similar to the one which reached the statute book on 23rd July 1860. This route left Llanidloes and the Severn southwards via the Afon Dulas (the route taken later by the Mid

Wales Railway), and out of the Dulas via little Cwmbelan and so to Llangurig and the Upper Wye, escaping thence via the Tarenig. Transfer to the Myherin Gorge would be effected by 1¼ miles of tunnel, and so the line would have been directed to Devil's Bridge.

The next stirring of a scheme for a major railway system, which could have brought Devil's Bridge and the adjoining farmland into direct contact with the rest of Wales and England, came in 1852 as the North and South Wales Railway, which was planned to pass the Kingside Mine at Cwmystwyth, and so it would have captured all the revenue from transporting the output of one of the greatest and richest mines of all. By a variation in route advanced in 1853, the line was to run closer to Devil's Bridge, and such a situation would hardly have left a sound basis on which to promote an independent narrow-gauge line from Aberystwyth.

In the following year there was yet another threat to the future lein fach in the form of the pretentiously-named Direct Manchester & Milford Junction Railway. This was projected from Pencader to Oswestry as a 7 ft gauge line. It was entirely in defiance of the Gauge Commission's fiat of 1846 that no further extensions to the 7 ft gauge could be allowed. Possibly the promotors had expected without good cause that for them this ruling could be overruled. What sort of scenic mayhem this project would have wrought in the gorges of the Myherin and of the Mynach we shall happily never know. In 1858 the Manchester & Milford promoters started looking at a more southerly route via the Ystwyth.

The greatest and most nearly-realised threat came in 1860 when the Manchester & Milford Railway actually got its bill through Parliament for the construction of its railway over what may be conveniently termed 'the northern route'. The Engineer was Hamilton Fulton with James Weekes Szlumper (of whom we shall read much more later) as his assistant, and his subsequent successor.

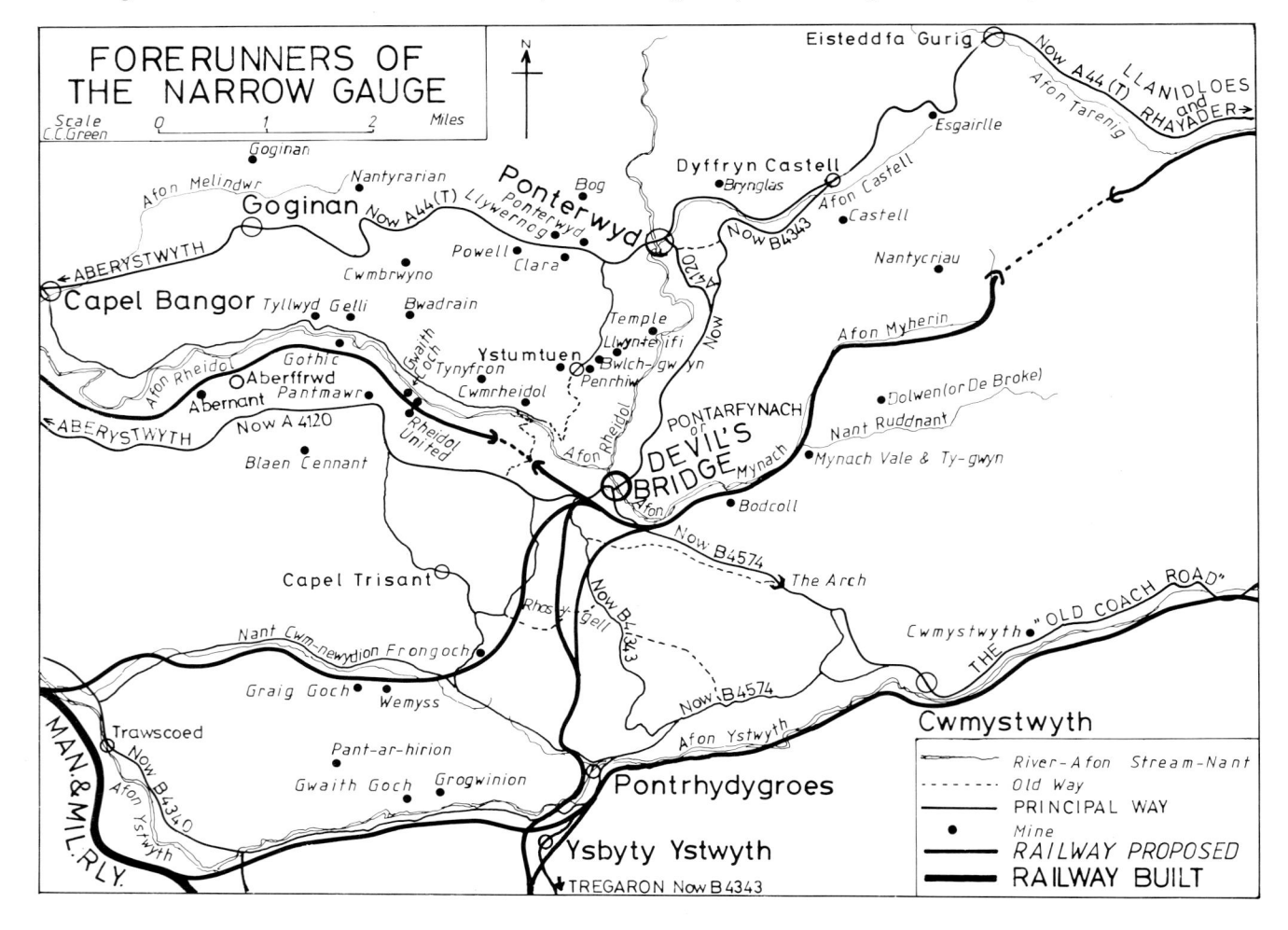

Railway No. 1 was duly drawn up in contract form and was built by Beeston from Pentponbren Junction with the Mid Wales Railway following the original northern route out of the Dulas Valley via Cwmbelan to Llangurig. Apart from the contractor's traffic, only one token train steamed its way to the temporary terminus in a small rock cutting in 1864. By this time the contract for Railway No. 2 had been let and work had started. Beeston built one bridge over a side-road in Llangurig and completed his formations for about five-eighths of a mile west of the cutting, and this work is still visible from the A44 west of Llangurig. Even more alarming for the prospect of a narrow-gauge line along the Rheidol was the work of an advance party who had gone up Nant Ceiliog and made the pilot cut into the hillside for the tunnel through to the Myherin. Worse still, the little expedition had gone over the mountain and had cut the second pilot run into the steep slope for the exit of the tunnel into the Myherin Gorge.

It was a near thing, only $4\frac{3}{4}$ miles from Devil's Bridge. A buzzard wheeling above Draws Drum can sight both cutting and Devil's Bridge in a single sweep and a crow going directly about its business can flap its way between the two places in only $8\frac{1}{2}$ minutes.

This line was to have bypassed Devil's Bridge to the south in cuttings, to turn away across Rhos-y-gell, down to Pont-rhyd-y-groes, whence it was to have climbed out of the Ystwyth Valley and away down the Teifi – all in all quite a geographical assault course. In addition it was to have sent a branch away west down the Rheidol to Aberystwyth. This would have required some pretty ambitious embankment or viaduct construction to have got away from Devil's Bridge, or the engineers may have had a tunnel in mind to break out down to Nant-yr-fynwg. Then a goodly tunnel would have been needed to get past Rhiw-fron and so down Allt-ddu. Aberffrwd would never have been the same again.

The Manchester & Milford's plans for sole commercial occupation of the region had included a branch from Llangurig down the Wye to Marteg in Mid Wales territory, which provoked the Mid Wales into counteraction. So the Mid Wales Railway advanced a new scheme, in opposition, for its own direct line to Aberystwyth. This was to have ascended the Elan Valley and the Claerwen Valley to get into and descend the Ystwyth Valley. This was tabled in 1861 with the addition of its own obstructive branch up the Wye in 1863. In 1864 the Mid Wales was at it again with a Llangurig Branch up the west bank of the Wye from Marteg, with a direct thrust towards Aberystwyth up Nant Dernol as a means of gaining the Ystwyth Valley and the sea.

Having got its northern route effectively into Llangurig, the Manchester & Milford Railway then sought a Deviation Bill to take its line out of the Tarenig, up Nant Troed-y-esgair, and more directly into the Ystwyth Valley and so abandoning the work already done towards Railway No. 2. This route kept to the original concept by turning south at Pont-rhyd-y-groes to pick up the original Teifi route to Pencader; and of course with a branch going north to Aberystwyth. It was even more of an assault course than the northern route it replaced, but now Devil's Bridge and the Rheidol were safe.

The Deviation Bill did not get parliamentary assent and at long last common sense was injected into the scheme of things. The Manchester & Milford and the Mid Wales Railways actually came into amicable agreement as to which should build what. Each obtained fresh powers in Acts of 1865, and the Manchester & Milford Railway was enabled to construct and operate its well-known line from Aberystwyth to a junction with the Carmarthen and Cardigan Railway at Pencader. By mid-1864 Hamilton Fulton had been dismissed from his post of Engineer and young James Weekes Szlumper had been appointed in his place, and it was he who got the line built. So the Llangurig Branch was left to subside into morass and the two tunnel cuttings were left for the Forestry Commission to conceal in its plantings of the 1940s.

The Mid Wales got its Western Extension Act for a junction with the Manchester & Milford via the Nant Dernol and Ystwyth Valley route down to Trawscoed, which included some quaint restrictions designed to protect the beauty of the Hafod Estate. It failed to construct.

As a last comment on this bewildering array of scheme and counterscheme, one of the engineers, probably James Szlumper, has left among the Manchester & Milford relics a 1 inch Black Electro ordnance map dissected on canvas of $c.1860$. On it is pencilled the most alarming array of squiggles, possibilities and alternatives, including a line as yet unmentioned. South out of Devil's Bridge it would have been run, past the great mines of Frongoch, Wemyss and Graig Goch, along Cwmnewydion and so to a junction with the Manchester & Milford just north of Trawscoed. And in 1871 the *Mining Journal* reported the publication of a prospectus for the Devil's Bridge Railway Company's line of $6\frac{1}{2}$ miles in length from a junction with the Manchester & Milford. Like motorway construction units, railway engineers never gave up until the last ditch, and usually only because the money ran out.

The whole business was beyond the comprehension of Mr. G. F. Cruchley, publisher $c.1870$ of a set of Railway and Station Maps designed to help the would-be railway traveller. On his map of South Wales he has shown Aberystwyth to Pencader correctly as built with a connection from Llancerrig to Strata Florida and with a cross-connection between Trawscoed and Sputy Ystrad Merric, the latter two being under construction.

Towards Incorporation 1871 to 1897

After all the foregoing one might well imagine the Vale of Rheidol settling back into a period of quiet rural peace. Actually nothing would have been further from the facts. Then the population was more than three times what it is today, and it was a very busy, noisy place with much coming and going.

At the top of the valley was the racket from the great Tynyfron and Cwmrheidol mining complex with its tramways, crushers, rolls and buddles. The ore went down the stony valley road in heavy carts with the attendant clop-clopping of hooves and the grating, grinding noise of the great iron-bound wheels. Further down, across the other side of the valley, the Rheidol United group of mines threw out its quota of similar noise, to be augmented by the Caegynon Mine right opposite. Here for some eight years or more there were clouds of noxious dust, and the gritting slither of shovels endlessly throwing the newly-valuable blende spoil downhill to the dressing-floor at the Gelli mine, and so forming The Stag. The thump and clank of the massive twin flat-rod drive system and great water wheel which sent power out of the Rheidol and over the crest of the hill to the Bwadrain Mine in the next valley, was not silenced until around 1876. Abernant, Bwadrain South, Pantmawr and Tyllwyd all added their little contributions to the never-ceasing background of rumble and thud.

Nor was the Victorian farming the quiet and peaceful matter it was supposed to have been. Much more of the land was under the plough and the fields across the river far below Devil's Bridge were seen to be growing corn in the Vale of Rheidol Railway's own publicity pictures. The jingle of harness and the shouting at the turns of the short fields went on for at least forty times as long as a modern tractor would be chugging steadily up and down without check. Also one does not have to shout at a tractor; albeit this practice is not unknown if it won't start and the writer has heard of strange Welsh ancestries or lack of them on such occasions.

Underlying the noise mentioned there was a more insidious one, the ringing of axes cutting tree after tree to make props for the mineshafts and cheap firewood. By the time the line would come to be built, whole miles of the upper section would be cut along the bare slopes of denuded woodland.

By the 1890s farming was quite vigorous and all the old water mills were still at work, augmented in places where there was no handy water supply by modern horse gins for grinding corn and fodder. Later, the mines presented a very different scene. A combination of falling prices and failing lodes had put all the smaller ones out of business. Caegynon and Rheidol United were at their last gasps and of all the Rheidol mines only Cwmrheidol was the one with any significant future. Fortunately for the promoters of the railway, support would also be forthcoming from the owners of the Cwmystwyth and Frongoch Mines whose ores could be brought to Devil's Bridge by road.

Such then was the general background when folk began to lobby for the construction of an independent railway line up the Rheidol Valley. The moves towards a vigorous form of democratic local government had been slow to have any effect around Aberystwyth despite the Reform Act of 1867 (Workers' Franchise), the Act of 1872 (Secret Ballot) and the Local Government Acts of 1887 and 1890, which had set up the town and county councils, and the influence of the church, the college and the gentry was still very strong. One private undertaking, The Aberystwyth Improvement Company, had been set up but it was regarded as somewhat of an alien outsider. However, it did get the Cliff Railway built in 1896 besides several other useful tourist amenities, and, of much greater interest, it mooted the idea for a standard gauge railway up the valley via Devil's Bridge to New Radnor. George Green, the owner of the Cwmrheidol Mine, was on the Board of Directors and so he had a strong interest in pressing for a connection. He also owned the largest foundry in Aberystwyth, and was using his position and influence to have the idea reduced to that of a simple line up the floor of the valley and terminating at his mine. If so built the line would have been quite unviable, and no others would support Mr. Green so the whole idea was dropped.

Earlier on in 1880 the *Mining Journal* had borne a very interesting yet tantalisingly uninformative little paragraph about a 'possible 2′ gauge railway in Cardiganshire'. It may not have been referring to a first stirring of the narrow-gauge concept up the Rheidol, but, where else in Cardiganshire could a 2 ft gauge line have been remotely viable? Ultimately, by 1896, all the interested parties had got themselves together and had arrived upon a scheme which the majority regarded as workable.

These interested parties were –

1. The mine owners who wanted cheaper and easier transport.
2. The Aberystwyth foundries who wanted transport to the mines for their manufactures.
3. The Aberystwyth Improvement Committee on general principles.
4. Mr. Thomas Waddingham, who saw the line as an outlet for the timber off his great Hafod Estate. He had been a pioneer in replanting with European Larch and much would shortly be ready for cropping.
5. A few (and only a few) of the local people who foresaw Aberystwyth as having a future in tourism and holiday-making.
6. The benefits to the local folk and the farmers were mildly supported by one or two of the landowners who had other interests in parallel and who were to prove helpful when the line was later under construction.

All were later to have one tendency in common – a great reluctance to put *their* money down on the table.

Here James Weekes Szlumper comes back into the story as a Knight and as a railway engineer of considerable repute. He had already surveyed the Manchester & Milford Railway's standard gauge route along the valley and he had his attractive house, Sandmarsh Cottage, in Aberystwyth at the end of Queen's Road. He had an interest in the Aberystwyth Improvement Company and in 1895 had been appointed Consultant Engineer to another 2 ft gauge railway, the Lynton and Barnstaple. He had even before that surveyed another 2 ft gauge proposal for a line from Llandyssul to Newquay. In short, he was obviously the right man in the right place at the right time.

He re-surveyed the old route in accordance with the lesser requirements of the narrow gauge and got out the land-purchase maps and his estimate of the costs of construction. With the addition of preliminary and formation of company costs, he estimated that the scheme could be built with an authorised capital of £39,000. At such an estimate the scheme was obviously practicable, or so all thought, and John Francis, Walter Taylor, Hugh Lowe and others went ahead with the obtaining of an Act of Parliament for the construction of the railway from Aberystwyth to Devil's Bridge.

The decision to go for the 2 ft gauge (fixed later as 1′ 11½″) was obviously a very sensible one since the traffic estimated so optimistically would never have covered the costs of a standard gauge line which could well have been at least four times that of the slender little substitute. Not far away was the splendid example of the Festiniog Railway of similar length whose officers could be and were consulted. The Festiniog was in the process of refurbishing stock and equipment and its passenger traffic was on the increase from that new source of revenue, the holidaymaker.

There was, from a quite different source, an absolutely mind-boggling suggestion as to selection of suitable gauge and an extension of route. Thomas Molyneaux, the Lancashire financier behind the Plynlimon & Hafan Tramway, in correspondence with Mr. Pryse, son of Sir Lewis Pryse of Gogerddan, hoped that Sir James Szlumper 'would adopt our gauge of 2′ 3″ for the Devil's Bridge line' and envisaged a connection between the two lines. The 2′ 3″ gauge would certainly have increased the cost of the Rheidol line by enlarging the minimum radius on curves with the extra embankment costs that would entail; but think of that commercially useless extension. Certainly a very expensive line could have been built up to Llyn Craigypistyll, 1,059 feet above sea level at map ref. 856720, but where would it have gone from there? To sink down to Pont Geifr some 700 ft below would have called for the most magnificent Welsh mountain specimen of a set of Darjeeling–Himalaya reversing stages such as would have gladdened the heart of every railway enthusiast. But if there could be such a thing as a Welsh grey mountain 'white elephant', then that would have been one.

Parallelling these preliminary activities was a complementary scheme for a branch line down to Aberayron which seems to have 'hatched' just a little time after the main plan. This is where is encountered for the first time the interesting admixture of Act and legal authority which was to be the distinction between the formation of the Rheidol Company and that of most of the other lines.

Thus, on the 3rd March 1897, there was a Board of Trade enquiry held in Aberystwyth Town Hall to resolve the differences of opinion as to the route, etc., of the Harbour Branch. The promoters had been unable to reconcile the opposing views of the fishermen and the Town Council. This was legally under the umbrella of The Regulation of Railways Act 1868. Exactly one month and one day later, and in the same building, the Light Railways Commissioners acting under their brand-new powers derived from the Light Railways Act of 1896, held their enquiry

INCORPORATION AND EXTENSION

into the desirability of authorising a Light Railway to Aberayron. Of course the new work was best pursued under the newly-available legislation, while time was to be gained by proceeding about the main scheme under the old, but it did lead to complications. It seems probable that the initial impetus for an extension to Aberayron came from a desire to please certain landowners to the south, e.g. the Powells of Nanteos so that their support for the principal portion might be expected to continue. Strangely, the expected opposition from the Cambrian Railways did not materialise.

Success came on 6th August 1897 as the Vale of Rheidol (Light) Railway Act 1897, 60 & 61 Vict Ch clxxiv. (1897 spanned years 60 & 61 of the reign of Queen Victoria and 174 is the Chapter of Parliament.)

Acts, Order and Amendment

In the preamble the Act cites itself as 'An Act for making a light railway between Aberystwyth and Devil's Bridge in the County of Cardigan and for other purposes.' Being a light railway under the Regulation of Railways Act 1868, the plans and sections had to be deposited with the Clerk of the Peace for Cardigan County Council. Also it gave the title of the company as The Vale of Rheidol (Light) Railway Company with brackets around the word Light which the Company proceeded to ignore. The Act consisted of 15 pages of an old size known as sixmo (257 mm × 177 mm) and was printed for T. Digby Pigott, Esq., C.B., the Queen's Printer of Acts of Parliament, by Eyre & Spottiswoode. It could be bought for one shilling. In terms of today's (1986) money it would cost £2.10 or thereabouts.

The significant and the quaint and more interesting provisions of the Act were as follows. Where quoting verbatim the portentious capitals and long unpunctuated pronouncements have been retained.

Para 5   Two railways were authorised.
Railway No. 1 eleven miles five furlongs and six chains in length. This was the main line to Devil's Bridge. Railway No. 2 three furlongs and 7.65 chains in length. This was the Harbour Branch.
Note   The basis of survey was the surveyor's chain 22 yards of 100 links. A link was 7.92″ or 201.168 mm. In metric the 22 yard chain was 20.1168 metres.
A furlong was 10 chains or 220 yards or 0.201168 kilometres.
The British system of measurement completed itself as 8 furlongs to one mile or 1.609344 kilometres.
To read deposited plans and railway length diagrams this system has to be invoked.

Para 6   Permitted axle loadings of up to 8 tons and speeds of up to 25 miles per hour.

Para 7   'The railway shall be made and maintained on a gauge of two feet' with provision for increase to standard gauge.

Para 8   The authorised capital to be £39,000 in £10 shares.

Para 12   Each share could be divided by vote into half each of the classification Preference Shares and the second half to be Deferred Shares or, as we would term them, Ordinary Shares.

Para 20   A further £13,000 might be raised by borrowing. Half could be raised after half the formation had been built and the remainder after completion of formation.

Para 30   Powers for the compulsory purchase of land to cease after the expiration of three years from the passing of the Act.

Para 31   Of the three bridges intended to carry public roads over the line the inclinations of the approach ramps were to be:–
At Llanbadarn 1 in 12 and 1 in 20.
At Nantyronen 1 in 6.
At Aberffrwd 1 in 7.
How physically they could have been built defies logic. The one at Llanbadarn would have needed a long S-shaped affair winding between the Cambrian main line and that of the Rheidol. They were picked up in advance by Her Majesty's Ordnance Surveyor for his next edition. He did omit the one from the map at Llanbadarn and got the one at Aberffrwd *under* the railway, which was after all the only practicable solution.

Para 32   The width of the bridge roadways was specified at 15 feet.

Para 33   Required a Board of Trade Enquiry into the route of the Harbour Branch. It permitted deviation to run clear of high water mark, thereby saving embankment and bridging.

Para 34   Protected the interests of the Manchester & Milford Railway where the Rheidol line would pass under at the water's edge.

Para 36   Required the consent of The Local Government Board before compulsorily acquiring more than ten houses tenanted by persons of the labouring class, which were defined as 'means and includes mechanics artisans labourers and others working for wages hawkers costermongers persons not working for wages but working at some trade or handicraft without employing others except members of their own family and persons other than domestic servants whose income does not exceed an average of thirty shillings

The Armorial Device   **The Company Seal**

Para 37	a week and the family of any such persons who may be residing with them'. *Note* Thirty shillings in 1897 would have a purchasing power of around £63 in 1986.
Para 37	Required a deposit of 5%, £1,560, to be placed with the Paymaster General for and on behalf of the Supreme Court for compensations in case the line was not completed and to be returnable if no claims were made.
Paras 47–50	Ensuring proper performance of works below tide level. This requirement would be called for in respect of the exit line from Aberystwyth station where it skirted the Rheidol tideway.
Para 39	'If the railways are not completed within five years from the passing of this Act then on expiration of that period the powers by this Act granted to the Company for making and completing the railways or otherwise in relation thereto shall cease except as to so much thereof as shall then be completed.'

On the 13th of August 1898 the newly-empowered Light Railway Commissioners granted the company The Vale of Rheidol Light Railway (Aberayron Extension) Order 1898. This was a larger affair than the Act and printed on foolscap sized (320 mm × 201 mm) paper. Its seventeen pages cost only 2½d. This time the plans and sections were deposited with the Board of Trade. The Order was much better laid out and indexed than the Act had been and was much more clearly referenced to other applying legislation.

Para 4	Conferred the power to make a railway sixteen miles, three furlongs or thereabouts 'commencing in the parish of Aberystwyth in the County of Cardigan by a junction with the railway authorised by the Act of 1897 twenty-two yards or thereabouts south of the point where the said railway authorised is intended to cross under the Manchester & Milford Railway' and 'terminating at Aberayron in the parish of Llanddewi-Aberarth in the said county at or near the southern corner of the enclosure numbered 898 on the 1/2500 Ordnance map of the said parish'.
Para 5	'The railway shall be constructed on a gauge of two feet and the motive power shall be steam or such other motive power as the Board of Trade may approve.' Gave also the power to have the gauge approval increased to anything not exceeding two feet six inches.
Para 7	Provided that the power to acquire land compulsorily should lapse after three years from the date of the Order.
Para 11	The conventional limitation on the acquisition of more than ten houses tenanted by members of the labouring class.
Para 12	An interestingly-worded one for 'Saving the Rights of the Crown' commencing 'Nothing contained in this Order shall authorise the Company to take use or in any manner interfere with any land or hereditaments or rights of whatsoever description belonging to the Queen's Most Excellent Majesty in right of her Crown and under management of the Commissioners of Woods without the consent in writing of the Commissioners of Woods on behalf of her Majesty first had and obtained for that purpose (which consent such Commissioners are hereby authorised to give)'.
Para 14	Gave only three years for completion from the date of the Order.
Para 15	While mainly dealing with permitted deviation of route, gave the power to reduce curves to a radius of not less than three chains.
Para 16	Provided for one bridge across a road in the parish of Llanychaiarn to have a minimum headroom of only ten feet with twelve feet to the spring of the arch.
Para 17	Provided for the building of two bridges carrying main roads and being twenty-five feet in width and five lesser ones only fifteen feet in width. (This does highlight the fact that the application must have been drafted before the advantages of proceeding under a Light Railway Order had been properly appreciated and understood.)
Para 18	Provided for gates to be maintained at all times at level crossings with keepers as otherwise permitted.
Para 22	Protected the Manchester & Milford Railway where the Extension Line bridged across that Company's line.
Para 24	Prescribed at least one month's notice in writing to the Board of Trade of the intention of opening the line for passenger traffic, and ten days notice of it being the opinion of the Company that the line is sufficiently completed for inspection and opening 'for the safe conveyance of passengers'.
Para 25	Permitted a loading of 9 tons per axle and a speed limit of 17 miles per hour. Further restrictions were 10 miles per hour around curves of less than three chains in radius and 6 miles per hour over facing points not interlocked with a fixed or permanent semaphore signal or otherwise properly fastened.
Para 27	Laid down the provisions for use of motive power other than steam and including electricity.
Para 28	Regulated the construction, insulation and use of 'electric lines and circuits' (meaning cables and wires) and with the quaintly-worded exception as to when 'Such power is entirely contained in and carried along with the carriages'.
Para 29	Over a page in extent protecting the Postmaster General's installations against damage, unauthorised moving, and, if electric motive power was used, against induction. (The motive power then available was by Direct Current which has far greater inductive power than the modern Alternating Current).
Para 32	The company's authorised capital to be increased by up to £63,000 to be accounted for separately as 'extension shares' and 'extension capital'.
Para 36	Provided that 'extension shareholders' had no voting rights over main line affairs and that shareholders under the 1897 Act could not vote upon extension matters.
Para 37	Borrowing might be increased by up to £21,000.
Para 40	Defined very distinctly the financial separation of the two undertakings.
Para 45	£2,000 to be deposited with the Paymaster General for good performance and protection of other people's rights.

The Order terminated with a schedule detailing the Board of Trade requirements as to construction and operation.

The Schedule

Permanent Way The rails used shall weigh at least forty pounds per yard. If flat-bottom rails and wooden sleepers are used, –
a. The rails at the joints shall be secured to the sleepers by fang or other through bolts or by coach-screws or by double-spikes on the outside of the rail and
b. The rails on curves with radii of less than three chains shall be secured on the outside of the outer rail to each sleeper with a fang or other through bolt or by a coach-screw or by double spikes with a bearing plate and
c. The rails on curves with radii of less than three chains shall be tied to gauge by iron or steel ties at suitable intervals or in such other manner as may be approved by the Board of Trade.

Turntables No turntables need be provided.

Signals No signals other than those at the junction of the line with a passenger line of the railway authorised by the Act of 1897 need be interlocked with the points.

At places where under the system of working for the time being in force trains may cross or pass one another there shall be a home-signal at or near the entrance points. If the home-signal cannot be seen from a distance of a quarter of a mile a distant-signal must be erected at that distance at least from the entrance points.

Home-signals and distant-signals may be worked from the station by wires or otherwise but every signal-arm shall be so weighted as to fly and remain at danger on the breaking at any point of the connection between the arm and the lever working it.

Electrical Communication If the Board of Trade require a means of electrical communication to be provided on the line the Company shall make that provision as the Board of Trade direct.

Platforms &c. Platforms shall be provided to the satisfaction of the Board of Trade unless all carriages in use on the railway for the conveyance of passengers are constructed with proper and convenient means of access to and from the same and to the level of the ground on the outside of the rail.

There shall be no obligation on the Company to provide shelter or conveniences at any station or stopping place.

INCORPORATION AND EXTENSION

The title of the second Act dated 30th July 1900 was The Vale of Rheidol Light Railway Act 1900 and so the brackets had been removed from the word (Light) legitimately. It was also on sixmo and cost 9d.

It repeated a number of the provisions of the 1897 Act and the significant additional provisions were:

Para 5	Extended the time for compulsory purchase of land to 5th August 1905.
Para 7	Enabled the line to be worked by electrical or other motive power as well as by steam.
Para 8	Enabled the company to take a supply of electricity from any undertaking or person.
Para 9	Laid down precautions and restrictions as to the safe use of electrical power.
Para 10	Protected the installations of the Postmaster General.
Para 12	Authorised an increase of £12,000 in the amount which could be raised as share capital.
Para 17	Increased the borrowing powers by £4,000.

On 1st August 1902 the Board of Trade, acting for the second time under the Light Railways Act 1896, confirmed that much-needed Vale of Rheidol Light Railway (Amendment) Order 1902. It's significant provisions were –

Para 3	'The railway of 1897 may be constructed and worked as a light railway under the principal Act.
Para 4	Extended the term for the acquisition of land for the Aberayron Extension by three years to 12th August 1904, and the time for completion of same was extended by four years to 12th August 1905.
Para 5	Dispensed with the bridges at Llanbadarn, Nantyronen and Aberffrwd and most of those on the Aberayron Extension.
Para 6	Required gates at any level crossing of a public carriage way where the Board of Trade may require gates.
Para 7	Required cattle guards at all ungated crossings, and speed-limit warning notices three hundred yards from the crossing in both directions, and in addition public warning notices along each roadway sited fifty yards from the crossing in both directions.
Para 9	Relieved the Company from the liability of maintaining diverted roads on the Extension after only one year.
Para 12	The County Council became empowered to advance or lend up to £18,000 towards the cost of the Aberayron Extension scheme.

So, by means of a foolscap-sized document costing only 1½d the Company was relieved of a useful bit of construction expense as well as maintenance and operating costs.

The Policies and Machinations 1897 to 1910

Now the promoters had a company with a legal identity of its own, a company with the power to raise money and a company with the power to build a railway; what more could they wish for that they had not got? The short answer was shareholders. From 1897 onwards there was a struggle to get the allegedly-interested parties to put their money down and to help in the search for other people who would also subscribe. So they just had to get under way with only a few shareholders plus the borrowing of the authorised £6,500 out of which they had straightway to find the Paymaster General's £1,560.

At the same time they were voluntarily tying the proverbial albatross around their necks in the form of the Aberayron Extension. This produced its own warning in the form of construction costs of £3,850 per mile overall compared with the £3,250 per mile cost of the principal venture. The effects of the Boer War were beginning to bite and costs were rising. Advisedly they re-examined the cost estimate and came to the conclusion that capital under the 1897 Act needed increasing by £16,000 and the necessary application was made which resulted in the Act of 1900.

While this was in process, the promoters still went hopefully ahead and eventually, by the efforts of an action syndicate assembled in 1900, enough practically-interested parties were found. In terms of actual spending power, the sum now required of £68,000 would be like having to raise £2,500,000 in 1986. Using modern excavating machines and diesel-powered locomotives it might just be possible to get somewhere near building the railway for such a sum. It would be very interesting to find out.

By now the roll-call of principal parties had changed to a remarkable degree. The leader and Chairman was Mr. H. H. Montague Smith, a director of the Central London Railway (the tuppenny tube), supported by Sir W. T. Madge, the proprietor of *The Globe* and *The People* newspapers, and only Mr. John Francis remained of all the mining proprietors. Of the gentry none were left and local support had dwindled to a few tradesmen, professional folk and widows who had faith that the line would be a good thing for Aberystwyth. Also about to assume very prominent roles were Sir James Szlumper, the Engineer, and Mr. A. H. Pethick, the Contractor, each of whom would be accepting shares in lieu of fees and contract instalments in anticipation of increased benefits in the future. This was a regular practice in the building of small railways many of which could otherwise never have been built at all.

Apart from a glitch in 1899 when they havered once again over the motive power and considered the use of hydro-electricity, the new consortium managed to get over all their financial hurdles and had arranged for the capital needed by the close of 1900 and held their first Board meeting on the 10th of January 1901. Construction could now become a reality but, before going on to that especially fascinating part of the history, it might be as well if the remainder of the background work of the Board was considered first. Particularly would they be continually bogged down by the abortive Aberayron Extension.

That first meeting of the Board had to ratify all that had gone before, place everyone properly in their appointments, and set the pattern for the future, all of course by careful pre-arrangement.

Mr. H. H. Montague Smith was elected Chairman, and his offices at 28 Victoria Street, Westminster, were to be the Company Office and the venue for the meetings of the Board. Sir James Szlumper and his half-brother, William W. Szlumper, were appointed Consultant Engineer and Resident Engineer respectively. Mr. Arthur J. Hughes, who had earlier been one of the original promoters, became the Aberystwyth Solicitor, with Lumley and Lumley handling affairs at the London end. The Chairman and the Engineers were authorised to confer with the Contractors and the Chairman was authorised to arrange for notice to be served upon the Manchester & Milford Railway concerning acquisition of the bit of land under their bridge across the Rheidol. Finally the 'Approved Seal' was produced and formally adopted as 'The Company's Common Seal'.

At its second meeting the Board authorised the opening of an account with the North and South Wales Bank in Aberystwyth. Next it accepted Pethick's offer of reducing costs by supplying second-hand rail and accepted the pre-arranged tender to construct the line for £45,000.

On 28th February 1901 the first Ordinary General Meeting was convened to do a lot more ratifying. The shareholders approved Mr. H. H. Montague Smith as Director and Chairman, and appointed as the other Directors Sir W. T. Madge, the newspaper magnate, Mr. John Francis from the mining cadre, Mr. Charles E. Cottier, the Pethick family's Solicitor from Plymouth, and Mr. Francis J. Ellis. Now they were really a properly constituted Board of Directors with the powers to do what they had already done on the 10th of January, but they forgot to pass a retrospective minute ratifying that position as well.

The shareholders fixed the remuneration of the Chairman at £100 guineas per annum. This might be worth around £4,500 of 1986 money. They put the other Directors on expenses only until the line had started running. Finally, they formally authorised the exercising of the borrowing powers.

After assuring themselves that they could raise all of the £68,000 a fresh correspondence was started with the Light Railway Commissioners which would result in the easement of construction requirements under both the 1897 Act and the 1898 Extension Order. An approach was also made to the Treasury for a grant towards the capital cost of the extension on the grounds that it was intended to serve an impoverished rural area. The Treasury turned the application down at first on the mistaken grounds that the company did not then exist. A second application was made in which the error was pointed out and the Treasury came back with the masterly and irrefutable 'That the case was not one in which they could properly make a grant'

in May 1903. The basis for the decision this time was that the line could never be regarded as a principal trunk route. A month or so later Mr. Montague Smith announced that if the County Council would find £18,000 the company would be able to raise the remainder of the cost of the extension.

On 26th February 1903 the Board re-affirmed its intentions 'to continue its endeavours to carry out the Undertaking of the Aberayron Extension' and appointed an Independent Aberayron Extension Committee of four members. Of the remainder of this chapter much will be given over to the bright ideas it managed to put forward. The real force behind this phase must have been the Pethick family. By taking shares instead of cash, they had built up their power within the company and at the half-yearly meeting held on the same day a third Pethick had been elected to the Board of Directors and a scrutiny of the register of shareholders would have revealed eight Pethicks voting. They wanted the extension contract and were not going to let up until they had secured it.

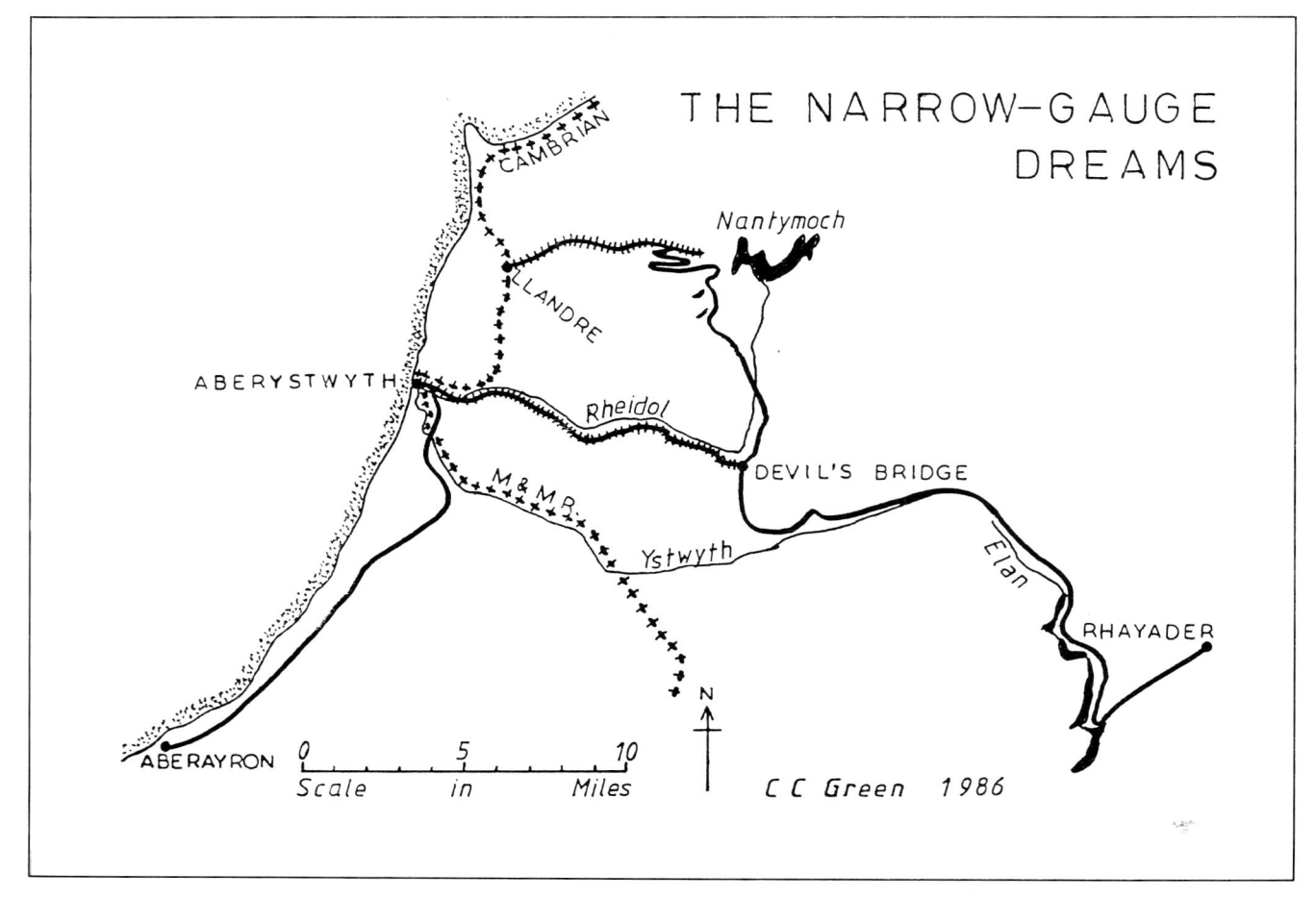

The County Council had got the necessary power to become a shareholder to the extent of £18,000 under the Amendment Order of 1902 and had promptly paid over £600 for expenses. Then the Council had passed a resolution in May 1903 voting the rest of the £18,000, but with the stipulation that the company must raise the rest of the money within the next six months. Sir James had approached the Council with the request that the time be extended to twelve months. Mr. Pethick had already pledged £10,000 and the *Aberystwyth Observer* reported optimistically that there was now every prospect of the line being built.

On 25th February 1904 Mr. Montague Smith retired from the chair and on 15th June from the Board on grounds of ill-health. He would still attend the half-yearly meetings both as a shareholder and as a representative of that faithful little group shareholder, the Works Syndicate. And guess who was elected Chairman in his place? Mr. A. H. Pethick, of course, and now the Pethicks reigned supreme.

So, in July 1904 they put out the first of their startling ideas. The Board should seek power to increase the gauge of the extension to 4′ 8½″ and when built The Cambrian Railways should be invited to operate it. Mr. A. H. Pethick as Chairman announced to the Board that the Cambrian were most anxious to see the route extended in standard gauge to Newquay and would be prepared to work it in perpetuity. Furthermore, they would do the same for the line to Devil's Bridge if that too was rebuilt to the standard gauge.

By 9th August 1904 the *Aberystwyth Observer* was back with a gloomy editorial warning 'unless something is done the whole scheme will fall through. The Board of Trade should make a grant of £40,000 because of the impoverished condition of the countryside'. This was because on the 2nd August the Board had authorised the sending of a letter to the Cardiganshire County Council admitting that it would be impossible to raise the capital, and this was just the capital for the narrow-gauge scheme. On 12th August 1904 the power to buy the land expired. Everyone seemed down in the dumps for at the next half-yearly meeting no quorum turned up and after one hour the meeting had to be adjourned.

Down for a time the Board may have been but the Pethicks were still far from being out. The *Aberystwyth Observer* had piled on a bit more gloom on the 11th August, writing that the scheme would probably be dropped, but still offering the hope that it might be taken over by the Cambrian who might construct it as well. By no means could the editor possibly have forecast the reality of the next wildcat scheme of 1908.

By this the main line was to be extended from Devil's Bridge to Rhaiadr (then known as Rhayader). With the Aberayron Extension the routes combined would have rivalled the old plans of the North Wales Narrow Gauge Railway for their ambitious little empire across North Wales, but entirely without its mineral potential. Naturally the owners of the Cwmystwyth Mine would have liked it but unfortunately they were much nearer to collapse than anyone suspected. The line could have reached Cwmystwyth, but only at fantastic cost, and it would have had to have been carried across the unstable mine workings to hold height to get up to Ffosllwyd at the crest of the Ystwyth/Elan watershed. Thence it would have been a fairly simple matter to have descended to the terminus of Elan Valley Railway No. 4 and to have used the Elan Valley Railway's formations to make a massive detour to get down to Rhaiadr. It had to be only talk.

There was a last and final fling at the Aberayron Extension in 1909 when the Extension Committee actually put it out to tender. When a Glasgow firm undercut the Pethick tender, the rest of the Board intimated that Pethicks would not be accorded any preferential treatment and that the contract would not be given to them. And that, finally, was that. In a combination of pique and the wish to salvage what they might out of the Rheidol affair the Pethick family commenced negotiations with the Cambrian. This resulted over the next twelve months in their shares being offloaded to nominees of the Cambrian, and a Cambrian takeover of appointments on the Board.

Now we have dwelt overlong in the stuffy atmospheres of boardrooms and committees and it is time to step outside into the fresh air of the valley.

ABERYSTWYTH

T. ROWLANDS,
FAMILY BUTCHER,
6, BRIDGE STREET, ABERYSTWYTH,

Begs to announce that he has always in Stock Primest Beef, Pork, Mutton, Veal and Lamb (when in season).
TRY OUR CELEBRATED SAUSAGES.
All Orders promptly Despatched to any Address
Your Patronage & Support is respectfully solicited.

GOGERDDAN ARMS
AND
LION ROYAL HOTEL,
ABERYSTWITH.

The "Old County House."

First-Class Family and Commercial Hotel.
ESTABLISHED OVER TWO HUNDRED YEARS.

THIS HOTEL is close to the Castle and Clock Towers, and within three minutes' walk of the Railway Station. The Hotel is now replete with every comfort. Spacious Ladies' Coffee Room. Well-Furnished Sitting Rooms and Bedrooms.
HANDSOME BILLIARD ROOM,
CONTAINING TWO TABLES.
Wine and Spirit Stores attached.
OMNIBUS MEETS ALL TRAINS.
FIRST-CLASS POSTING, STABLING, AND LOOSE BOXES.

Breaks leave the Hotel every morning for the Devil's Bridge at 9-30; Fares, 4s.

TARIFF ON APPLICATION.

JOHN ROBERTS,
Proprietor.

WYNNE'S
Dispensing Establishment
7, PIER STREET.

AND FOR
Pure Drugs, Chemicals, & Patent Medicines

The Aberystwyth that awaited the coming of the Lein Fach. Illustrations include: The newly built Pier Pavilion where James Rees would place his railway's posters *(E. R. Gyde)*. A beach scene *(believed J. Valentine)*. Aberllolwyn's milk cart — milk was measured into your jug at the front door from a gleaming churn *(Courtesy Mrs. Margaret Evans)*. A Cambrian Railways dray delivering supplies in the town. Sails in Aberystwyth Bay *(E. Rudolph Gell)*. The other steam railway. An engine with a vertical boiler pumped water up into the tank of the descending car *(Aberystwyth Cliff Railway)*. Mr. Phillips who, offering tours to Devil's Bridge, was about to experience a considerable drop in his income *(Courtesy Mrs. Margaret Evans)*. Culled from 'Aberystwyth Yesterday' by Howard C. Jones, from 'Born on a Perilous Rock' by W. J. Lewis, and from Cambrian Railways timetables.

CHAPTER TWO

CONSTRUCTION
10th January 1901 to 21st December 1902

First on site had to be Sir James Szlumper and he staked out the course of the contractor's work. The use of the original standard gauge survey as modified for the narrow gauge ran him into difficulties, and he owned up to none of them. The standard gauge included some gradients steeper than the now-desired 1 in 50 and in 1897 the cavalier treatment of houses and farmsteads which was usual in the 1860s was no longer socially acceptable. The hugging of contour lines, not possible with standard gauge, gave the narrow gauge the advantage on the upper section of a longer route, by reason of the incurving and reverse curving, and so Aberffrwd to Devil's Bridge did just work out correctly. Aberystwyth to Capel Bangor presented, of course, no problems, and all the problems lay in the middle bit from Tan-yr-allt to Aberffrwd. For economy the line was kept low until Tan-yr-allt to save lane diversion. At Ty-llwyd the line was held above and behind the farmhouses which settled the levels at Nantyronen. At Aberffrwd the route was kept above and clear of the village, and level to provide for the expected future station.

By allowing virtually no transition from level to incline at Tan-yr-allt, the first lift was held at 1 in 50. To get up to Nantyronen the next piece of slope was pitched at 1 in 40. To get out of Nantyronen, the trains have to rush a brief length at 1 in 36, levelling off to 1 in 45, with a draggy reverse curve at the upper end – all of which Sir James blandly set down on his gradient diagram at 1 in 50. The Cambrian were aware of the one discrepancy up to Nantyronen, and the Great Western did redraw the gradient diagram to show this incline as 1 in 48. All of this became evident only when trying to draw out a neat gradient diagram to scale off Ordnance Survey maps. That middle bit refused to fit the map.

Pethick's first move was to erect a sound brick-built site office and stores behind the future buffer stops on Smithfield Road (later Park Avenue). Later they were to buy a good dormitory hut from the Elan Valley scheme and erect it at Devil's Bridge, where it still stands as a trim bungalow. In advance of starting, they had written from their Laira Bridge, Plymouth address, asking the Festiniog Railway for 'particulars of the locomotives, passenger carriages, goods trucks &c used on your railway which we believe is a light railway 2' gauge'.

They started cutting formation from Aberystwyth and around Capel Bangor, where such little spare rural labour that there was could be readily got to work. By April 1901 they claimed that a £3,600 call on their shareholding was more than covered by the work done, which the company refuted in a letter stating that this claim 'scarcely agreed with the report of the Resident Engineer'. Then the company threatened legal proceedings if the call was not paid by 11 o'clock on 15th May.

On 29th May 1901 the Board set up a Finance and General Purposes Committee to acquire rolling stock and equipment and generally to do everything necessary to get the line running. The acquisition from the Hafod Estate, belonging to Mr. Thomas Waddingham, of the site of Devil's Bridge station and yard and of the top section down to Nant-ar-fynwg, meant that work could be started down from the top. Now Sir James and the contractors would start to clash in real earnest.

Sir James wanted 3'6" of firm ground clear on both sides of the 6' wide carriages, and, because of the need for continuous drainage ditches at the lower end, he was getting his way with little bother.

On the expensive ledges Pethick's instruction to his gangs was '7' into the hillside and not one inch more', and if he could sneak a scarcely-detectable bit of down hill fill into that cross-measurement he was willing. Most of the work was done by pick, beetle and wedge, and crowbar and sledgehammer. There was a reluctance to use expensive dynamite where cheap labour could be substituted. It is ironic then that the only casualty was a shot-firer who fell off a cliff-face while fixing a charge.

Not until mid-June did Sir James issue his first certificate of work completed to his satisfaction, for only £3,000. Realising that the long summer working days of 12 and 14 hours, as was usual in those days, would soon be shortened by the onset of autumn, he wrote a hastening letter about 'poor progress through the contractors not having enough men on the ground'. Pethick countered that he was 'already paying higher rates than those obtained in the district' and that there was 'a real scarcity of labour until harvest time was past'. On 30th October Mr. John Pethick was summoned before the Board in London and he still maintained that he could complete the construction in time for the Board of Trade inspection on 31st March 1902.

After that things seemed to have bucked up a bit, and by December rails were arriving at the Stone Quay, and the Harbour Branch had been laid. Probably Pethicks had been able to augment their workforce with navvies discharged from work on the dams in the Elan Valley. Their arrival certainly stirred things up in the valley, the girls were delighted and their parents were alarmed. The total lack of the grog shops to which they had been accustomed caused drinking clubs to be set up and these made matters worse. They were usually only temporary huts, 'shebeens' the valley folk termed them, and after the scandalising goings-on had gone beyond what the good folk could bear, the police were called in. The organisers and servers were arrested and sentenced at the Quarter Sessions although some were warned and got away in time to escape punishment. This measure only curtailed the roughest of behaviour a bit, but the gambling and fighting still went on and the valley was not the same until the entirely nomadic elements of the workforce had completed their task and been paid off.

From W. G. Bagnall & Co Ltd, Pethicks had bought *Talybont*, a 2-4-0 tank, which Bagnalls had repurchased out of the bankruptcy of The Plynlimon and Hafan Tramway, and had re-gauged to fit the Rheidol track. From the company they had on hire ten end-door wagons which the Midland Carriage & Wagon Co Ltd had re-possessed for non-payment from the Plynlimon & Hafan. When they started to complain that progress was being delayed by shortage of wagons, the company brought and hired five more to the contractors.

By 16th January 1902 the *Aberystwyth Observer* started to take notice of events up the valley and reported that the rails would have reached Rhiwarthen (Capel Bangor) in a few days and 'Mr. Pethick says the railway will be complete to Devil's Bridge by the end of March'. On 27th February they reported that the rails had been laid for six miles. Progress was satisfactory and the ground for Aberystwyth station was being fenced and filled in. Mr. Smith, the Chairman, stated that the Board of Trade would be asked to inspect the line during the third week in April and that it was hoped to have it opened for Coronation Day. That event was to have been on 26th June but Edward had fallen ill with appendicitis and the ceremony had to be put off until 9th August. Even this postponement was not to be of any help because what the infant company needed was the start of its income to pay all the outgoings. Incidentally, the makers of china souvenirs were not doing so well either with all those dated mugs and chamber pots to smash up; at least the cutlery trade could melt down their silver spoons.

And while the verbal reportage seemed to augur well and Mr. A. H. Pethick had just been elected to be a Director, an event occurred which quite literally blew the lid off. At the end of March Sir James and the Chairman spent five days on a detailed inspection of the work. Pethicks received a very strongly-worded letter 'to forthwith put upon the Works such additional plant and men as will enable the construction of the line to be completed for inspection by the Board of Trade as early as possible'. Pethick replied that their engine was insufficient for the work and that they had tried unsuccessfully to hire one. Davies and Metcalfe had one engine completed and this was hired direct to Pethicks on terms 'at no detriment to the Company'.

This measure did bring some improvement in progress and only a few weeks after the delivery of *Prince of Wales* onto the line the *Observer* sent a reporter up the line, who wrote at the end of May, 'There being no Pullman car we seated ourselves in an open truck preferring that to standing room on the locomotive. Behind us were a couple of trucks loaded with rails'. He commented that the line had been completed for about half the distance and that rails had been laid for about 10 miles. The remainder would be finished early in June. Alas even that was not to be.

In June the Board, starting off into another state of alarm over the lack of a firm completion date, had a letter sent to Sir James on the 17th averring that the Engineers 'might have taken such steps as they were under the Contract empowered to take to have ensured the Contractors completing their Contract by 31st March 1902 and the interests of the shareholders were suffering by reason of the line not being ready for opening'. A man of Sir James's standing and experience was well capable of seeing off a Board composed of little London business men, country hicks and contractors, and by the 25th they were apologising for the wording of their letter.

Completion was then to be expected by 12th July and the *Observer* duly reported that the rails had been laid to Devil's Bridge on 28th July. All that had happened was that the unballasted rails laid down from Devil's Bridge by Burridge's gang had met the last bit of unballasted rails going up laid by Jenkins' gang, hard by Nant-ar-fynwg. It was hoped, too, by the *Observer* that passenger trains would be run on 15th August. There had been an unofficial inspection by the Board of Trade just before the link-up and this had uncovered many shortcomings which would have caused the refusal of the certificate on an official inspection. Rock ribs must be trimmed back where curves outward were oversharp, and much ledge section required cutting wider where the firm formation was too narrow. Mr. Dutton Junior, the son of the Managing Director of Mackenzie & Holland, was on that train and recorded that the engine was too rigid for the 2-chain curves and engine and stock derailed several times 'to the great amusement of the Inspector'. Both this train and its official successor would have been of the 4 ft wheelbase wagons with bench seats, and there were stanchions and a handrail fixed across the front of *Prince of Wales* for engineers and the Inspector.

On the 12th August Major E. Druitt, Royal Engineers, made the formal inspection, and, while much remedial work had been done, his fair and detached appraisal still revealed deficiencies which precluded the issue of a certificate.

After a few descriptive sentences he made his stand quite clear. 'The formation is for the last 7 miles cut from the side of the valley, and this is in some places precipitous, so that a derailment might be attended with most serious results'. The tablet instruments were working only as far as Capel Bangor. The run-offs at the sidings were over-sharp and certain of the traps (catch points) should have been double-tongue (a complete set of points). He ordered several to be turned more fully away from the main line and that the traps should be moved further along (Pethick had been saving on point-rodding). At Capel Bangor he had the down home-signal moved further away from the crossing so that it was not confused against the buildings and the signal-wire had to be properly protected where it ran across the road. He ordered additional fencing at many points.

He disliked the earth buttresses of the Rheidol Bridge held firm by only stake palisading but was reassured that all groyne and protective work along the entire river was made in this style and that it was effective. He noted carefully that the trestles were stated to be driven 12 to 14 feet into the river bed, and called for a drawing and for a proper deflection test on his next visit. By now, the Chairman, the one Director, the Consultant Engineer (Sir James), the Resident Engineer (his son W. W. Szlumper), and the Contractors must have been wearing pretty long faces, and Major Druitt had not seen the dreaded upper section yet. Before leaving the area of the bridge he condemned the unlocked ballast siding and ordered it to be removed.

Then he got down to his opinion of the track. 'The ballast is river shingle or broken stone from the cuttings. The permanent way is for the first five miles in pretty good order, but for the remainder of the line is in an unfinished condition, the sleepers are not sufficiently packed, and the rails in many cases not set

Sir James Szlumper (left) and Mr. John Pethick at Capel Bangor. The horizontal bar behind Sir James' back is mounted across the front of *Prince of Wales* for use when inspecting the line.
National Library of Wales

CONSTRUCTION

to proper curves. Much of the broken stone at present on the line requires breaking up before it will be suitable for packing the sleepers and for top ballast. Some of the sleepers are well below specified width'. Some sleepers were more than the required 3 ft 6 ins apart and on upper curves must be set at intervals of 3 ft. At all curves above steep slopes continuous check-rails must be added 'as a derailment might be attended with disastrous results'. At only 7 ft in width across the top, the Cwmdauddwr embankment beyond Aberffrwd was too narrow and in certain places the carriages were running too close to the rock. The small culvert at Llanbadarn was not satisfactory and his lengthy and carefully worded description of the 5 ft culvert at Nant-ar-fynwg amounted to 'wonky and dangerous'. Speed limit boards had not been erected at any of the crossings. He then placed the following speed restrictions: over the crossing at Llanbadarn 6 mph, over all other crossings 10 mph, and 10 mph along the entire railway beyond Nantyronen. He ended his report with:

'It will be seen from the above report that the railway is in an unfinished condition and the opening of the railway would in my opinion be attended with danger to the public using it. The matters which I have called attention to in paragraphs marked *a* to *i* all need seeing to before the line is fit for passenger traffic. I have the honour to be &c, E. Druitt. Major Druitt R.E.'

And so ended the dreadful day which all the parties had, through incompetence, impetuosity, stupidity in thinking that Major Druitt could be conned, and contractors' greed, brought upon themselves.

The notice of opening on 15th August was cancelled and the inadequate work-gangs were exhorted to work even harder than before, because for setting the rails to curves Pethicks had provided only two 'Jim Crows' over the entire works. Fortunately (or otherwise) the good Major had missed one important factor. He wrote from the information given to him that the rail was second-hand and weighed from 48 lbs to 60 lbs per yard. In fact much of it was very light in the upstand and footing and weighed only 32 lbs per yard. The haulier who was paid for carting rails to Devil's Bridge for use by Burridge's gang, had taken full advantage of this by picking as much 32 lb rail as he could find.

The only thing the Board could do was to authorise the Traffic Superintendent to canvass for the carriage of goods, and goods trains were run during the overhaul period with much value in settling the ballast. Actually, the 15th August date could not have easily been met for passenger traffic because carriages were still to be finished and delivered. Mr. Gibson, the editor of the *Aberystwyth Observer*, seems to have lost patience with the company and, despite a request for a good spread from his friend the Traffic Superintendent, all he would put was

VALE OF RHEIDOL RAILWAY
OPENED FOR GOODS TRAFFIC
This line is now opened for goods traffic.

Sir James made a placatory visit to Major Druitt in London and got his assurance that he could return to complete his inspection on 25th November and would accept notice given by the 17th as the statutory 10 days notice. Keeping up his less than helpful attitude, Mr. Gibson next reported after a trip up the line by goods train that the company were running goods trains to consolidate the track and had no idea when the passenger services would start.

In the middle of October there was an informal trip of inspection for the Directors and the line was declared to have been practically completed, and only a few men were left at work tidying up. Then came another petty rumpus. Pethicks complained that the engines were too rigid and had damaged their track and that they could no longer be held responsible for its condition. Once again Sir James proved equal to an awkward situation. He enlisted the support of no less a personage than the President of the Institute of Civil Engineers, Mr. Hawkshaw, the Principal also of the well-reputed firm of Hawkshaw and Dobson. He sent the following letter.

Dear Sir   *Rheidol Valley Engine.*
Referring to your call a few days ago in respect to the above engine. We have carefully gone into the question of alleged damage to the permanent way by the same. The engine has ten wheels, six wheels coupled, and we have been unable to discover anything in the drawing that would lead us to believe that any damage could be ascribed to the engine.

The rail weighs about 56 lbs per yard and is therefore strong enough to carry much heavier axle-loads, and as the rigid wheelbase

Quarry Cutting, showing the steep sides before opening out by rock falls and ballast removal. Note the waney sleepers, and the lumpy ballast objected to by Major Druitt. *Railway Magazine*

The first official train at Devil's Bridge on 5th November 1902. *Courtesy E. Savage*

Dignity at Devil's Bridge, probably the full party of 5th November 1902. *The National Library of Wales*

CONSTRUCTION

57153 RHEIDOL RAILWAY, DEVIL'S BRIDGE *Copyright Frith's*

Down train leaving Quarry Cutting. Note the wide spacing of the sleepers. *Frith's Series*

is only six feet the Engine ought to be able to travel with ease round curves of three chains radius, although it might be better as is customary if the flanges of the middle wheels were turned down thinner than those of the other wheels, but this is not shown on the drawing. This would give additional clearance.

It is possible that the permanent way may require fresh alignment as it is often found that curves are disturbed by slewing and are often sharper than originally set out.

Yours faithfully
Hawkshaw & Dobson.

The Board resolved 'that the allegations of the Contractors are not capable of being sustained or proved'. Even then the lightness of the rail did not come to light. Were they all pretending that the rail was up to specification and not daring to admit that it was not? So faces were saved all round and Davies & Metcalfe's prides and joys were substantially vindicated. Nevertheless the Board passed one of those annoying self-protective resolutions instructing the Engineer 'to see that the Engines comply with all the requirements of the specification'. They concluded that meeting hopefully, with a minute recording that after getting the line passed by Major Druitt they could open the line for passenger traffic, but pessimistically deferred the likely date to 1st January 1903.

Then, as if to cheer themselves up, they ran a special private trip on 5th November 1902, which became indeed a merry affair during which several members had to be leaned up against the engine to hold them still for the photograph. The party consisted of the Chairman, directors, contractors, officials, County and Town Councillors, local landowners and shareholders. And then they had to endure many speeches of which Mr. James Rees, the Traffic Superintendent has left some extracts. Mr. H. C. Fryer, Clerk to the County Council, declared that the railway would add greatly to the amenities of the district, for whereas hitherto hundreds had gone by road to enjoy the beauties of Devil's Bridge, thousands would be able to go by rail. Major Pryse Lewis said that he had travelled a good deal abroad and declared that he had not seen anywhere from first to last a more beautiful stretch of scenery than that along the line of the new railway. Alderman E. P. Wynne affirmed that the trip had been a revelation to the guests and that the railway would prove a priceless asset to the town, and several more were in similarly eulogistic vein. Mr. Gibson relented a little and the *Observer* carried a short account of the trip, noting that there were stationmasters at Aberystwyth, Capel Bangor and Devil's Bridge, but not at Nantyronen. Aberffrwd had the status of a halt but a station could be provided if the owners would give the land.

After the VIP train had returned, it went back up for a second time with employees, wives and friends for an even jollier do. 'There was drink enough for all those who wanted it and we did not have to hear all those speeches.' The train was four coaches and a van, and the last coach derailed at that place of fate Nant-ar-fynwg. Tom Savage, the Foreman-Fitter who was driving, unhitched and took the party on to Devil's Bridge in the three leading coaches and returned to sort out the mishap and bring the other two vehicles up to reunite the train.

On 25th November Major Druitt returned and completed his re-inspection. His hand-written report, which survives as a jelly-

Edward VII **posed with a rake of newly arrived carriages. Note Pethick's office behind the train.** *Courtesy E. W. Hannan*

block facsimile, starts: 'Sir, I have the honour to report for the information of the Board of Trade that in compliance with your instructions contained in your minute of 17th November I have re-inspected the Vale of Rheidol Light Railway No 1 constructed under the Act of 1897 as amended by Amendment Order of 1902.' He had the bridge tested and noted scouring around the third trestle 'which should be carefully watched'. Five checkrails were still needed 'which the promoters promise to lay forthwith'. He closed with: 'The permanent way is now in very fair order for a new line and subject to the additional check rails being provided I can recommend the Board of Trade to sanction the line for the use of passenger traffic but the following speeds should not be exceeded viz Between Devil's Bridge and Nantyronen 10 miles an hour except over some sharp reverse curves between $8\frac{3}{4}$ and 9 miles where speed should be reduced to 6 miles an hour.'

Other than returning on 26th August 1903, Major Druitt had played his part correctly without fear or favour and the line was a whole lot safer than it would have been without his authoritative presence. On that last occasion he passed the Manchester & Milford, the Exchange and Rhiwfron sidings. On that occasion he was not wined and dined by the Chairman but there was a little entry in the minutes approving the drawing of a cheque payable to Mr. Rufus Williams, 'Lunch BOT Inspector £2–15–6', so he had been well looked after.

The line would be opening more than eight months later than had been anticipated, and financial difficulties were overwhelming the slender resources which were only finally set into a workable financial state by a very interesting set of monetary juggling. To improve the status of their ordinary shareholdings, the Pethick family sent a cheque for £13,210 thus taking up all the unissued Debenture Stock which was registered in five separate Pethick names. The Engineers then settled Pethicks' Contractors account. Pethicks had lodged a claim for extra payment for work done in excess of that covered by contract, of which some would be for increased prices of materials specified in the price-adjustment clauses. Finally, a last certificate for £4,500 was issued and calls of £1,900 on Pethick-held Ordinary Shares were deemed to have been paid. In consideration of being released from the obligation of maintaining the track for a period after completion, Pethicks were to surrender back to the company £2,000 in Pethick-held Ordinary Shares. It was thereby made possible to pay Davies & Metcalfe for the engines, the Midland Carriage & Wagon & Co Ltd for the rolling stock, and all other various suppliers of equipment. So at last the Vale of Rheidol Light Railway owned all of its undertaking with reasonable prospects of being able to operate it, while Pethicks went on to other activities including the widening of London Bridge.

CHAPTER THREE

ADMINISTRATIVE HISTORY

The Independent Board. 22nd December 1902 to 24th February 1904.

The Traffic Superintendent, Mr. James Rees, persuaded the Chairman to override the Board's decision to start running on 1st January, and the passenger service actually commenced on 22nd December 1902. This was typical of the enthusiastic and extrovert Mr. Rees who had answered an advertisement for a Welsh-speaking officer at a salary of £200 per annum and had been appointed since 1st May 1902 to put together his office and staff. His salary would have the spending power of around £8,000 of 1986 money. As Goods Manager of the Manchester & Milford Railway, he had built up a sound reputation and his custom of taking his young wife out with him on away trips gave rise to the saying that M & MR stood for Mr. and Mrs. Rees. As was the custom in those days, he had to pay for his own fidelity bond in the sum of £250. He worked unpaid for a while and later was able to catch up the deficiency by using the petty cash when there was any. He started with the telegraphic address REES ABERYSTWYTH which was soon altered to VALE ABERYSTWYTH by the London-based Secretary, Mr. John Wood, who was not going to let the man on the spot get too much power into his hands.

Initially he was receiving instructions from the Finance & General Purposes Committee and doing much of the spadework in making arrangements for the Postmaster General, in letting yard space at Devil's Bridge, and in discussing a suitable basis for the Cambrian transfer siding while still running the railway. He also set up the Works Syndicate so that employees could buy small shareholdings and so partake in the future prosperity of the company. All this was too much for the Secretary and the Accountant, Mr. William Pascal Keeling FSAA, who felt that little regard was being accorded to their offices and appointments. Accordingly they got the Board to pass a minute defining the terms of reference and limitations of the office of Traffic Superintendent. Upon him was laid a whole new list of duties, procedures and obligatory weekly returns to London. The list contained some very restrictive omnibus clauses.

He was under no circumstances to 'enter into any agreement which may bind the Company directly or indirectly without proper instructions from the London Office' and 'the duties of his office shall be strictly limited to the conduct of the passengers and goods traffic upon the line, employing and being responsible his staff of men required therefore' and 'all such matters that are incidental to the working thereof and not intended to embrace anything connected with the administration, management or policy of the undertaking'. What a set-down for a hard-working and effective man! Only one tangible good thing came of all this officialdom. Mr. Keeling had his clerk keep a detailed journal made up from James Rees' returns and where he did not understand what the item was or where it would be charged, he set it down with great care in full detail; and so unintentionally he has given us a valuable insight into much minor detail of what had to be bought to run a railway. Only one item has defied interpretation. They frequently bought 'Brobs', which may only have been a form of patent firelighter or even the first 20th century equivalent of a detergent.

So James Rees just had to swallow the insult and get on with the job. By now he had sorted his men out adequately and made his best staffing adjustment by picking out and upgrading driver Thomas Savage to be Locomotive Foreman, with Harry Millman as his assistant. There were none better at their craft. Only one of his station masters was to let him down and get the sack for dipping his fingers into the takings. He never had a deputy and did much of his overseeing by personal visitation. Neither the station masters nor the gangs knew when a door of a slowing train would fly open and disclose their lord and master about to take a running leap to the ground to see what they were about.

Once James Rees had got all working reasonably smoothly, it was realised that something ought to be done about getting publicity from the press. The Chairman and Sir James persuaded a celebrated journalist, 'Sub Rosa' of the *Morning Leader* (Mr. Spencer Leigh Hughes MP), to visit Aberystwyth with his photographer to take a ride up the valley. As Chairman of the Press Gallery, he carried a lot of weight and he wrote a stylish panegyric extolling the virtues of the line and the beauties of the valley. The *Daily Express* lauded both town and valley and 'The King' declared that the Vale of Rheidol Railway was 'The lion of the place'. Ernest Rhys, author, poet and writer for the *Manchester Guardian*, too was liberal in his descriptions and praises. The company kept up a local poster and timetable handout campaign and the bid to obtain tourist traffic was under way. Nor were the postcard firms lagging, and dozens of versions

---

"THE MANCHESTER GUARDIAN" says:

"Leaving Aberystwyth the line does not at once produce its best sensations or offer its true novelties. For a couple of miles it follows much the same route as the Cambrian Railway. It makes its first stop at Llanbadarn Fawr—a place with the rare old towered Church where one of the rarest of mediæval poets lived when he was not wandering all Wales, Dafydd ap Gwilym, the flower of all way-taring minstrelsy. Llanbadarn is a mile-and-a-half from Aberystwyth. Three miles further, and the next station, Capel Bangor, is reached. Now the engine puffs valiantly up one incline after another into the wild recesses of the Vale. At Nantyronen, the next station, six miles-and-a-half from Aberystwyth, the adventurousness of the line, and the delights of the scenery, and the peculiar wayward-ness of the Rheidol must affect even the most callous of railway travellers. And the train goes slow enough to let every point — river, copse, rapid, and rocky falls—be seen and appreciated. It takes about an hour to do the whole twelve miles from Aberystwyth to Devil's Bridge. In that run it climbs at its highest pitch to nearly 800 feet above the sea level. It gives one an indescribable glimpse of the Rheidol Falls en route, and dodges an apparent precipice here and there with much nonchalance, and shows the notorious "Stag" carved in a natural piece of sculpture a little above the Rheidol Falls, and then lands one at its upper terminus, so close to Pont-y-mynach—Monk's or Devil's Bridge, the terms are not interchangeable—that the uproar of the falling waters easily drowns the complacent panting of the engine, its twelve miles climb over.

Extract from the *Manchester Guardian* used in the company's own timetables. *Author's collection*

Devil's Bridge c.1903, possibly the earliest photograph before the flowerbeds were dug or the weighbridge installed. Already the engine crew have been provided with tiny seats (resting on top of the cab) so that they could 'sit out' and keep cool; the engines were little infernos. The message on the back to Mr. H. L. Hopwood reads 'What of the P.W. here?'

Courtesy J. I. C. Boyd

ADMINISTRATIVE HISTORY

Down train on the newly formed Cwmdauddwr embankment c.1903.
Courtesy J. I. C. Boyd

Prince of Wales **posed on the Derwen curve for a publicity photograph. A piece of joist on the top of the tank may be for the ganger. From a hand-coloured print c.1903.** *J. Valentine*

of the train approaching Devil's Bridge along the upper ledges were on sale. Extra trains became necessary and longer trains were put on with *Rheidol*, the small engine, piloting one of the Davies & Metcalfe engines. Up at Devil's Bridge refreshments and other amenites were being considered but not arranged.

On the passenger side, things looked pretty rosy but, just as all the sidings and yards were properly connected and organised, there were signs that the expected goods traffic was never going to match the forecasts. Also this first Board was not particularly adventurous and James Rees could not get them to agree to his suggestions for additional stations and halts, and, quite suddenly, boardroom politics took advantage of the ill-health of the Chairman and that first Board was replaced by one of a totally different character. The effect of the shares taken in lieu of remuneration by both engineers and contractors had been creeping up on the original Board for some little time and now had come the reckoning.

The Pethick and Szlumper Board 25th February 1904 to 4th October 1910

With A. H. Pethick as Chairman and two more Pethicks and Sir James as Directors, control of the company was about as completely sewn up as it could be. It was obviously likely to be a much more go-ahead Board than its predecessor and, apart from a tighter financial control, better things would be in store for the Traffic Superintendent whose better ideas would get adopted. The London offices were moved to those of the Contractors at 115 Victoria Street, and the Secretary resigned 'because it would not be convenient for him to attend at the new offices', and Mr. Massey Sharpe was appointed in his place. Now that construction was complete, the Chairman's fee had already been reduced to £250 per annum, and Sir James bowed out as Consultant Engineer. W. W. Szlumper had also left and Sir James' son, Charles D. Szlumper, was appointed Engineer for the future.

James Rees tried for promotion to the status of General Manager and failed. Mr. Ellis was hanging onto his Director's Gold Pass which Mr. Massey was trying to recover to hand to Mr. N. F. Pethick, and Mr. Montague Smith had duly handed over two keys to the company seal when they found out that he was secretly trying to hang on to yet a third. Mr. Sharpe only got

Train approaching Quarry Cutting. There were many other versions published, including this one retouched to convert it into a snow scene for Christmas. In another the engine, lost in shadow, was retouched to look like a 4—4—0. *Courtesy of D. C. Clayton*

A wealth of detail at Devil's Bridge c.1907. Most noteworthy are the chance views of ex-Hafan wagons Nos. 16 (a bit of one end) and No. 10, the end of a drop side-door wagon and of the flat truck cut down from one of the Hafans. *E. T. W. Dennis & Sons*

ADMINISTRATIVE HISTORY

21

The service was in reality far from perfect and a local cartoonist soon seized on its slightly erratic character.
Courtesy J. I. C. Boyd

£28 per annum, payable quarterly, which would be something below £1,000 of 1986 money.

James Rees soon got his authority to open the additional stations and halts and the refreshment facilities. Also timber trade was looking up and he got the derrick crane at Devil's Bridge (secondhand from Pethicks). Besides these good things, he got something not so good, a descent from on high by the new Chairman and Sir James for a detailed look at his records and systems. That one station master was dismissed, the Traffic Superintendent really got his knuckles rapped, and a load of extra precautions and returns was laid upon him. They ended 1904 by removing his power of settling increases for the staff and by refusing his own application for an increase.

For 1905, arrangements were completed for the carriage of mail, and the Postmaster General agreed to a payment of £120 per annum provided that one special mail train ran each day. And so began those little early morning and evening runs of *Rheidol* with one coach and a van and sometimes two coaches in the summer.

In 1907 James Rees had another visitation; this time the Accountant, Mr. Keeling, examined his records and reported to the Board that they were satisfactory. By the end of 1907 the amounts borrowed were due for repayment but the Debenture Holders refused to accept Debenture Stock in lieu of repayment and it was agreed that the Debentures be renewed until 1910. Dividend had dropped from 3% to 2½%. In 1908 there were distinct signs of panic and an even more stringent financial control was introduced. Nothing could be paid without the authority of the Board itself, cheques could only be signed at Board meetings and the bank pass book was to be produced at each meeting.

On 6th July 1908 the Board met at Aberystwyth for a change, and had a full tour of inspection along the Harbour Branch (one coach and *Rheidol?*) and then all the way to Devil's Bridge. They stopped specially at the ballast siding to discuss the complaints of Mrs. Anne Morgan (see under Geufron Siding). Also the Traffic Superintendent had reported the disagreement he had been having with the farmer at Troed-rhiw-felen. His stockmen had been leaving the gates open to save the bother of opening and shutting them each time cattle were driven up from the lower fields for milking. Nobody was taking Mr. Rees too seriously and

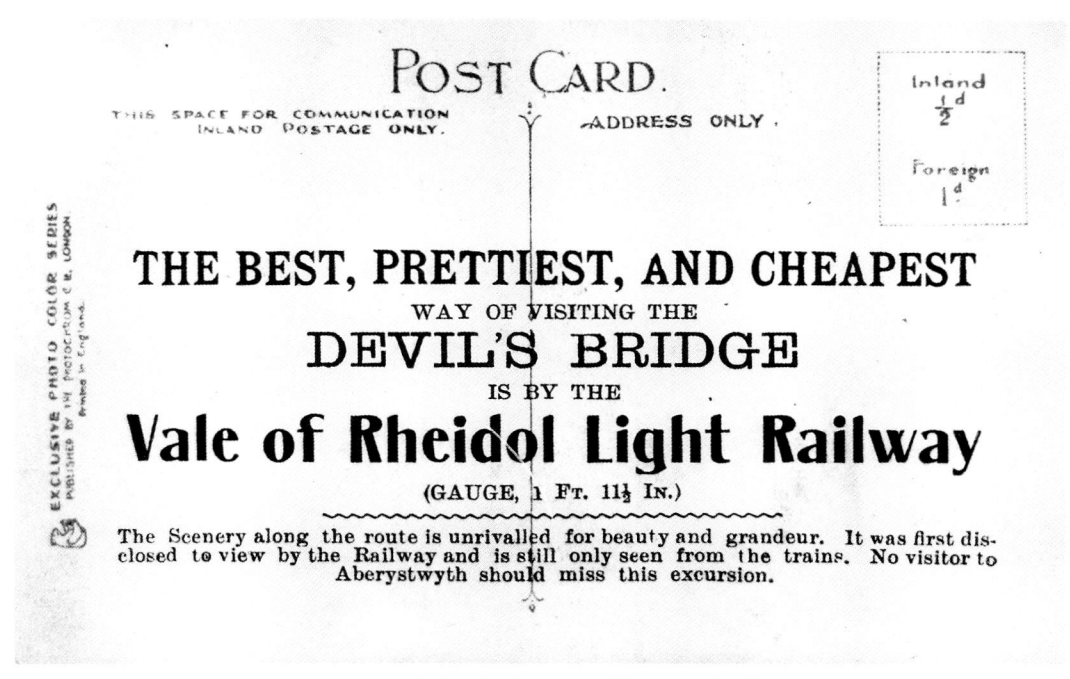

Advert on the back of a postcard (see page 158).

Rheidol about to leave Aberystwyth, showing station and awning, c.1910.

A. J. Lewis

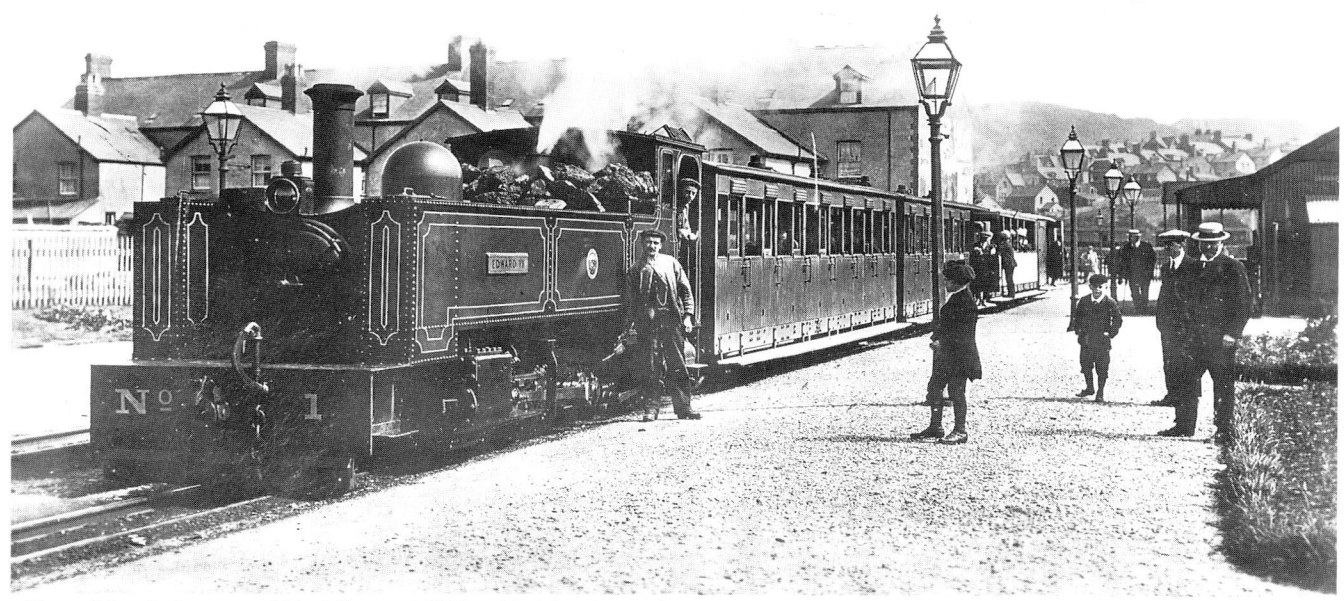

The striking dual green and black livery of 1910, with driver Evan Lloyd Jones and fireman 'Jack Bach' Davies. *Kingsway Series*

the farmer protested in all assumed innocence that none of his men would be so careless or so lazy. And when that little unscheduled early morning special came puffing up there were the open gates and a collection of red faces.

At 10.30 a.m. the Board solemnly jammed itself into the Traffic Superintendent's office and held the meeting. A most strongly-worded letter was to be sent to the farmer at Troed-rhiw-felen re 'the malpractices of his servants'. As he had also been trying to bring a claim for stock injured because of the poor state of the fencing, he was told that the Board considered that the gates and fencing were in good repair and that no additional work was needed.

On 5th May 1909 Mr. Rees received the well-merited title of General Manager and a £20 per annum increase in salary, and in June the contracts of the Engineer and Secretary were renewed for a further three years, all of which suggest that the event which was so totally to alter the company next year was as yet unforeseen. The Board visited Aberystwyth again to look at the Cambrian Railways' proposal that the Vale of Rheidol should extend its terminus into the main Cambrian station. Then it was discovered that the Great Western Railway Company's power to acquire land between had just lapsed and the proposal was dropped.

It was during the last few years of this Board that the potential of making open-air vehicles from which the tourists could appreciate the lovely fresh air and marvellous high-level views was understood. Two timber trucks were made into 'toast-racks' during the summers and three bogie coaches were also opened up for the hardy. To take care of the increase in local trade and in the timber trade, six convertible dropside/bolster wagons were put on the line. Also two closed carriages had adjustments made to provide first-class accommodation. 1910 was the first year in which the Territorial Army was encamped at Lovesgrove and this led to gas generators being placed in the three vans and

---

GEORGE BORROW,

The Famous Scholar and Traveller, having visited

DEVIL'S BRIDGE,

declared it to be

"One of the Most Remarkable Localities in the World."

IT CAN NOW BE REACHED BY THE

VALE OF RHEIDOL RAILWAY.

Full particulars and pamphlets gratis can be obtained on application to

JAMES REES, General Manager,
ABERYSTWYTH.

One of James Rees' publicity notices. *Author's collection*

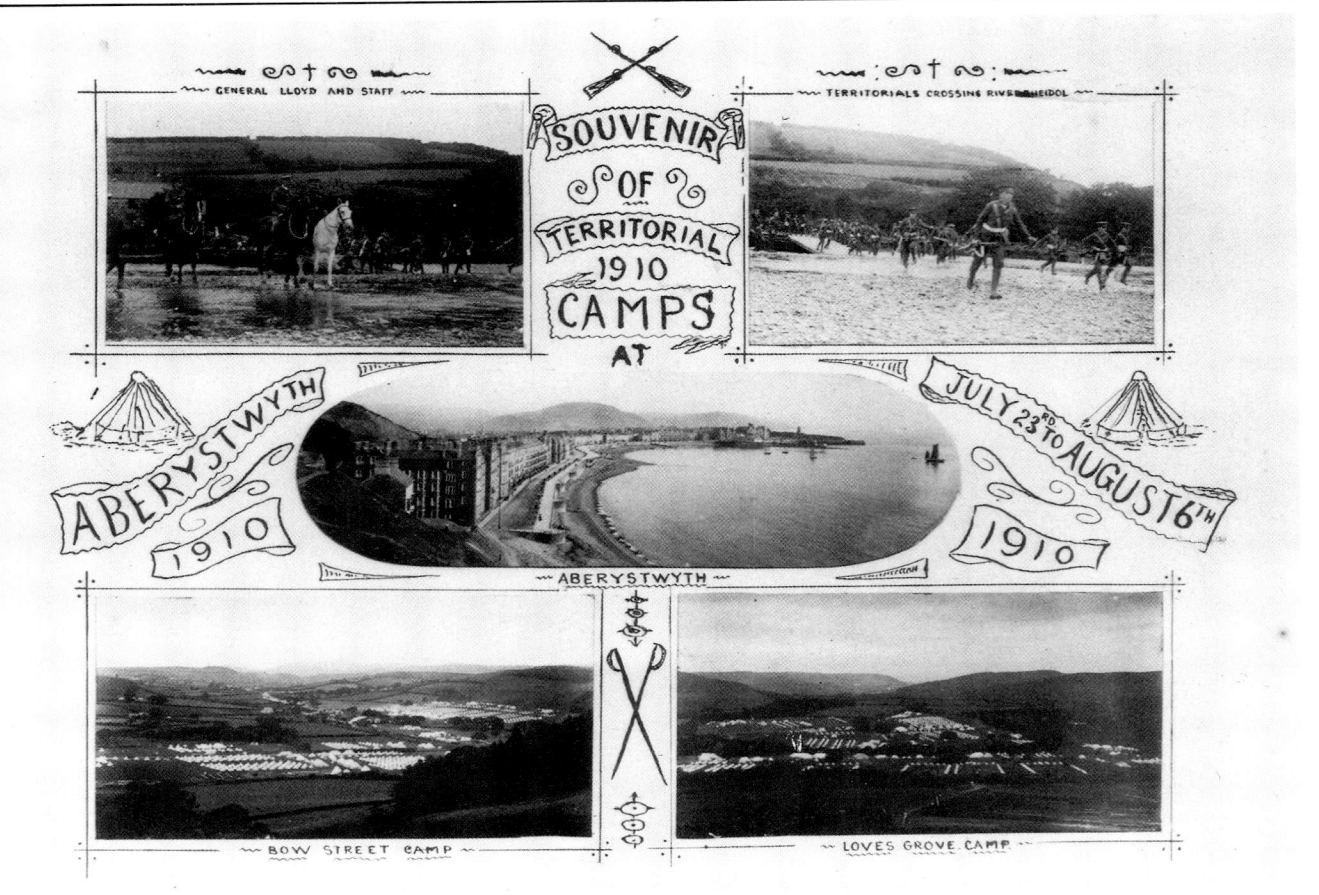

In this souvenir card of 1910 the lower right picture, taken from the hillside above Lovesgrove, shows the three pontoon bridges in situ. The two top views show them in use for training in river crossing by assault.
A. J. Lewis

to gaslighting in all the coaches. The General Manager was complimented on the manner in which he had dealt with the extra military traffic and was granted an honorarium of twelve guineas, which would be about £400 in 1986, so it was quite a generous award. It was the Board's last showing of their appreciation as the storm over the other Directors not siding with Pethicks over the Aberayron Extension Contract was about to break.

The Cambrian Board 5th October 1910 to 30th June 1913

On 5th October 1910 the company found itself once more effectively under entirely new management after the Pethick family had agreed to transfer all their holdings to nominees of the Cambrian Railways Company. All the Pethicks retired from the Board and in their places appeared the Cambrian Chairman, John Connacher, as Chairman, and as Directors there appeared Mr. Thomas Craven, DL, JP, who was the Cambrian's Deputy Chairman, and two more Cambrian Directors, Mr. Alfred Herbert and Mr. Charles Bridger Orme Clarke. Mr. Clarke would become the Chairman's assistant in Vale of Rheidol matters. Later Alfred Herbert, who was Chairman of the Cambrian-backed Aberystwyth Queen's Hotel Company, would take over as Chairman when Connacher fell ill.

The venue for meetings shifted to the usual Cambrian place, the Euston Hotel. Fire insurance was shifted from the Alliance to the Ocean, Accident and Guarantee Corporation, and boiler insurance was terminated as the Cambrian carried it under their own arrangements. An account with Hoares Bank was closed. Other share transfers took place and the dividend fell to $1\frac{1}{2}\%$. The connection with the Great Western via the Manchester & Milford siding was ripped out. Mr. Keeling was allowed to stay on until the end of 1911 by reason of his agreement but he was 'relieved of his duties forthwith'. The Secretary was instructed to 'forward to Oswestry all books, documents, papers etc., the property of the Company'. On and from the 5th April 1911 the minutes appear in the beautiful professional copperplate handwriting of the Oswestry clerical staff, as the Cambrian Secretary, Mr. A. S. Williamson, was to be Acting Secretary to the Rheidol Board. More shares were being registered in the names of John Connacher and Alfred Herbert. Pethicks gave the newcomers a nominal push by issuing notice to the Board to quit the use of the Pethick offices at 115 Victoria Street. Rheidol accounts had to be produced to the Board certified by the Secretary before any cheques might be sent out 'as circumstances permit'.

When it was found that the Great Western had taken over the local motor coaches, the Cambrian sought to hire from another source (for tours from Devil's Bridge).

The first out of the ordinary item they had to deal with was a letter from Principal T. F. Roberts of the University College of Wales and from the Reverend F. Warburton asking for no trains to be run on Sundays. The Board agreed to curtail 'as far as possible' and not to run any during October 1911. The search for another motor hirer was successful and an agreement was entered into between the Cambrian and Commercial Car Hirers Ltd of London. On 3rd July 1911 they held a Board tour of inspection which passed off without comment.

As from 1st January 1912 the net was drawn tighter still. Supervision of locomotives and rolling stock devolved upon the Cambrian's Locomotive Superintendent, Herbert E. Jones. H. Warwick became also Superintendent of the Line to both Cambrian and the Rheidol, and the Cambrian's Engineer, George C. MacDonald, relieved Szlumper of his duties. One matter arising directly from this was an approach to Bagnalls for revisionary designs for the valve gear of the two larger locomotives. This followed the Board's call for reports on the condition of locomotives, rolling stock and permanent way. Then a prominent electric traction company volunteered a fully-costed scheme for building a reservoir and running the line by hydro-electrically generated motive power. No details as to where the reservoir etc. were to have been have so far come to light but nothing came of this last way-out idea and in any case it could never have been paid for. More practicable was a proposal for three new open coaches, for tourism was definitely booming, and less so was the expense of buying a fourth locomotive. To help to carry the additional and now regular military traffic, the six dropside/bolster convertibles were coupled in two rakes of three, with vacuum piping and seats. When returning empty these proved most popular with the tourists. For the 1912 season the Chairman was authorised to hire a locomotive from the Festiniog Railway for the first time. After the death of John Connacher, his place on the Rheidol Board was taken by another prominent Cambrian celebrity, Lieutenant-Colonel David Davies MP. On 11th June 1912 Samuel Williamson was formally appointed Secretary and 'Registered Officer under the Railway Companies' Securities Act 1866 and Company's Authorised Agent in Bankruptcy Proceedings'. The lein fach was about to become properly recorded, controlled and, alas, regimented. Foreman platelayer Fred Stanton was given three months notice but luckily he found employment with the Great Western. The public were not to be affected by the impending changes for James Rees was still at Aberystwyth looking directly after their comfort. The Rheidol's last independent bank account was closed and the balance of £1,800 was paid into the Cambrian Company's account. Meetings of the Rheidol Board were to be held immediately after a meeting of the Cambrian Board.

So, on 6th November 1912, proposals for the formal absorption of the Rheidol undertaking were considered. The monetary offer was £15,022 Cambrian A Debentures for £16,900 of Rheidol Debentures, and £12,715 of Cambrian A Debentures for the £51,000 of Rheidol Ordinary Stock, or less than a quarter of the money put in in 1898. Amalgamation would be effective as from 1st July 1913. There was a special Proprietors' General Meeting at the Euston Hotel on 14th February 1913 attended

The shed gang c.1910. Left to right: Bert Walton, boilersmith from Swindon, borrowed via old M & M connection to work on *Rheidol*, driver Evan Lloyd Jones, driver J. E. Davies, fitter Harry Millman, carpenter William Evan, foreman Tom Savage, guard Nat Humphries.
Courtesy E. Savage

Devil's Bridge c.1912 showing three of the box-timber trucks converted as troop carriers.   *Courtesy E. W. Hannan*

by the Cambrian's nominees and Sir James Szlumper armed with all manner of proxy votes. There was one dissenter, a Mr. E. J. Evans who disapproved by threatening 'I shall object and get local bodies to do so unless my shares which are 180 and my friends shares 70 are acquired by the Cambrian Railways at full price'. Of course he did not stand a chance and the motion of acceptance was easily passed. And when the time came for settlement he had to confess that he had lost his certificate, and didn't Samuel Williamson rub his nose in it? Of him was required a full Form of Indemnity countersigned by the Manager of the National Provincial Bank. In vain he protested, but had to submit or lose his money. There was another objection in the form of a letter from a former Cambrian General Manager, Mr. Charles Sherwood Denniss, who seemed to fear that issue of additional Cambrian A Debentures on (for then) such a scale would depress the market value of his own holding.

The Great Western Railway insisted on the insertion of clauses protecting their traffic with the Rheidol line, but since this was by now almost non-existent re-connection of the Manchester & Milford siding was not insisted upon.

And so the arrangements for the extinction of the Vale of Rheidol Light Railway as an independent entity were complete.

There was a final Half Yearly Ordinary Meeting of the Rheidol Company on 12th September 1913 and the last dividend paid was four-fifths of one percent. So died a valiant little Railway Company and with it foundered more than three quarters of its ordinary shareholders' money. Of the original promoters, only John Francis remained true to the end, plus a handful of people in Aberystwyth. A surprising loser was the great firm of Brunner, Mond & Co Ltd who had bought shares in 1909 when they leased the Cwmystwyth Mine. Strange to relate, but that astute accountant, Mr. William Pascal Keeling, who held shares originally as a matter of protocol, had sold all his somewhat earlier. Also someone seemed to have got the Works Syndicate out of it.

A Branch of the Cambrian Railways. 1st July 1913 to 31st December 1921

The Cambrian Railways Board had set up a special Parliamentary Committee which met first on 11th June 1912 to settle the general scope of the proposed Bill and again on 6th July at the Castle Hotel, Brecon, for the convenience of Lieutenant Colonel David Davies. This second meeting instructed the General Manager to prepare the scheme for the acquisition of the Vale of Rheidol undertaking which would be incorporated into the Cambrian Railways Act 1913, which took effect on 1st July.

Henceforth Rheidol matters would be dealt with by the Finance Committee or, more often, by the Traffic and Works Committee, and there would be no more entertaining boardroom shenanigans. A highlight of future four-day annual tours of inspection by the Board and Committees would be the journey along the Rheidol Branch. There was a last spate of money-saving adjustments to insurances, including the discontinuance of the Workman's Compensation Policy as the Rheidol

Up train on Rheidol Bridge in 1921, showing the Cambrian abutment which replaced that old timber protection disliked by Major Druitt.
W. L. Good

Group at Devil's Bridge in 1921. Left to right: Richard Jones, Will Jenkins, ganger Isaac Jenkins, guard Owen Hopkins, Edward Davies, John Morgan, L. F. Jones, driver J. E. Davies.
Courtesy J. E. Davies

VALE OF RHEIDOL RAILWAY.
Time Table, Tuesday, July 1st, to Tuesday, Sept. 30th, 1913.

UP TRAINS.		WEEK DAYS.								SUNDAYS.	
	a.m.	a.m.	a.m.	a.m.	a.m.	p.m.	p.m.	p.m.	p.m.	p.m.	p.m.
Aberystwyth, dep.	7 0	8 b 30	9 50	10 50	12c30	2 0	3 0	6 30	8 45	2 15	3 d 0
Llanbadarn ,,	7 5	8 b 35	9 55	10 55	...	2 5	3 5	6 35	8 50	2 20	3 d 5
Glanrafon ,,	7 10	8 b 40	...	11 0	...	...	3 10	6 40	8 55	2 25	3 d 10
Capel Bangor ,,	7 20	8 b 50	10 10	11 10	12c50	2 20	3 20	6 50	9 5	2 35	3 d 20
Nantyronen ,,	7 30	...	...	11 20	...	...	3 30	7 0	Mon., Wed., and Sats., during Aug.	2 45	3 d 30
Aberffrwd ,,	7 38	9 b 8	10 28	11 28	...	2 38	3 38	7 6		2 53	3 d 38
Rheidol Falls ,,	a	...	a	a	...	a	a	a		3 4	...
Rhiwfron ,,	a	...	...	...	...	...	...	a		a	...
Devil's Bridge arr	8 0	9 b 30	10 55	11 55	1c30	3 5	4 5	7 30		3 20	4 d 0
DOWN TRAINS.	a.m.	a.m.	p.m.	p.m.	p.m.	p.m.	p.m.	p.m.	p.m.	p.m.	p.m.
Devil's Bridge, dep.	8 15	11 5	1 40	3 c 15	4 25	5 25	7 45	Mon., Wed., and Sats., during Aug.	5 0	7 d 0
Rhiwfron ,,	8 20	11 10	1 45	3 c 20	...	5 30	7 50		...	...
Rheidol Falls ,,	8 30	11 20	1 55	3 c 30	4 40	5 40	8 0		5 15	7 d 15
Aberffrwd ,,	8 40	11 30	2 5	3 c 38	4 50	5 50	8 10		5 25	7 d 25
Nantyronen ,,	8 45	11 35	2 10	3 c 43	4 55	5 55	8 15		5 30	7 d 30
Capel Bangor ,,	8 55	11 45	2 20	3 c 53	5 5	6 5	8 25	9 15	5 40	7 d 40
Glanrafon ,,	9 5	11 55	2 30	4 c 5	5 15	6 15	8 35	9 25	5 50	7 d 50
Llanbadarn ,	9 10	12 0	2 35	4 c 10	5 20	6 20	8 40	9 30	5 55	7 d 55
Aberystwyth arr.	9 15	12 5	2 40	4 c 15	5 25	6 25	8 45	9 35	6 0	8 d 0

a—Calls when required to set down passengers on notice being given to the Guard of the train at the preceding stopping station. b—Runs August 4th to 8th only.
c—Runs July 21st to September 15th. d—Runs July 6th to September 14th.

Pink card timetable of the first services to be run by Cambrian Railways. Author's collection

employees would now be covered by the provisions of the Cambrian's own fund. There was, too, a nasty little instruction to the General Manager 'to resist any attempt by Vale of Rheidol staff to gain parity with Cambrian employees'.

Generally the company and its staff were pleased with the idea of running the now celebrated little line and some quite good plans for improvement were drawn up, but, as was usual with the Cambrian, they were a bit slow off the mark, and these good ideas were overtaken by the 1914–18 Great War. Having found they could hire an engine from the Festiniog meant that neither was there a fourth engine nor new valve gear for the Davies & Metcalfe engines, and the three new open carriages never turned up either. Instead there was a string of fresh and tighter measures for financial control and economy, and when the Rheidol costs appeared first in the returns, Herbert Jones found himself having to explain why there had been an increase in wages, locomotive running costs and coal.

Mr. Rees was dismissed from his post of General Manager because the branch was now 'being controlled from Headquarters and can in future be supervised by the District Inspector and canvassing be done by the Coast District Agent'. He went on to a sound post as District Goods Manager at Oswestry, but still looked on at what was happening to his railway with considerable sadness. In time there arose a fresh 'Mr. Rheidol' in the person of Lewis Hamer who as station master was still caring for it in the 1950s.

During the war passenger services were cut to the limit, but there was a good income from timber cut for pit-props. Also the Cwmrheidol Mine came briefly to life once again, and on the bend at 9¾ miles the Erwtomau Mine was opened up to tap the lodes of the Rheidol United complex. Track was allowed to deteriorate into an appalling state and the only modifications to the locomotives were the setting-back of the brake handles to give more room for the fireman and an increase in coal capacity to enable enough of the Cambrian's poorer quality coal to be carried to be sure of completing the run.

When the attempt to sort out the parlous state of the country's railways by forming 'The Big Four' was made in 1922, the Rheidol, along with the rest of the Cambrian, dropped into the hands of the Great Western Railway Company, and once again the original shareholders got done. Having already lost on a basis of one for four, they got only two GWR for three Cambrian shares.

A Branch of the Great Western Railway Company. 1st January 1922 to 31st December 1947

The GWR already had a large number of Welshmen on the payroll and the Cambrian and Rheidol men only just missed the chance of taking part in an Eisteddfod held inside Swindon Works in the previous November. The new area was first called The Cambrian Division, but it was soon realised that this was a tactical error which would perpetuate distinction and the area was rapidly renamed The Central Wales Division. Now pinstripe trousers, spats and bowler hats would get right up to Devil's Bridge and the branch would be run to as near main line standards as possible. The entire GWR hierarchy took their new little acquisition to their hearts and gave it all in their powers they could give. Without that sudden surge of first-class attention the line could never have survived to be re-opened in 1945 after the second world war.

The men fared less well initially, and their earlier service would not be credited towards their pensions and the GWR scheme of that time was not liberal. Eventually they were raised to parity with the main line employees and the loco crews would go onto the main rotas and be seen on footplates at Pwllheli, Carmarthen, Shrewsbury and Birmingham. Of the Cambrian middle management, most received golden handshakes, but C. M. Colclough took his knowledge of and regard for the Rheidol locomotives to a good promotion at Swindon Works. His father, E. Colclough, stayed at Oswestry to become Divisional Superintendent so the Rheidol still had old friends in both places who, now that money was available, would be able to see done what they would have wished to do under the Cambrian régime.

The GWR's Chief Mechanical Engineer, C. B. Collett, received authority to construct two brand-new locomotives of a design very like that produced originally by Davies & Metcalfe

About to leave the old terminus c.1924. Coach No. 15 has been repainted in GWR style with garter crest, arm and wing. The second coach is still in Cambrian livery.
F. Moore

which were put onto the rails at Aberystwyth in 1923. Earlier on he had sent the works photographer to Aberystwyth to take a photograph which would convince the management that new open carriages were also urgently needed. The result was authority to build four new open carriages which were given the delightful designation of 'Summer Cars' and these, too, arrived in 1923. Then in 1924, under the guise of a heavy repair, Collett turned out a third brand-new locomotive to the same drawings. One of the original Davies & Metcalfe engines was rebuilt and kept as a spare and the second and little *Rheidol* were scrapped.

In the 1926 rebuild of Aberystwyth station, the line was extended across Park Avenue so that the new point of departure lay alongside Platform 5 the old M & MR bay. Access was across the back of the bay, and tickets were henceforth bought at the main ticket office. When Sir Felix Pole, the GWR's General Manager, wrote to the Mayor advising him that he would be visiting Aberystwyth to inspect the progress of the new work, his letter was ignored, so he ordered the omission of all non-essential finishing work. If the Council couldn't be bothered to take an interest in the improvement of the town's facilities he wasn't going to be bothered to spend any unnecessary money on them. Fortunately he did not suspend any work on the Rheidol. The permanent way, too, was undergoing that much-needed replacement of sleepers by the thousand.

Cattle trucks were a new innovation, but traffic was being captured by road transport and the line was closed for goods traffic as from 1st January 1927, the cattle trucks being re-gauged for use on the Welshpool & Llanfair. The closed carriages became steam-heated. Regular passenger services were withdrawn after 31st December 1930. The GWR publicity system did the Rheidol Branch quite well and, as run for tourists only during the summer, the line was showing a profit. As a result,

the management were able to justify the building of twelve new coaches on steel underframes in 1938, the year in which they tried to enforce their ridiculous edict that no working instructions should henceforth be given in Welsh. The line was closed during the war from the end of the 1939 season. In 1940 a new work was completed that was to have a far-reaching effect on the line nearly forty years later. A 210 ft long engine shed was built as a replacement on the same site as the demolished old Cambrian 150 footer.

During the war the three locomotives were kept under cover in the sheds and the carriages were sheeted over, but anti-deterioration maintenance was carried out regularly and there were no problems when the time came for re-starting the service on 23rd July 1945 on weekdays only. The track was still in good order.

By application of the Transport Act 1947 the GWR passed into history and yet again the old shareholders were defrauded on transfer.

Part of Western Region. 1st January 1948 to 14th July 1963

Now the tiny line was well and truly somewhere in the bottom layer of an enormous pyramid. It was a unique situation for a railway based entirely on tourism. Its character should have assured it accord as a national asset of Wales, a status worthy of its own preservation order. Management was based at Shrewsbury, with Oswestry responsible for general mechanical maintenance. Some carriage-painting would be done there while the locomotives would still go to Swindon for all work other than running adjustments. The man on the spot was still the station master of Aberystwyth, Mr. Lewis Hamer, and he was as keen as ever to

On the 6¼ mile curve in September 1959.

have his beloved lein fach running effectively. Someone had the good sense to adopt the maroon and cream livery, usually reserved for gangwayed passenger stock, at the first repaint of the carriages, which suited them very well and they still showed up at a distance on the mountainsides.

After the abolition of the Railway Executive in 1953, the Chairman of the British Transport Commission announced the comprehensive plan for the modernisation of British Railways which included the upgrading of the track and civil engineering works so that trains could be run at 100 miles per hour. Unfortunately, nobody seems to have told the two Rheidol gangs about this or even have taken care that they were given enough sleepers to keep the track in the condition in which British Rail had received it from the GWR.

Indeed, in 1954 came strong rumours that the Rheidol was not considered to have any place in the bright new future of BR and that it was to follow the Corris into oblivion. A number of railway enthusiasts took notice and wrote letters to magazines and newspapers. The locos were repainted in splendid style once again, full Western Region express green with lining, and the coaches reappeared in a version of the old GWR chocolate and cream. This was arranged without formal authority by Oliver Veltom, a quiet Cornishman who had adopted Wales as his home and the Vale of Rheidol as his special railway. VOR was from then on held to mean Veltom's Own Railway.

With something fresh to show, the publicity took a brighter turn and things really looked up from the 1957 season on. That Easter the author was waiting by the bridge for a photograph but at the due time there was no warning whistle in the distance. Minutes passed and it was half an hour before the whistling for the Park Avenue crossing was heard, then for Plascrug and lastly for Llanbadarn. A large plume of steam betokened an engine working hard, and patience was rewarded with a photograph of an immaculate seven-coach train. Back at Aberystwyth, also immaculate as always, was Mr. Lewis Hamer with his gold braid spotless and shining and a beautiful rose in his buttonhole, but almost dancing with delight. 'Did you see the train Mr. Green? Four coaches I had to put on, then we had to set back for two more, and then we had to go for another.' The Rheidol might not be getting the personalised care and attention which was being lavished on the preserved railways like the Talyllyn or the Festiniog, but it was once again receiving the best attention the professionals could give it.

While all seemed to be going well down at Aberystwyth, from elsewhere came three unpleasant warnings. In 1955 the new motorways construction programme was announced, in 1956 BR disclosed its first outright loss of £16,500,000 under the new accounting procedures, and the other nationalised narrow-gauge railway, the Welshpool & Llanfair was closed.

The publicity campaign was kept up and returns still seemed to be keeping up with costs. By 1959 Lewis Hamer had retired and Mr. Harry Rees, the Senior District Relieving Station Master, took over as 'Mr. Rheidol'. A keen railwayman with a great interest in and knowledge of the history of the railways of Central Wales, he arranged the first of the modern photographic publicity displays on Aberystwyth station.

Then the Gillebaud Committee recommended an 18% increase in the wages of railwaymen and, against a background of rising costs, decreasing custom and extending motorways, the government announced further new measures. As is customary when something nasty is about to happen, names were changed yet again. Away went the British Transport Commission and it was replaced by the British Railways Board, presided over by Dr. Richard Beeching. He had been head of the BTC since 1961 and had been mainly responsible for the Transport Act 1962. Against this background the Rheidol jogged quietly on with some slight improvement in receipts until rationalisation of areas supervened and the influence of Western Region was withdrawn from Central Wales.

In the deep cutting beyond Cwmdauddwr, in June 1955.

Rheidol approaching the Cwm-yr-ogos Horseshoe Bend, c.1906.

Courtesy J. I. C. Boyd

CHAPTER FOUR
THE PERMANENT WAY

In case readers used to the more conventional accounts of such matters may imagine that some of the ensuing must be figments of the author's imagination, it was his privilege to have known men who worked for Pethicks and many of the events can be verified from Minutes and Reports.

The releasing of Pethicks from all their contractual obligations as to maintenance of the formation and track, thrust a great load upon foreman platelayer Fred Stanton and his four gangs. Admittedly, the preliminary Board of Trade inspection in July 1902, with its attendant derailments, had brought about the correction of the over-sharp bends, but both inspections had not revealed many less-apparent insecurities in the formation. River-polished stones and Silurian flinders were a most unsatisfactory combination as ballast, and the Cwmdauddwr embankment, a curve round a rock bluff at $10\frac{1}{4}$ to $10\frac{1}{2}$ miles, the Nant-ar-fynwg bend and the embankment carrying the line into Quarry Cutting, were constantly settling and needing repacking.

Also there were hundreds of yards of formation where, in measuring the 7 ft only ledge to be cut away from the hillside, Pethicks had included the scanty and fragile layer of vegetative covering lying thinly on top of the rock. After being loaded with the material cut and used to widen the visual ledge, it would shear away leaving long cracks parallel to the rails and just under the sleeper ends as soon as the first heavy rains fell. The gangs had to tamp narrow ledges a few feet downhill and try to build back upwards until the sleepers were once again fully supported. Only a narrow rebuild at a time was feasible; too much and it would promptly shear off gaining them nothing. In particular, the three embankments and the bad patch went on settling and spreading their bases. Again and again the culverts at Cwmdauddwr and Nant-ar-fynwg had to be lengthened a little, and they had to burrow into the bank below Quarry Cutting to get some lateral drainage in. When a ledge settled really badly trains were flagged across slowly and coaches were seen to lean outwards.

Nor were these the gangs' only problems; there was all that second-hand rail. Sir James may have convinced Major Druitt that 'The permanent way consists of second-hand flanged steel rails of weights varying from 48 lbs to 60 lbs per yard' and that the sleepers were 'Baltic timber or local larch $4'6''$ long $\times 9'' \times 4\frac{1}{2}''$,' but the gangs knew differently. There was very little at 60 lbs per yard, a lot at 32 lbs per yard and some below 30. There were cripples with damage to flange and web, there were hollowbacks and there were hogbacks. There were many differing cross-sections of the same weight and much variation in the quality of the metal. A skilled ganger could assess the feel of the rail with a tentative first tightening of the 'Jim Crow', that would tell him what he had got, and just how much to over-tighten, so that when the rail had sprung back it would have settled into the required curve. Mr. Isaac Jenkins has left a written account of all this in which he has reckoned that in all there were over thirty variations of weight, section and quality in that sorry lot of contractor's rubbish. There was even a bit of old plain iron. They really must have scoured the abandoned sidings of half Devon and Cornwall to find it. The points were new from Thomas Summerson and Sons at approximately £10 a set, but these had been bent up to give a gap of $1\frac{1}{2}$ inches at the checkrails with an over-generous allowance for settlement.

So they finished at nearer 2 inches gap which did little to steady the 4 ft coach bogies, leaving an over-long drop at the vee which later on *Palmerston* was not going to like one little bit.

The sleepers were a mixture of oak and larch, and Pethicks' instructions as to the use of waney and half-log was 'Chisel 3" to bear', and this without soleplates and mostly only two dog-spikes per rail, or only four dogspikes to hold both rails down and to gauge in any one sleeper. The only trace of coach-screwing was at $4'' \times 2''$ clips on either side of joints. Mr. Waddingham had given all the sleepering needed down to the edge of his estate just above $11\frac{1}{4}$ miles, and an agricultural steam engine and sawbench were set up there to provide them newly felled. Many a dogspike fractured in that fresh dense sappy timber.

Some places in the formation could need repacking only three days after the previous attendance, and, besides all that, the gangs' duties included signal maintenance, building maintenance and new work, as well as standing in for staff shortages in any other trades. Mr. Isaac Jenkins has recalled that when Aberffrwd station was newly opened, he issued and collected tickets and worked the tablet instruments from 6 o'clock in the morning until 9 o'clock at night, and while there was nothing happening in particular he went back to digging out the recess in the hillside to house the water tanks at the east end.

While this intensive programme of recovery from contractors' shortcomings was going on, the problems arising from the use of insecure ballast on a mountain railway were beginning to cause another sort of trouble. When a train is ascending and is working hard, the engine in gripping the rails is trying to drag the track downhill towards the train and only the ballast can prevent it. Similarly, when a train is coasting downhill with brakes on, the entire train is trying to take the track down the hill with it which again only the ballast can prevent. With the poor quality of the ballast, curves round rock-faces were being dragged nearer to the rock, and baulk strutting had to be placed between sleeper ends and the rock. Where the bend was an incurve, the movement was towards the edge of the formation and the gangs had to dig up all the shingle and replace it with the best they could contrive by widening the Quarry Cutting. The incurable enemy on a mountain line is climate. As the sun warms the rails they expand downhill. During the chill of the night the rails contract, but never creep back quite to the old position, especially when there are only two dogspikes and no soleplates. This the gangs had to remedy by loosening a range of fishplates and by crow-barring rail after rail uphill and back into place. Of course, what with the poor quality of some of the rail and with mild iron fishplates, both snapped frequently. No ganger on dawn patrol went without spare fishplates and bits of spare rail to bridge any gaps. No wonder four gangs were needed until 1908. These fishplates were extra-long and were drilled at one end only. Rail breakages only took place across the weakest point, the lower of the fishplate boltholes. So the damaged bit was taken out and a suitable piece put back clasped by the long fishplate. The train would be flagged over the temporary repair and the full gang would repair the break properly later on.

Later still, uneven wear on the sleepers would start the rails canting and the whole lot would have to be lifted, re-faced and set back with packing plates. Mostly, and almost entirely because of the devotion to the job on the part of his staff, the Traffic

Superintendent managed to keep things rolling without having to appeal to London for assistance. Only occasionally did he expend money rather than time which was much cheaper, such as when small quantities of explosive were bought. One lot was for rock for shoring up the river bank above the $1\frac{3}{4}$ milepost and there was '2 lbs Nobel's Dynamite for Station Repairs 2 shillings from the Rheidol Mining Co.'. Looking at the quantities taken out of Quarry Cutting the gangs, several of whom had been miners, had their own ways of getting a bit of explosive when it was needed.

In 1904 the gangs had to raise Plascrug Crossing some 18 inches at the complaint of the Borough Surveyor despite his having passed it at the level constructed on the deposited plans. Once they were on the job, which was designated 'fettling and lifting', they were made to raise all another 15 inches to get level with the Cambrian track before the Council was finally satisfied. At the same time complaints were received that the low banking was causing flooding of fields on the uphill side of the line around Llanbadarn but the only landowner to get extra drainage was the University College of Wales at what is now the Blaendolau Playing Fields. Mr. Richardes of Aberffrwd wanted a sheep bridge and extra-fine fencing mesh; but he did not get the bridge. The fencing must have been inadequate since on three occasions up to 1905 the Company had to pay for sheep and lambs killed by trains. 10 shillings was the going rate for a sheep and at one instance six lambs were run down.

Already, after only three years, 600 sleepers had to be bought locally to remedy defects, and in 1905 the Engineer had to put in an urgent order to Sisterson's for 5 tons of new rail which would amount to about 220 yards of single rail. 1906 was a year of trouble. First there was a collapse in Quarry Cutting which did give the gangs a bonus of 350 tons of rock for ballast. Then the decay of the green sapling and brushwood Pethicks had used to stabilise the Cwmdauddwr embankment caused it to subside and fracture the culvert. The gangs put in a concrete arch cast over an arch-form of old rail. William Hughes claimed successfully for cattle killed through getting onto the line because of defective fencing. Farmer Richardes involved his claim for loss of stock with his unsettled claim over purchase of his land and also won. Mrs Anne Morgan was making trouble too as the

Double-headed train approaching Rheidol Falls, with Mr. Sheraton, W. H. Smith's agent, on the footplate. Note the casual staggering of rail joints, 2 bolts only per fishplate, and rails laid bare on the deteriorating loggy sleepers held by only 4 dogs per sleeper. *A. J. Lewis*

gangs discovered when they went to Geufron Siding for more shingle ballast; which was still being used on the straighter stretches up to Capel Bangor.

By August 1908 the spread of the Cwmdauddwr bank called for a lengthening of the culvert at a cost of £10. Another 1200 new sleepers were necessary and another 5 tons of new rail had to be bought. The County Council called upon the company to provide stiles and gates where the Geufron footpath crossed the line; this was also probably the handiwork of Mrs Anne Morgan. In 1909 more sleepers were bought, for 1/6d each from the Hafod Estate, but authority to buy more rail was refused because of shortage of money. However, James Rees persevered and got the gangs another 5 tons by the end of the year.

Before 1910 was out both Cwmdauddwr and Nant-ar-fynwg banks were in dangerous condition and more land to the south had to be bought from Richardes so that the culvert could be lengthened. Also the gangs needed another 500 sleepers and 15 tons of new rail which was authorised by the Cambrian Board. By this time the gangs were down to three and were still working long hours while doing their utmost to overcome the defects in that niggardly construction. One interesting piece of expertise adopted was the ironing-out of the abrupt changes of direction by introducing into the middle of reverse curves a 30 ft length of straight track so that the coaches would settle before being jerked in the contra direction. Such a measure is not necessary on sound track but it did improve riding over that shaky lot. Also in the making-up of the tender spots, the gangs had been collecting a lot of fertile top-soil from the uphill sides to interlard with the infertile mineral rock and vegetation was creeping over the slopes and binding them. Up to the time when the Cambrian took over, the gangs under the Independent Boards had held their own.

At the end of 1911 Cambrian influence made itself felt in the person of Lewis Jones, the PW Inspector from Machynlleth. He took a good look around and it seemed that better days were coming. It was not to be and the Cambrian Company put the line on a diet of second-hand sleepers and part-worn rails and failed to supply both. So they still had to carry on as best they could, only those green sleepers of 1902 laid mostly bare on the ground were older and were rotting faster. They collected all the old scrap rail and, when it had been priced at £30, permission was reluctantly given for the purchase of £30 worth of new.

Being of a more independent nature, as folk of farming and mining stock might well be, the gangs put in for an increase of pay in 1914, unsuccessfully of course, but it is the tone of the application that is so revealing. 'We beg to apply for a little increase in our wages. As we understand the Platelayers on the other sections of the Cambrian Railways are having more wages than we have, we feel justified in making this application'. They were only asking for 18/6d instead of 17/- for platelayers and for the same 1/6d for gangers who got 20/- and 21/- per week.

By the end of the 1914/18 war, Cambrian neglect was giving rise to trouble everywhere. Loss of gauge was treated on the spot by extra spikes or by rebedding sleepers askew. A retaining wall below the bad bit above $10\frac{1}{4}$ miles was sliding downhill and the south face of the Cwmdauddwr embankment was spreading again. The stream at Nant-ar-fynwg was burrowing askew under the bank and lump stone had to be placed to check the erosion. The River Defences around the Manchester & Milford bridge had started to get scoured away but the Cambrian managed to defer action until the GWR inherited all the responsibility for rectification. A rebuild of the timber-protected abutments of the Rheidol Bridge had to be put in hand before the westmost span fell in and this was well done in concrete. Much damage left along the upper stretches by felling of timber by careless workers had to be put right, along with smashed fencing and telegraph poles.

Derailments were not infrequent, mainly through gauge-spreading. On one afternoon Isaac Jenkins stood aside for the 3.0 p.m. up train to pass in the wet cutting leading out of Aberffrwd where there is an underlying seam of clay. The leading pony wheels dropped between the rails and were squeezed back on again; so he begged the farmer's permission to cut down a sapling, notched it to fit the flanges of the rails, and slipped it under. The returning train was checked and flagged safely across the temporary expedient. As soon as possible the wet section was reinforced by three bits of old channel iron which Isaac had by at Nantyronen, and similar gauge-holding notches had been laboriously sawn and cold-chiselled out of the thick old iron. A few soleplates were provided to try and check the downhill slipping of the rails along the upper section, but there were never enough. The sleeper allocation for 1919 was 2,000 'For Light Railways' to be shared with the Welshpool & Llanfair. 1920 was marginally better, 1,261 six-footers and 4,000 of 4'6". On 21st December 1919 came the most serious flooding on record and a lot of the track up to Capel Bangor was under water and no trains could be run. Luckily, damage to the formation was slight and all was well four days later, trains being flagged along from Christmas Eve onwards. Ballast was almost impossible to get because they had cut away the rock from Quarry Cutting right back to the line of demarcation and fencing, as had also been done at many spots lower down to scrape a bit of precious stone away to pack some needy spot.

Commentary on the Cambrian era ends on a very odd note. In 1921 the Ministry of Transport had appointed a Light Railways Investigation Committee. In its return to that committee, the Cambrian claimed that the sleepers were laid on 4" of gravel and that the rails were of 48 lbs and 60 lbs weight. It owned up to some gradients of 1 in 48 with 1 in 50 as ruling. It slipped up by giving curves of 2 chains radius with 3 chains in sidings. It gave the maximum booked speed as 12 mph which was undercut only by the North Wales Narrow Gauge.

In 1922 Inspector Woosnam of the GWR required to be shown the line. (The Woosnams were an old M & MR family). He and ganger Jenkins went up on the last train with, as was so often done, the man-rider trolley hooked on at the back. They set out on their clattering journey and it had been a very wet week; even under the negligible weight of two men and a trolley, the joints flexed at the worn fishplates and the rotten sleepers pumped down and up, drenching them with muddy water. By the time they were near Aberystwyth Inspector Woosnam was a very thoughtful man indeed. At parting he said, 'If you will let me know how much is needed I shall find a way to supply you'. Also there was an old friend coming back on the scene under Inspector Woosnam. Fred Stanton, whom the Cambrian Board had dismissed in 1912 when the gangs had been reduced to two only, was foreman platelayer once again and became responsible for his old railway once more. When he had the list he looked it over and said, 'Isaac, you say you want sleepers, and I will choke you with sleepers'. And so it was.

Good treated half-sleepers arrived by the thousand and with them came fishplates, bolts and spikes to match. Also came $1\frac{1}{2}$

DEVIL'S BRIDGE, ABERYSTWYTH. 10057.

The approach to Quarry Cutting c.1930. Isaac Jenkins' way of adding a skimming of topsoil is succeeding and the rail is now bedded on new Great Western sleepers and ballast. All is stable and sound at last.
J. Salmon Ltd.

miles of new rail of 48 lbs weight, but as yet no soleplates; Swindon had not as yet got down to making them. So that first renewal had to be started with the rails bare to the sleepers, but this was soon put right. First attention was given to places where the gauge was at risk; then the poorest remaining of the old Pethick rail was lifted, the best being moved and relaid to match, and the staggering of the joints was re-arranged where patchy renewal had left some opposite to one another or nearly so. This was the first stage of restoration towards a standard that C. E. Spooner could have approved – and with new, clean, sharp ballast as well. This came first from Wern, near Portmadoc, and later from Nantmawr and Llanddu. The Engineering Committee had voted £2,000 for ballast 'for ballasting and making up cesses on the Vale of Rheidol Light Railway'. Other items were £460 for flood culverts, £212 for extra drainage works and a total of £1,417 on rebuilding the river walling by the engine shed and beyond the M & M bridge. A further £990 was voted for a 'Rip Rap' which was an additional defence against river erosion. All was voted in bits to avoid going to the Board as was necessary for items exceeding £1,000.

The PW gang checking points and track at Devil's Bridge in the 1930s. Note the weighted point lever holding the switchblades for the crossover movement. *W. E. Hayward*

The whole of the Gwaith Coch ledge was reformed and the 10¼ mile weak spot was given a lasting reconstruction. Old rail was pile-driven deep into the hillside below, the rock was drilled and cross-rails were concreted in and bolted to the piles. Wallings of long sleepers completed the job by forming a solid secure breastwork below the formation 75 ft long. The Cwmdauddwr culvert was entirely rebuilt with a further lengthening to the south and an impressive mass-concrete face to the north, having '1.2.1924 GWR' incised over the lintel. The wet bank on the north side of the cutting was rock-walled up and could no longer subside onto the newly drained track. Having built three heavier locomotives, the GWR was providing the track which would carry them safely.

Early in 1929 the formation slipped just below Rheidol Falls and a piling of second-hand rail was put in at an estimated cost of £105, the job being completed at the end of 1930 with a further expenditure of £225 which included cutting back the rockface. In 1931 another £600 had to be spent in protection work to the river walling between the shed and the M & M bridge, and in 1934 the same spot swallowed another £400. All in all, that bit of line took more than £100,000 of today's money before it was finally stabilised, so the Cambrian knew what it was about when it fobbed off any commencement of work on this stretch until it become no longer responsible.

At Nant-ar-fynwg in 1935, the stream was directed past a heavy mass-concrete wall in a concrete bed which deflected it smoothly into the culvert and the whole was reinforced by a pair of heavy flying buttresses strutting the upper face of the wall. Much drainage was reformed and wet places like the start of the incline at Tanyrallt were remedied. In all the line has pipes across the ballast at 69 places of which 12 are twinned pipes of up to 18 inches in diameter. Over the next six years another nine miles of 48 lbs rail was delivered and laid on good sleepers at 2 ft 6 in centres instead of 3 ft, and down to 2 ft at joints, entirely on soleplates. This time rail saws were provided together with several powerful 'Jim Crows', of which one was ultimately set up on a concrete stand at Plascrug for use by both standard and narrow gauge.

So were laid the countless bogeys which had afflicted the gangs since the rails were put down in 1902. No preservation society has ever done it better and no other railway has benefited from an almost total reincarnation only 20 years after construction.

Arched flying buttress upstream of Nant-ar-fynwg embankment in 1959.

The ganger, Arthur Jenkins, watching the behaviour of a train in 1960.

THE PERMANENT WAY

The gang who cleared the viewing bays. Left to right: Evan Davies, ganger (or track chargeman) Arthur Jenkins, Jack Tanyrallt (John Jones) and Emrys Evans. *Courtesy Owen Jenkins*

The gangs, later numbered 61 and 62, and whose lengths abutted at the $5\frac{3}{4}$ mile post, were set for a long period free from untoward incidents. Of course, expansion and contraction still went on, and occasionally a fishplate would go, and they did try heavy forged fishplates. This resulted eventually in a snapped rail and the idea was abandoned along with the use of oil-shale as weed-proof topping which also did not work out as well as expected. One or two sleepers were perhaps not as well bedded as they should have been and it was a mole who gave the game away by popping up through a bolthole left in one of the second-hand but sound half-sleepers.

There was still difficulty at points and, after a careful study, these were renewed with checkrails clearing by $1\frac{3}{4}$ ins, and some chanelling at the frogs. It was considered, and rightly so, that accuracy of gauge was more important than dragging at the backs of the wheels of short bogies.

Another extensive work became necessary by the $2\frac{1}{2}$ mile post where a bend brought the river scouring against the formation. A row of old rails was driven vertically into the river-bed and held up a breastwork of sleepers, a bit like the work above $10\frac{1}{4}$ miles. Later, when the weights of the engines caused the piles to cant outwards, the line was moved 6 ft away from the river so that the new shear line was more at the base of the piles, hence that odd little bit of reverse-curving that the author calls 'the 6 ft jink'.

One day Isaac Jenkins found that the timber semi-bridge over a mineshaft above $9\frac{1}{2}$ miles had given way, along with shaft timbers below leaving a deep hole which could not be plumbed by Mrs. Jenkins' clothes line. He reported the matter and soon a truck consigned to him appeared in the yard. In one corner was a small heap of sand and in the other one 1 cwt bag of cement. To say he was put out by the stupidity of those in authority above him was a bit of an understatement. So he begged some old rails from the scrapheaps and cut them to make a fresh bridge, slabbing them over with rocks. Then he carefully built up the formation and, with the help of his two boys, dug out some oak saplings with permission from a farmer and trolleyed them to the site, setting them to grow and anchor his work. His improvised repair lasted for nearly fifty years until 1979.

GWR Engineer's inspections were a bit rough on a ganger. They were an annual occurrence every spring before the trains were allowed to run. A trolley was put up at Devil's Bridge by pushing, which took two days. The Engineer arrived at Devil's Bridge by car and the journey started. It was generally all right as far as Capel Bangor; then (often in the rain with the great man sitting under his umbrella) Isaac had to push the trolley all the rest of the way to Aberystwyth.

During the 1939/45 war the one man was left to keep a watch over the entire line, help being drafted in if needed. There was but the one major piece of damage when the culverts became

The man-rider trolley, Aberffrwd in 1955.

Checkrail close-up, with 'trackdaw' and calling card. Note GWR standard 4-dog soleplates on the far rail and the staggered rail joint. The provision of check rails required special soleplates.

blocked at Nant Llettys below Devil's Bridge and the entire bend was washed away, leaving only the sagging rails across the gap.

Western Region maintenance policy was reasonably sympathetic but, as the allocation of expenditure of both time and materials had become bound up with that of the main line, requests for large allocations of material were beginning to be refused. About 1950, as an experiment, a trolley was fitted up as a weedkiller with spray nozzles but it proved inadequate as the handpump could not build up enough pressure, making it a dreadful chore. The wild strawberries along Allt-ddu have never been the same since. Between 1952 and 1959 some second-hand 70 lb rail from the Aberayron Branch was allocated for replacement work, and, where there was re-sleepering, rails were held down by a sprung type of dogging. As part of their training a detachment of Royal Engineers did a good job of reinforcing the Rheidol Bridge.

A solution was devised for keeping the track stable across the old mine shafts. A long piece of standard gauge bullhead rail bolted down between or outside the sleepers formed an excellent and extremely strong bridge. Three places are now stabilised in this manner most effectively and at no great cost.

Under London Midland Region the atmosphere became much less happy. As mentioned in the historical section, there was even less money to go round and under the enforced economy measures the little line really suffered. To quote but one instance, ganger Arthur Jenkins had succeeded to his father's old post. He was on good terms with the landowners and considered that the passengers had come to see the valley from the train and were entitled to some good views on the way up. With the permission of Miss Stevens, he had some viewing bays cleared below Rhiwfron and also cut to ground level all the obscuring trees on the Cwmdauddwr embankment; this latter partly to give a view and partly because he feared that they were getting too big and might be plucked out in one of the winter gales, thereby wrecking the formation. When his superiors found out that he had done this they were furious and the time allotted to Rheidol work was severely cut. Later, when BR management was taking a more enlightened view, the land had been bought by a less-enlightened owner who wanted an impossible sum per tree felled.

Replacement sleepers were cut to 400 per annum, quite insufficient to meet the rate of decay, and spot-sleepering to hold gauge was once more the order of the day, as was the slewing of sleepers. It was never quite as bad as 1921 but it was much less than ideal. On occasions, Arthur Jenkins resorted to poaching ballast once more from the better spots to patch up the worst

Left: Utility version milepost (probably WR) in 1956. Centre: Original Vale of Rheidol milepost in 1956. Right: Original Vale of Rheidol level post at Nantyronen in 1956.

THE PERMANENT WAY

spots, just as his father had had to do. On one or two occasions, and this troubled him greatly afterwards because to him it was the equivalent of stealing, he did take ballast from piles intended for the standard gauge, such were his problems.

Nowadays all that is in the past, and the Rheidol track is being given its third reincarnation. Most of the rail is good and the curves at Cwmdauddwr and Nant-ar-fynwg got new rail in the 1970s. The principal new work is resleepering in hard Jarrah and entire renewal of ballast. The sleepers are prepared at Aberystwyth with bolted-down gauge-retaining plates and the rails are set on cushioning pads, a standard never before seen up the valley. Fresh ballast is brought by road from Hendre Quarry near Strata Florida and is piled at Capel Bangor or at Devil's Bridge, whence it is scooped up and dropped into the little wagons by a hired JCB. A wagon is filled in four massive bucketfuls and the train is back at the working site in no time at all. All this started in 1982 and the abutments of the Rheidol Bridge were overhauled in 1983 as well. The only problem now is that of keeping this renewal programme going at a pace to outstrip the rate at which the second-hand sleepers, put down by the GWR in the 1920s are coming to the end of their time.

The gangs were always the providers of stakes, peasticks and beanpoles for the once-extensive railwaymen's allotments and some wondrous loads have been seen descending the valley in

A hurdle and bit of wire, and there's safe winter grazing for you. The mile post is standard GWR pattern. Photographed in 1954 before the season opened.

an odd wagon tacked on at the back of the train and on the tops of the engines. Sleepers and other small items often went up on the tank tops, and telegraph poles would be lashed to the footboards on the south sides of carriages, those doors being locked. Messages would be handed up or down from the engines in cleft sticks and might read anything from 'Drop two sleepers off the 2.30 at $9\frac{3}{4}$' to 'Expecting you all for tea on Sunday'.

Looking at minor lineside items, the mileposts were of a distinctive pattern. The GWR reset them with some replacements measured from the new terminus, 584 ft further to the east. All bar one are GWR and BR replacements as in 1985, and as long as they serve as useful reference points they are not likely to be moved to measure from the terminus in the station, which is around 469 ft nearer to Devil's Bridge than was the original terminus, i.e. they are all 1053 ft out, but this could change yet again if the terminus suffered another disturbance.

Platelayers huts were not liberally provided up to Capel Bangor but there were plenty along the inhospitable upper stretches. They were very necessary in the days of open trolleys and the canvas-sided Wickham, but the fine new Permaquip Personnel Carrier, which was first seen at the end of 1985, is literally a mobile and comfortable gang hut, and possibly the old sleeper-built huts of GWR origin will be allowed to decay away. The old Rhiwfron hut survived at Quarry Cutting until about 1963 and the hut at $8\frac{3}{4}$ has a little shuttered window facing east. This was the pay hut, and when the guard handed down the pay tins, ganger Jenkins would close the door from the inside, open the little shutter and, vested with the full authority of a representative of the GWR, formally pay his gang and friends with whom he was on Christian name terms all the week.

Arthur Jenkins with his gang and a visitor on the J.A.P.-engined Wickham trolley, below Devil's Bridge c.1963. *Anon*

'No. 10 Downing Street' is, or was, worthy of note. Sited above the Cwmyrogos Horseshoe Bend beyond the 10 mile post, it was where all the decisions were made, particularly in bad weather when the gang was to be formally 'laid off'. Besides, it was the hut the Army abandoned at Lovesgrove when it marched away at the outbreak of the 1914/18 war. All the upper huts had one very important thing in common. All were sited close to springs or streams not noted for running dry.

Old Rhiwfron Mine hut shown in use beyond Derwen in 1956. This can be seen at the entrance in Quarry Cutting in the picture on page 36.

Crossing and 10 mph limit sign at 6½ miles, looking towards Devil's Bridge in 1954.

Edward VII approaching Nant-ar-fynwg with a mixed train c.1905.

Author's collection

CHAPTER FIVE

RUNNING THE LINE

Regulations

Before commencing to operate a passenger service at the start of the 20th century, the first thing an infant railway company had to have was a set of Bye-Laws approved by the Board of Trade 'For regulating the Travelling upon and using the Railway belonging to that Company' and also 'For maintaining Order in and regulating the use of the Company's Railway Stations and the approaches thereto and for other purposes with respect to which the Company has power to make Bye-Laws'.

The opening paragraph lists the reference numbers of certain succeeding paragraphs which all define the various ways of incurring a penalty not exceeding £2 for the first offence and £5 for any subsequent offence. These were:

4. Travelling past the due station plus full recovery of fare.
5. Defacing one's ticket.
6. Selling or buying used tickets and half-used return tickets.
7. Entering a carriage or compartment which is already full.
8. Being a person of male sex over 8 years entering any compartment reserved specifically for persons of the female sex.
9. Mounting on engines, carriage roofs or footboards.
10. Entering or leaving carriages when trains are in motion.
11. Travelling with an Infectious Disorder (including the same penalty to be enforced against a companion).
12. Being Intoxicated.
13. Using Obscene or Abusive Language.
14. Taking a dog, a bird or other animal in a carriage. The Public Notice version states that these 'will not be suffered to accompany Passengers in Carriages, but will be conveyed separately and charged for'.
16. Smoking anywhere in parts of buildings or carriages not specifically set aside for that purpose.
18. Hawking or selling goods on railway premises &c.
19. Bookmaking, wagering or betting on railway premises.
20. Wantonly, maliciously, or negligently throwing or dropping bottles or other dangerous objects from trains.
21. Being a driver, conductor and person in charge of any ombibus, cab, carriage, waggon, or vehicle on railway premises and not conducting himself in an orderly manner.
22. Spitting anywhere on the Company's trains or premises.

The equivalent in 1986 of £2 would be in the order of £85 so it was a fairly stiff penalty. A higher penalty of £5, or around £210 in 1986 was reserved for:

15. Taking into, or placing, or causing to be placed, or having in or on any carriage or vehicle using the railway, or premises &c. – any loaded firearm, gun, or weapon, – and any cylinder, tube or receptacle containing any inflammable, explosive, or corrosive gas, spirit, or liquid. There was however an exception clause which would allow a gentleman a hip-pocket flask.
17. Wilfully, wantonly or maliciously breaking, cutting, tearing, soiling, defacing, damaging or removing any carriage or vehicle &c. with a lot more detail about minor thefts including number plates &c. as if anticipating the depredations of the modern collector of railwayana.

Entering upon the railway or carriages without a ticket at all invited merely removal by the duly authorised servant or agent of the company.

The foregoing bye-laws were not deposited and so regularised until 24th November 1905 but a simpler broadsheet public notice had been deposited with the Board of Trade on 8th August 1902. This included at the foot certain ominous notices.

1. The Penalty for Fraud did include travelling without a ticket. £2.
2. Obstructing the Officers of the Company, Penalty £5.
3. Injuring Notice Boards &c. Penalty £5.
4. Sending Dangerous Goods unmarked without prior notice and these included matches under the designation Lucifers £20.
5. Trespassing on the Railway £2.

To make it look more impressive, £2 on the public notices was expressed as Forty Shillings. Items 1 to 4 were cited under the Railway Clauses Consolidation Act 1845 and Item 5 under the Regulation of Railways Act 1868.

Rules and regulations as to arrangement of goods and mixed trains were frequently broken under the independent company, less frequently under the Cambrian, and scarcely at all under the GWR régime. Practices related to specific places are stated in the place history.

Generally goods trains could propel wagons but passenger trains could not, but are reported to have done so. The Cambrian prohibited the attaching of wagons behind a mixed train up from Capel Bangor to Devil's Bridge in 1921 and limited to four the number permitted behind the van between Aberystwyth and Capel Bangor. Another practice forbidden from the beginning was the transporting of long timber on bolster wagons by mixed trains.

Goods Traffic

A railway intended purely for the carriage of goods did not require a Board of Trade certification before it could commence running trains, and technically therefore goods could be conveyed as soon as rail connection was complete. Major Druitt, for that reason, as stated in his report, did not inspect the Harbour Branch. Being denied the right to run passenger trains, the company did the next best thing to start the flow of revenue by opening for goods traffic as soon after 12th August as it took to advertise and get the first consignments.

The rates which could be charged for merchandise (which meant large bulk consignments of over 500 lbs in weight) were fixed in the provisions of the Railway Rates and Charges No. 6 (Festiniog Railway &c) Order Confirmation Act 1892. They worked out at 2/3d per ton for coal and lime to Devil's Bridge and for ore to Aberystwyth. There was an additional transhipment charge of 3d per ton for ore etc. loaded onto the standard gauge. This is stated to have been less than one fifth of the charges levied by local carters.

Small parcels were controlled as to charges for conveyance by passenger train, which meant of course that they went up in any convenient van. The rates were: Up to 7 lbs – 3d; 7 to 14 lbs – 7d; 28 to 56 lbs – 9d. Above those weights the company was at liberty to fix its own rates. Parcels could be consigned to halts provided that somebody was waiting there to receive them, but not merchandise.

The mineral traffic started well enough with about 600 tons being sent down each month once things had got into their stride but this soon started to decline as ore veins became less economical to work or became completely worked out. By 1913 traffic in ore was below 25 tons a month and the anxiety of the Board was expressed regularly in the minute book as their main source of revenue failed without much hope of revival. The principal mines which sent ore were the Cwmystwyth which sent to Devil's Bridge, mainly by pack pony, the Frongoch using the same means, and the Cwmrheidol, which loaded at Rhiwfron

No. 1213 on a PW train c.1923. No genuine goods train photographs have yet been discovered. *Mr. James*

from its own aerial ropeway. Smaller amounts came from the Bwlch Gwyn and the Llwynteifi by pack pony to the foot of the ropeway, down the old public way from Ystumtuen, and from the Dyffryn Castell or West Esgairlle by pack pony to Devil's Bridge. The Cwmrheidol and the two Ystumtuen mines sent mainly lead ore and the others could produce both lead ore (galena) and zinc ore (blende). A small shaft about half a mile east of Dyffryn Castell sent relatively minute quantities of copper to Devil's Bridge. All were failing by 1910 and the Cwmrheidol had closed down, leaving bills for carriage of ore unpaid. The mines in the Ystwyth Valley faltered on during the war and a new source of ore onto the railway was created by opening a back way into the veins of the Rheidol United mine from Cwymrogos which was called the Erwtomau mine. After 1918 only the Cwmystwyth carried on until 1921, with a slight addition from Hodgkinson-Carrington's revival of the Cwmrheidol which lasted up to around 1925. The bulk of the ores went to the transfer sidings to go on to Swansea and to Padeswood but some went to the harbour for shipment to Antwerp. There was a little traffic in the crude sulphurous deposits removed from the flues of the smelting works and in other forms of sulphur by-products which were shipped to Arklow in Ireland where Nobels had a munition works. Cement, coal, iron and timber were taken to the mines.

Fortunately, the output from the mines was not the only source of goods traffic or the company could well have been bankrupted by 1908. The *Aberystwyth Observer* on 4th September 1902 was telling enthusiastically of the 'Goods Traffic exceeding all expectations' and forecasting that the company would have to provide more wagons. Other sources wrote of the transporting of the produce from farm, garden and orchard down to market at Aberystwyth, not omitting that from the henroost. Traffic in the up direction consisted of groceries, building materials, fertilisers, fuel and liquid refreshments. The wagons had to make two round trips each day and the first up goods had to shunt all sidings as necessary and make sure that all empty wagons came back on the 12.30 down trip. Claims for loss in transit were made by D. Lloyds in 1903 for a sack of oatmeal lost between Stone Quay and Devil's Bridge, 9 shillings; by James in 1905 for £7, (split between the company – one third, and the GWR – two thirds); and Lloyds recovered £2 6s 0d in 1906 for goods lost at Devil's Bridge.

In 1904 James Rees tried to start his own private war against the Cambrian by asking that all the company's loco coal should be specifically routed up the M & M because the Cambrian were refusing to issue day return tickets up to Devil's Bridge. This was not approved and in 1906 he was concluding arrangements with the Cambrian to tranship timber at the transfer siding, and the Cambrian agreed to send a travelling crane whenever required. That there was a traffic from timber to replace the loss of the ore traffic was entirely due to the foresight of Mr. Thomas Waddingham of Hafod, who had pioneered the planting of European Larch and his first plantations were just coming into maturity. Poles were 51 ft in length, allowing for 50 ft nominal and slight bruising at the butts and tops. These were carried on the two pairs of bolsters aleady described and were never allowed to go in mixed trains. Sometimes Box Timbers or side door wagons, with the sides and ends removed and the bolsters in place, would be brought into use as carriers of long timber coupled together by chains. The odd 60 ft oak log could give loading and transhipping problems.

In 1907 Mr. Rees was called upon to report on and explain the fall in revenue and to continue to do so in each of his weekly returns. It was of course the commencement of the decline in the output from the mines, assisted by a diminution in the sending of stone for road improvements around Devil's Bridge. In 1909 the GWR undertook to give the company a rebate on the charges for transporting coal, thereby striking a blow at the Cambrian. In 1911 the Board made a bad mistake in agreeing to a credit account for 'Mr. Gammon's traffic'. Mr. Gammon was the then owner of the Cwmrheidol mine and he ran up sizeable arrears before closing the mine.

The 1914/18 war caused an extraordinary boom in the timber traffic. The Ministry of Works set up a steam-powered sawmill in the yard at Devil's Bridge for pit-props to be cut on site to the requirements of various collieries and Driver Edwin Davies wrote of 'thousands of tons' being loaded away in the box wagons. The destinations were collieries at Aberdare, Treharris and away in Yorkshire, all arranged by local agents Anderson & Anderson and John Lloyds. Pit-props could be anything from 3 ft strutting up to 13 ft posts. The shorter stuff was stacked in the wagons either loose on the floors or end-stacked. The longer posts were stacked butt down and downhill from 12 to 16 per wagon and the end-door ex-Hafans had to be on rail with the doors also downhill to get the weight on the stronger fixed end. The freight rate was 10/- per ton, of which 2/- was costed to the Rheidol Branch. The gross revenue in 1916 amounted to £4,000 per month in some months and 250 tons could be got away during a single Sunday. To enable the transporting of such quantities, the bogie open car was stripped down as already described and pressed into the service which earned it the nickname 'The Lusitania'. 6'6" props were laid transversely at the ends, with 6 fts to complete the load in the middle, to preserve clearance on tight curves, and this unfeeling treatment caused her to sag in the middle when fully overloaded, just like a torpedoed ship, the men said.

Entire stretches of hillside along Pantmawr and Allt-ddu and above Nantyronen were denuded, and the resulting props, cut by hand or by the use of portable engines, were loaded directly into the little trucks placed wherever the stacks happened to be. As a strategic asset in wartime the Rheidol Branch and its staff played a magnificent part. Loading from the stacks was all done by manpower down baulk timber 'bridges', using ropes, chains and levers; they were men after a style not seen today.

The tree fellers, particularly those working for Anderson & Anderson, were a rough careless lot and were paid on piecework. Consequently it was nothing unusual for trains to be halted by a heap of timber across the line from a badly buttressed stack or by immense thickets of trimmings left unburnt and carried away by the winds. The railwaymen got their own back in a way, for they certainly did not clear the blockage by restacking the fallen lengths back uphill. The Welsh record for cabers tossed downhill is not known. Also Anderson & Anderson's men, instead of keeping to the openings made in the fence, wrecked 1½ miles of it. The Cambrian obtained a Writ of Injunction to halt the destruction, and in 1919 were awarded £25 plus £100 for damage to fencing and costs.

After this relatively big bang, goods traffic declined steadily and faded out with barely a whimper. The better-off farmers had their own motor lorries and some of those less well off brought their goods to market in 'tin lizzies' and similar cars. In common with other railway companies, the GWR was scoring 'own goals' by running a fleet of general carrier motor lorries from their own goods yards, and that at Aberystwyth was no exception. So, as from 1st January 1927, the goods service was withdrawn but nobody told the gentleman who compiled the timetables, for in the Service Time Table for 1946/47 were shown the numbers of wagons which could be run in mixed trains.

In the return made to the Light Railway Investigation Committee in 1920 details were given of the goods traffic for two years.

Goods Carried	Direction	1913 tons	1917 tons
Grain	Down	345	210
Groceries	Up	101	73
Pitwood	Down	4560	—
Ale & Porter	Up	26	19
Packed Manure	Up	20	27
Basic Slag	Up	33	32
Bricks	Up	31	25
Coal & Coke	Up	747	874
Lime	Up	148	220
Spelter	Down	244	1342
Lead Ore	Down	42	118
		6297	2940

Notes. Basic slag was a byproduct of blast furnaces much used as an agricultural dressing and fertiliser.
Spelter was zinc tainted with a small amount of lead.
Porter was a heavy, dark and sweetish beer which got its name from considerable consumption by the market porters.

The Passenger Services

The coming of the railway made a tremendous difference to the quality of the lives of the people living in and around Devil's Bridge. Much of the farming was at subsistence level on small semi-fertile holdings, many of which had sprung from an original 'ty'n nos', a one night house, enclosed between dawn and dusk out of the old common land. This implied a boundary made by a row of stones or a slender ditch one spade in width and depth, a rough lean-to bothy, and a stone fireplace and chimney which had to be smoking when the sun set. This established the right and all else could be made good later.

Transport down to the market was the monopoly of a small group of carters and was much too expensive for ordinary folk.

While the railways were still under debate, one woman regularly walked sixteen miles to market in Aberystwyth carrying her eggs and vegetables. From her selling she bought a bushel of wheat, carried all the way up the hills on her back, and left it to be ground at a mill on the Mynach; then she went to get the meal for her man and her children. The ground wheat would be used mixed with barley or oats to make bread or potes llaeth, which was a kind of milk porridge, or it could be mixed with buttermilk to make uwd. Folk lived very simply and cheaply in those days before 1900. The people down in the valley fared a little better for a farmer would take them to Aberystwyth for coppers in his market car, which has been described as a gipsy tent on four wheels. It was a long, slow, tedious journey for by no means could the horse ever be persuaded to trot until he was under Llanbadarn railway bridge. This 'ran' on Mondays only, and if anything was needed on any other day of the week it was a case of step and fetch it both ways.

No wonder at all then that the inhabitants of village and hamlet and hillside came to the station on that first day in traps, on ponies, or on foot to gaze on that little marvel that was to make things better for them in so many ways. Now they could get easily and cheaply to market and to the hiring fairs which had become accessible to farming folk who hitherto lived too far away to get there and back in the day on foot. Their household and farming necessities would arrive to be collected from the station at less than half what the carters had been charging, and the great influx of tourists would call into being tea places providing a few jobs for sons and daughters.

If the carters had been badly affected, what about the large cosy ring of charabanc proprietors down at Aberystwyth? No longer would there be convoys of five or more horse-drawn brakes and charabancs toiling up the hill behind Penparcau and along the upper road to Devil's Bridge, on to Parson's Bridge and Ponterwyd, and home through Goginan, a round trip which took nearly all day and stopped at only those places of refreshment with which the drivers had understandings. Their trade had vanished overnight, killed as surely by the Vale of Rheidol line as that of the sailors of Aberdyfi which had been killed overnight by the building of the Aberystwyth & Welsh Coast Railway (spelt Aberystwith in the Act).

The more enterprising of them plied from the station or from the Hafod Arms Hotel, offering tours of the countryside, and a few picked up some crumbs by being ready to take back to Aberystwyth those more timorous railway passengers who did not care to go back by rail. The line was a brand-new scar along miles of open hillside, the formation was still pretty narrow, and passengers could see straight down the hillsides to the river hundreds of feet below just as they could in the 1950s. James Rees recalled several specific cases. A highly-placed official of one of the leading British railways, who had a wooden leg, had his nerves so badly frayed that he vowed he would walk back to Aberystwyth rather than return by train, and another passenger was observed to show signs of much distress as the train entered the rugged country beyond Aberffrwd. He soon shifted his seat and sat where he felt safer gazing at the solid rock. It turned out that he was a colliery manager from Ammanford who descended daily into deep pits in a cage, which seemed safer to him than a ride on the lein fach. Here we must keep in mind that Mr. Rees, who had a very great sense of humour, was recounting years later when he was no longer responsible for encouraging people to travel on the line.

An early publicity photograph showing the halt for taking water at Nantyronen. Note the timber-sided water tank with angle-iron corner stanchions. The driver is Bob Morris and the fireman J. E. Davies.
Courtesy John G. Rees

Having got their railway, the next move on the part of the Board was to invite as much publicity as possible. Many reporters and article writers were persuaded to make the trip, and the result was a fair quantity of euphoria and hyperbole, not to mention the present day equivalents, enthusiasm and exaggeration. The Cambrian had been publicising Aberystwyth as the Welsh Biarritz and to this the *Railway Magazine*'s editor added 'The heart of Welsh Switzerland' when describing the arrival of the train at Devil's Bridge. The engines go along 'puffing bravely' and when approaching Devil's Bridge 'proceed through a few rocky chasms whose width or lack of width caused the wayfarer when he negotiated them to wonder what would happen if a man of fairly stout proportions was overtaken by the bustling little train that goes rattling through the cutting with but a few inches to spare on either side'. (The Quarry Cutting had not then been widened in the winning of all that ballast.)

That famous picnic in 1903. Left to right: Spencer Leigh-Hughes MP ('Sub Rosa' of the Morning Leader); his daughter Constance; Mrs. Leigh-Hughes; The Reverend Thomas Owen Evans, Curate at Devil's Bridge; Mr. James Rees; Mrs. Bowen, manageress of the Hafod Arms Hotel. The clean new decking was fitted to the trolley by Isaac Jenkins who was responsible for the control of the trolley.
Courtesy John G. Rees

Also worthy of special note was the visit of the Honourable Spencer Leigh-Hughes MP, who was the editor of the *Morning Leader* and wrote under the pseudonym of 'Sub Rosa'. He was accompanied by his wife and daughter and a cameraman. On the way down, the train was halted at the Horsehoe Bend at Cwmyrogos for a picnic. The table was a platelayer's trolley which had been specially replanked for the occasion, and the repast, which included a great plum cake, was provided by the lady who was the Manageress of the Hafod Arms Hotel.

James Rees in an early fit of enthusiasm had told the editor of the *Aberystwyth Observer* 'that it was proposed to pick up the passengers on the road just as trams or omnibuses do, only of course with the necessary restrictions', only of course things did not work out quite like that for two reasons. The first was the timetable listing the proper stopping places and the second was the table of fares.

Under the 1897 Act the rates for passengers were one penny per mile for 3rd class passengers and threepence per mile for 1st class passengers. 1st class could take 120 lbs of luggage at no extra cost, whereas 3rd class could take only 60 lbs of luggage. There was a minimum fare of three miles and each portion of a mile over that ranked as a full mile e.g. $5\frac{1}{2}$ miles ranked as 6. These charges applied to ordinary and express trains and the company could charge what it wished on special trains. The tourist return fare for 3rd class was fixed at 1/6d, less than half the horse-drawn charge of 3/6d. 1/6d translated in terms of inflation tables would be about £3.40 of 1986 money, so the actual fare charged for 1986 for the summer months only, with a long sterile winter term in between, does not look to be at all outrageous at £4.00.

Right from the start James Rees had his staff take a leaf out of the coaching fraternity's book by visiting hotels and boarding houses daily in the season to arouse interest and to drum up custom. The Board looked favourably upon 'A Petition from the Servants of the Company' and approved a system of staff privilege tickets between the Vale of Rheidol and the other and much larger railway companies.

For 1904 there were season tickets between Aberystwyth and Devil's Bridge for £15 per annum and reservations of compartments for parties on payment of five fares or more. Additional season tickets rates were approved at £2 for Aberystwyth to Llanbadarn, £6 to Capel Bangor and £10 to Nantyronen. It was from March 1904 that the 1/6d market return fare was introduced. Negotiations with the Cambrian resulted in an agreement for advertised through bookings and the Rheidol Board were to pay 5% of the advertising costs. Half-rate scholars' season tickets were approved to be issued on receipt of a certificate from the Headmaster. The Secretary of the Taff Vale Railway wrote asking that staff privilege tickets be issued to Retired Officers, Pensioned Servants (note the distinction) and their Wives, Children, etc. This too was approved. By September of 1904 tourist journeyings up the line had caught on, and there were many meetings and conferences which ended with a trip to Devil's Bridge, and the 1/6d return was extended to embrace half-day trippers as well. All of this had so alarmed the coach proprietors that they had started a whispering campaign, spreading rumours that the railway track was not safe. The Board resolved to do nothing and recorded 'let such matters take their course for the time being'.

1905 opened with the provision of one special mail train early each morning for which the Postmaster General was asked to pay £120 per annum. There was some dispute over the charge and in 1906 it was refixed at £60 per annum. In 1905 the company agreed to an arrangement with the Cambrian and the M & M that official passes should be valid over all three systems. On 18th April 1905 the conversion of carriages for the conveyance of 1st class passengers was approved. On 18th March several specials were run to Devil's Bridge for Gipsy Smith's revival meetings. Thos. Cook's became agents for tickets at 10% discount. This principle was extended to the proprietors of the Victoria Hotel and other boarding houses but at only 10/– per cent. Griffiths & Millington, a firm of advertising contractors who had taken up the right to display in carriages and on stations, gave notice to end the agreement; they could not get any business out of it. The receipts were down overall and the unfortunate Mr. Rees was told to go into his returns and offer an explanation. By September Sunday trains were running at a loss and the service was suspended at Mr. Rees' discretion.

In 1906 Mr. Rees was given an odd sort of commission to try and let advertising space at 10/– per cent up to £100 brought in and 15/– per cent for any business above that sum. A Pictorial Timetable Card was approved and Aberystwyth Corporation started subscribing £10 per year towards the cost of company posters. A kiosk was erected at the entrance to the pier as an enquiry and publicity office. Mr. Rees' commission proved extremely short-lived and in September W. H. Smith & Son Ltd became advertising agents at 50% discount. It was fortunate that the tourist traffic had boomed because the mineral traffic was showing a considerable fall-off, from which it never recovered.

Vale of Rheidol Light Railway

TIME TABLE

OF

LOCAL TRAINS

FOR

Saturday, May 21, to Thursday June 30, 1904

—o—

For the lover of excursions, long or short, Aberystwyth will be found a most convenient centre. The "lion" of the place is presumably the Devil's Bridge. No visitor should fail to make this excursion—"THE KING" for June 27th, 1903.

The sage-green cheap paper leaflet of 1904 (full size).
Author's collection

The scene at the newly constructed curve at Nant-ar-fynwg with Faen Grach, The Scarred Peak, in the background.

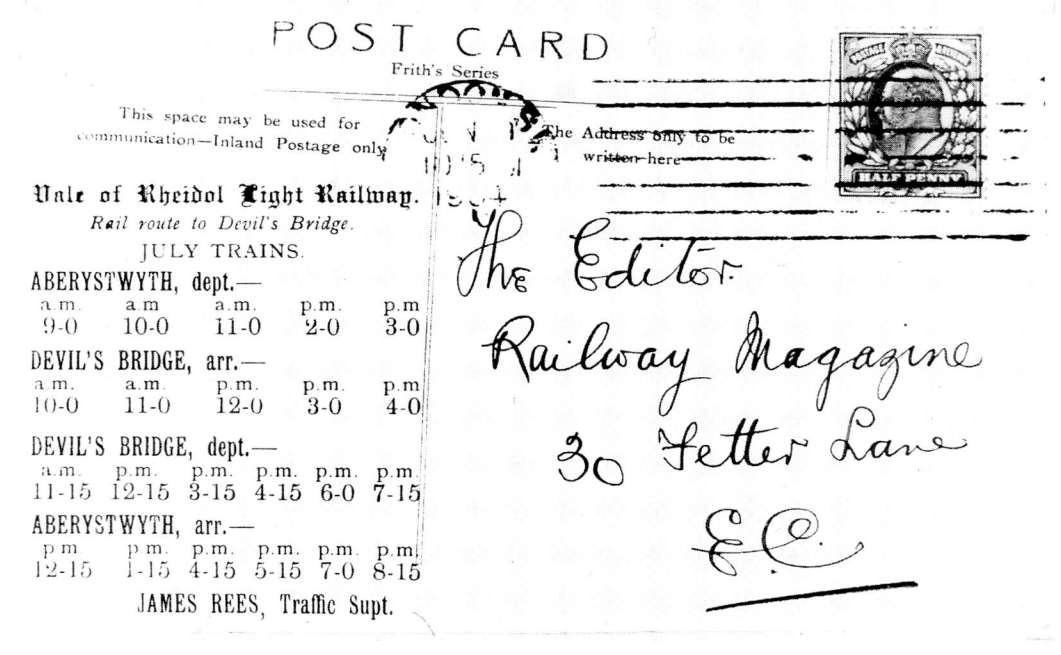

Vale of Rheidol Light Railway.
Rail route to Devil's Bridge.
JULY TRAINS.

ABERYSTWYTH, dept.—
| a.m. | a.m. | a.m. | p.m. | p.m |
| 9-0 | 10-0 | 11-0 | 2-0 | 3-0 |

DEVIL'S BRIDGE, arr.—
| a.m. | a.m. | p.m. | p.m. | p.m |
| 10-0 | 11-0 | 12-0 | 3-0 | 4-0 |

DEVIL'S BRIDGE, dept.—
| a.m. | p.m. | p.m. | p.m. | p.m. | p.m |
| 11-15 | 12-15 | 3-15 | 4-15 | 6-0 | 7-15 |

ABERYSTWYTH, arr.—
| p.m | p.m. | p.m. | p.m. | p.m. | p.m |
| 12-15 | 1-15 | 4-15 | 5-15 | 7-0 | 8-15 |

JAMES REES, Traffic Supt.

The Editor,
Railway Magazine
30 Fetter Lane
E.C.

A timetable of 1904 printed on the back of the scene shown in the previous photograph. Note the addressee.
Collection J. I. C. Boyd

RUNNING THE LINE

Devil's Bridge Train, Rheidol Valley, near Aberystwyth.

Double-headed train rounding the Cwm-yr-ogos Horseshoe Bend c.1910. Preceding the van is the fully open car No. 9 and the two converted timber trucks Nos. 16 and 17 are at the rear.
Courtesy J. I. C. Boyd

The lack of revenue from advertising was still a sore point in 1907 and even the Secretary was roped in on a commission rate to try and get some business in London. Rates were fixed at 1/6d per sq ft at stations and 3/– per sq ft in the carriages. Mr. Rees tried to get going with a combined rail and road tour with the GWR via Devil's Bridge and Trawscoed. It was approved that a page should be taken in the GWR publication *South Wales* at a cost of £10.

1908 was a good year for innovations. Mr. Lightfoot had opened his golf course at Devil's Bridge and combined rail and golf tickets were issued at 2/6d, of which the Rheidol took 1/6d plus 10% of Mr. Lightfoot's 1/–. The enterprising Mr. Lightfoot then took a charabanc for trips to Hafod Mansion and the combined facility cost 3/– return from Aberystwyth. Someone managed to persuade a Mr. Herbert Jones to pay £20 per annum for advertising rights in the carriages.

1909 was noteworthy for a minor crime wave; two passengers were caught travelling without tickets, one of whom apologised and was let off and the other was fined 6d and 24/– costs. The Aberystwyth Council was considering the provision of a town golf course and James Rees recommended a site between the Rheidol Bridge and Glanrafon. Mr. Herbert Jones defaulted in his payment for those advertising rights. There was a first class combined ticket issued at Devil's Bridge which included a show on the pier.

From 1910 the Rheidol joined the Cambrian Resorts Association which was formed as a publicity agency and this was the first year in which Territorials were encamped at Lovesgrove.

In 1911 the company hired for the first time its own motor charabanc for combined tours by rail and road to Hafod. Commercial Car Hirers Ltd of London undertook to provide a 20-seater provided that the contract was entered into by the Cambrian. As the alternative available was one from the GWR, the Cambrian agreed, wishing to have no truck with chocolate and cream. In the event an 18-seater arrived and the company cut the hire payment accordingly. The Hafod tour proved so popular that a further tour to Eisteddfa Gurig for a guided walk to the top of Plynlimon was added in 1912. Thereafter all proceeded happily until the outbreak of the 1914/18 war.

The oddity for 1912 was the granting of permission to the British Automatic Co Ltd for the placing of two additional Race Machines. The Company issued a $4\frac{3}{4}'' \times 8\frac{1}{4}''$ brochure entitled 'Devil's Bridge – How to get There', which listed all the motor tours linked with rail travel from Aberystwyth. Hafod Church cost 3/– 3rd class and 4/– 1st class, which included front seats in the motor. Plynlimon, including a guided walk to the top of the mountain, was 4/– and the Waterworks on Thursdays only cost 6/6. In addition a 'Well-appointed Motor' plied between Devil's Bridge and Parson's Bridge for 6d each way, so one could walk there and come back by coach etc. The brochure included its own little panegyric 'The little railway misses nothing' and 'Taken up in a series of curves on the steep hillside in such a fashion that, though itself unseen, its passengers always look out upon the scene below' and 'Rail has quite superseded the Road'.

The Cambrian minutes for 1914 reveal the charging basis for the Plynlimon car, which was £22 per week plus £20 for

Above the loco can be seen the rudimentary staithe from which the Erwtomau ore wagons were tipped. Photographed in 1935.
H. F. Wheeller

Passengers in one of the original coaches in 1936. Note the gaspipe stanchions keeping the roof from sagging, and the disused gaslights.
H. F. Wheeller

conveyance of car to Aberystwyth and back to London, the Cambrian Company to be liable for the first £10 of any insurance claim.

In 1922 the GWR was publicising Aberystwyth as 'The Queen of Welsh Watering Places' and produced a nice poster of Devil's Bridge without mentioning on it that they had a railway going up to the place. The Crosville declared war on the railway in 1924 by launching Route 601 Aberystwyth-Devil's Bridge-Ponterwyd and Route 602 Aberystwyth-Penparcau-Devil's Bridge. Later on, in 1931, they were to consolidate their takeover of passenger services up and around the valley with Route 610 Aberystwyth-Capel Bangor-Glyn Rheidol.

By 1928 the writing was on the wall; the conveyance of ordinary passengers going daily to and from work had nearly ceased and the weekly shoppers were using the buses too. It was time to look at ways of increasing the tourist side of the business. Accordingly a pair of ex-War Department cross-country motor vehicles was purchased and put onto an excursion, whereby the passengers joined the cars at Devil's Bridge and were driven right to the top of Plynlimon. At least, that was the theory of it, but many a time the car bogged down and people had to finish the way on foot to get back to Aberystwyth by Crosville.

Then, almost unnoticed, the regular carrying of passengers by fare stages was terminated on 31st December 1930, and the line was totally shut down until the following summer.

Tourists only

The GWR had the resources with which to carry a minor branch line which was no longer likely to bring in much revenue, and all concerned enjoyed the running of it. In effect, from the 1931 season onwards, The Vale of Rheidol line had become a preserved railway without change of ownership and without a long drawn-out period of attrition followed by dereliction. Usually the seasons commenced at Whitsuntide and the last train was run towards the end of September.

The beautiful poster picture painted in the cream and lake period of Western Region achieved one thing no driver has yet done — the tender engine is running down from Devil's Bridge chimney first — but it was still a great poster. *Author's collection*

In 1939 the season was allowed to run its course as advertised and the line was closed indefinitely until the war had ended. It reopened on 25th July 1945 with a much-feted initiatory train and the pre-war pattern of short summer seasons only was resumed. In the 1954 season a fresh approach became apparent. The posters became much more attractive and Sunday trains were restored, special evening excursions being put on for the school and industrial holiday period. A separate handbill in 1957 promoted one morning and one afternoon train during the whole of Easter 22nd to 27th April. The return fare was 2/9d and the author overheard a family agreeing that it had been the best

A party of Great Western staff were taken up to Eisteddfagurig for this photograph which was actually taken on the level with them all leaning forward to give the impression of being on a steep slope. The driver is C. H. F. Kent. *GWR Magazine September 1928*

No. 1213 on an extremely unusual train formation for the 10.00 a.m. to Devil's Bridge on 21st May 1930.
Ifor Higgon

2/9d worth they had ever had. The fare for the evening trips was 2/–. This bit of sparkle was short-lived and Western Region went back to short season patterns with uninspiring leaflets.

Operation

Prior to 1971 brake vans and brake 3rds were always marshalled at the rear and had to be shunted round at the end of each journey. The 4-wheeled vans always ran with the look-outs or the end windows at the Aberystwyth end. The first toast-racks and open cars were marshalled as far from the engines as possible with the four-wheelers right at the back.

All stock carries the coupling chopper at the Devil's Bridge end. Coaches run with the gangways on the south or rock face side except (as has happened) when they arrive back after overhaul the wrong way round. Excepting the two brake composites, all coaches run with the train alarm indicators at the Aberystwyth end.

Carriage doors were kept locked on the rock face side when on the move but at Llanbadarn the doors of down trains were unlocked on that side and the doors on the north side were locked ready for running into the left-hand side of the loop at Aberystwyth. The gates of the toast-racks and the doors of the open cars were always locked all round when moving, and passengers joining at the halts and stations on the way had to take seats in the closed coaches.

The guards examined tickets and collected singles on up trains at Aberffrwd before 1915 and until 1921 at Capel Bangor. Tickets were examined and collected off down trains at Llanbadarn unless the train was held and delayed in the loop at Aberffrwd or Capel Bangor, whereupon the guard might use his time there to avoid the halt at Llanbadarn. The guard was the person responsible for marshalling of goods wagons and for telling the driver if there was anything for Rhiwfron on the way up or down. The GWR reverted the collection of tickets on up trains to Aberffrwd at the height of the season for a few years. Otherwise all GWR tickets were dealt with at Aberystwyth and Devil's Bridge.

Apart from the last item the engine whistle codes were, and still are:

To leave loop onto main	One
To enter loop from main	Two
To enter or leave sidings	One long, two sharp
Call attention of guard	Three sharp
Apply brake instantly	Four sharp
Release brake	One long, two sharp
Approaching road crossing	Several long
Goods to be put off at Rhiwfron (Small items only, not coal etc which was shunted off on the way back)	Three long at $9\frac{1}{2}$ miles.

The 1897 and 1900 Acts contained no provisions as to speed limits other than a maximum of 25 mph without local restrictions, but the Aberayon Extension Order laid down a maximum speed limit of 17 mph and 6 mph over unlocked facing points. The 1902 Amendment Order added a 10 mph limit for 300 yds when approaching an ungated level crossing. Major Druitt imposed a limit of 10 mph between Nantyronen and Devil's Bridge and of 6 mph round the Cwmyrogos Bend. James Rees told the reporter from the *Railway Magazine* in 1903 that the speeds were 17 mph to Capel Bangor and 10 mph thereafter and he would know. The Cambrian raised the limit at Cwmyrogos to 8 mph. Major Druitt did add some rider limits round certain other bends but these seem to have disappeared with the provision of more checkrails and improvements to the track.

Train capacity up to 1922 was limited quite simply to everything the engines could move. *Rheidol* usually handled the morning Mail with a 1st 3rd composite and a van, and was quite good with two coaches and a van plus, perhaps, one toast-rack; more was a bit of a struggle, and never on a wet day. *Palmerston* was more effective and could handle three coaches and a van. The Davies & Metcalfe engines could easily take six coaches and a van and often seven and a van but, and particularly on wet days, an additional engine would be put on the longer trains to enable them to keep to the timetables. When the reinforcing engine on a long train was *Rheidol* or *Palmerston*, it was put at the front as a pilot engine. When it was one of the 2-6-2 tanks it went at the rear and banked (to avoid overloading the Rheidol Bridge).

There is one unusual story from those earlier days. On one sunny summer day in 1912 Driver Jack Davies was taking a normal train up with *Edward VII*. Just past the 10 mile post he and his fireman were amazed to hear a roar from the chimney and a mad whirling of wheels and rods. The train lost way immediately and, when they tried to restart, was actually losing ground. Mystified, the pair of them set the brakes and got down. The air above them was filled with the gossamer skeins of descending oak eggar moth caterpillars which were thick on the ground and over the rails. The plague lasted about a week and left the trees with bare skeletons instead of leaves. They tried fitting canvas sweeps held down to the rails with light timbers but this did not work very well. Quite the worst part of it was the appalling stench of gunge frying on the brake blocks when returning downhill.

That was the time of 'one engine, one crew,' but, as the crew could find themselves at the barriers with a roll of tickets slung round their necks, rules as to manning hardly worked in practice all the time. Driving and crewing in a main line rota system was initiated by the Cambrian and it provided a means of getting more men used to working on the narrow gauge and there was much less need for excessive working times.

The arrival of the three Great Western engines with their improved fireboxes and greater power, changed things a good deal; designed for Welsh steam coal from the start, they proved to be much more economical and were much easier for the men. It was said that a newly-drafted trainee fireman used to stoking 'Dukes' and Moguls had first to go to Woolworths. There he had to buy himself an ordinary domestic hand shovel for, instead of eight feet in which to wield the stoking tools, there was barely three uncluttered.

The technique which soon developed was to light up at about 05.30 for the 10.30 train, each fireman starting his own fire with newspaper and chopped-up sleeper. When the pressure was up to 40, the engines were walked out of the shed to be topped up with coal and water, and later the driver joined and topped up the lubricators on the motion, looking round to ensure that all was as he wished. As yet the fire was being pulled up sparingly and if the fireman found that he was not getting enough draught, the shedman would help with cleaning through the tubes. At

The Great Western passenger service from the service timetable 11th July 1927 to 25th September 1927.
Courtesy Roger Wilson

Heading for the hills in June 1956.

60 lbs psi the engine could be taken out of the yard to be backed down to the train and the vacuum braking could be tested, and checked again when backed onto the train. By then the fire had been built over 'deep and green' with a fraction of blower so that the full 165 lbs came on the gauge just before starting time. As yet the fire would be far from maximum heat.

During the run to Capel Bangor the fire was touched as little as possible, and on arrival would be nicely burned through all over so as to be ready for the hard work to come. So far the regulator would have been on first valve only with cut-off at 75% or even less. From Capel Bangor the regulator would be on second valve for the rest of the way with cut-off at 75%, and not more if it could be avoided. All being well, the climb to Nantyronen would go crisply, but on a wet day there would be wheelslip under the trees and a brief pause to use the blower to restore pressure could be necessary with a light tending of the fire.

At Aberffrwd the water tanks were replenished and the fireman would set the blower on full, make up and tend the fire to ensure leaving at full pressure, ready for nearly four miles of continuous 1 in 50. Any slacks in this gradient are all on curves which impart an additional drag. A good crew, used to each other's ways could, on a dry day and sometimes on a wet one, lift a seven-coach train clean up to Devil's Bridge without faltering once – and that is craftsmanship.

The climb to Rheidol Falls would show whether the fireman had got it right and many a crew had a brief stop around $8\frac{3}{4}$ miles for a bit more with the blower and a quick retend at the fire. The author put his foot in it well and truly down at the shed one morning in 1962. 'The 2.30 was having a bit of trouble yesterday wasn't it?' 'Eh? What was that?' 'Well we were walking on the hilltop opposite and he was stuck twice along the Cnwch.' 'The lying so-and-so, he told us they got up without stops.'

On a fine dry day about 200 gallons of water would be needed at Aberffrwd and up to 250 on a wet day, so for the first $7\frac{1}{2}$ miles the fireman would not have been too much occupied with the injector. The last four miles usually needed all of 250 gallons, and the water gauge and the injectors could not be neglected for more than a couple of minutes; small boilers cannot take in large sloshes of water at a time without chilling and losing pressure.

The return journey was made with the residue of the fire and with the regulator used only sparingly on first valve and with continuous soft application of the brakes. On test it has been proved that a six-coach train allowed to gather speed to 15 mph can be halted in its own length but great care is always taken to avoid such a situation and speed when descending is kept within known safe limits. The object is always to crawl down hill at the right speed for each part of the line. Returning takes less than 250 gallons of water all told and the time saved by not having to stop to pick up water is absorbed in careful descent.

Good handling on a dry day would get the train to Devil's Bridge and back on 8 cwt of coal but 9 to 10 cwts were more usual. The enforced use of the dustier Maltby coal after the line came under LMR caused a total rethinking about the entire principles of stoking. There could be no more deep and green firing, the fire just choked, and from then on it was a case of 'stoke and tend' from the time the fire was lit. Up the line, unless great care was taken, there would be black smoke and sparks and this was quite unavoidable with a bad lot of coal. There were no problems with lineside fires for the first 75 years and always the distant train could be marked by watching for the plume of white smoke; and now we watched for a plume of grey smoke. The funny thing about this 'stoke and tend' period was that a little less coal was required.

Coal for the engine shed was loaded into Rheidol wagons at the transfer siding at Plascrug. Once goods traffic had ceased, any old wagon that was handy was used until the GWR selected four of the end-door Hafans as marked 'LOCO'. Despite this the crews used the handier dropside wagons for preference when they could get them. Indeed, during the last few years of coal firing when coaling was done inside the former standard gauge shed, the side door wagons were by far the more practicable.

Stoking tools were naturally on a different scale to those provided for the standard gauge. Normally the pricker was only five feet long but of a heavier section to give it weight and there was an equally short slicer. There was an ordinary pan shovel for use when coaling and a stout little shovel on an 18″ long T-handled shaft for use on the footplate. Nevertheless some firemen preferred that which Woollies could supply. A most indispensable oddity was a three foot length of three-eighths rod with a loop at one end and a hook at the other which was used from the cab to pull the other tools to hand without having to climb up to get them. Another specialised tool was a stoking shovel on a shortened shaft and bent at right angles for scooping out the fire and ash at the end of the day. This was kept back at the shed. These are all things of the past, and it would have been nice if one set could have been kept and hung on the shed wall.

The upgrading of the track to GWR main line standards had enabled the speed limit between Aberystwyth and Capel Bangor to be increased to 20 mph and in any case the drivers had always exceeded the old 17 mph limit when there were goods to put off at Llanbadarn or at Capel Bangor. The GWR-permitted loads were 6 coaches and a van, 51 tons, up, and 10 coaches and a van, 75 tons, down. They restricted mixed trains to one passenger coach and one van, with six to nine loaded wagons up, and nine to fourteen loaded wagons down. If the wagons were empty, twelve could be taken up and eighteen down. These limitations were still solemnly included in the GWR Service Time Tables for 1947, so there is nothing new in the expression 'Well, nobody told us.' The general policy today is to keep the load down to six coaches to avoid over-pressing the engines, but they still pull more.

Under the GWR the Rheidol drivers moved further afield and could even be seen on holiday lodging turns at Tyseley shed on 'Dukes'. Jack Davies was the one who had the most difficulty in getting a turn outside. He pleaded and cajoled and in the end was allowed to drive standing on a little platform he carried everywhere so that he could see over the rim of a standard gauge engine's spectacles. Besides being known as Jack Bach, he also got referred to as Jack-on-the-Box. Later still the driver who took you up to Devil's Bridge could have brought you to Aberystwyth on the 'Cambrian Coast Express'.

Once, some time in the early 1930s, little Jack Davies had just got No. 7 back from Swindon with new motion bearings throughout. He was reassuring himself that Swindon had done their job properly by hanging head down over the side and listening. He failed to spot that the stay of a telegraph pole was coming up and it removed him, dumping him on the ballast, out cold. As he said later, 'I was the first to go in the new motor ambulance and I never knew anything about it.'

An unavoidable problem with all steam engines is the long slow softening of the rear driving axle springs where the heat from the firebox reaches them. Sooner or later most steam engines can get slightly light at the fore end if the springs are not renewed in time. Driver Gwilym Davies got himself into this brand of trouble, the front pony truck lifted off and he had to telephone for assistance. He relates that he could not raise an answer from the shed so he tried getting one of the booking office clerks to go down with a message, and the man seemed a bit slow on the uptake as to what he had to pass on. Eventually the duty shedman came on the telephone asking 'And what is all this nonsense about you having trouble with a donkey cart?'

Coal-fired footplate of No. 9 in September 1957.

THE VALE OF RHEIDOL LIGHT RAILWAY c 1984

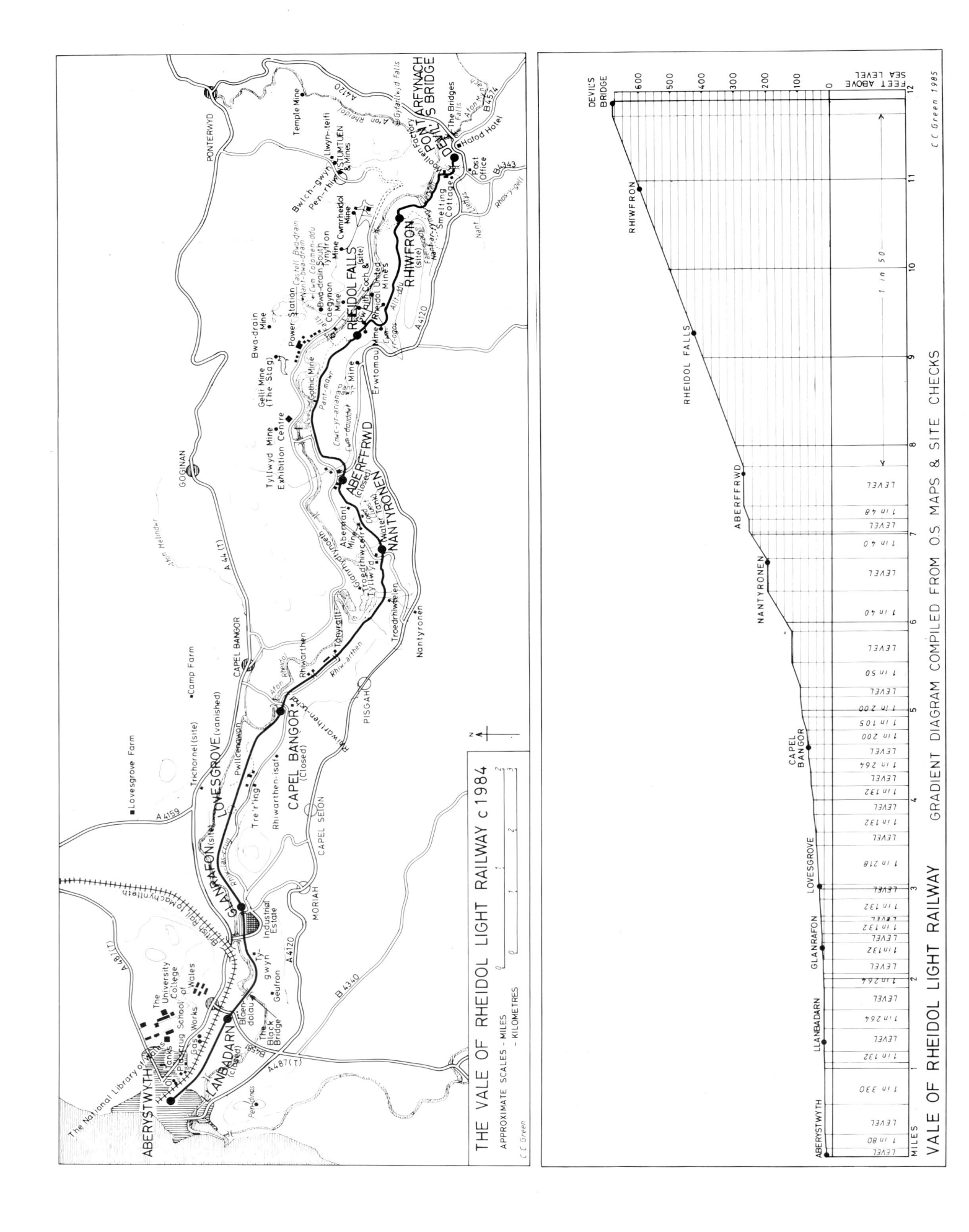

APPROXIMATE SCALES - MILES
- KILOMETRES

VALE OF RHEIDOL LIGHT RAILWAY

GRADIENT DIAGRAM COMPILED FROM O.S. MAPS & SITE CHECKS

C C Green 1985

CHAPTER SIX
THE JOURNEY UP THE VALLEY

After all the proper Welsh names the author has given equivalents in English, in the hope that they will make the descriptions more interesting. They will not all be precise as very often no exactly suitable expression can be found.

The previous Aberystwyth termini and the line's original route away from the town are described elsewhere. Today the trains depart from the floor of the old standard gauge Manchester & Milford Railway Company's northern terminus, between Platforms 4 and 5, as they became known later, and rejoin the original course of the line at Llanbadarn.

When sitting in the train going up, north is on the left and south is on the right, and north and south will be used in all descriptions because they will hold good equally on the down trip.

Waiting in the terminus, the view to the south is blocked by the old station wall which has been enlivened by an interesting mosaic of the valley and the line, designed and applied by the students of Coleg Prifysgol Cymru (The University College of Wales). Beyond the wall are the car and coach park and the cattle market. To the north east behind the oil terminal, the view of Aberystwyth is dominated by a building crowned by a small cupola above a central pediment. This is the Chemistry Department of the UCW, built in 1907, with its modern extension on its right. Further to the right and closer is the building which houses several Government departmental offices described to the author, perhaps a little unfairly, as 'the abode of the awful taxman'.

As the train draws out to the ends of the platforms, the cliffs of Constitution Hill and its steep funicular railway come into sight further to the west. Platform 5 still curves away to the south towards Pencader and Carmarthen but the old yards and main line are now a car park. To the north is the old standard gauge steam shed, which now houses the Rheidol engines, carriages and repair facilities. Beyond are the narrow gauge sidings holding spare carriages and the few wagons needed for moving ballast and sleepers. Once clear of the railway clutter, a glance to the north shows that magnificent building Llyfrgell Genedlaethol Cymru (The National Library of Wales) which, from its portico, possesses the finest view to be enjoyed from any library in the world. Behind the library are the campus buildings of the UCW and the tall column is the best-designed chimney in the whole of Dyfed.

To the south, across overgrown allotments which were once the pride of many railwaymen of the pre-television era, the long hill of Pendinas (Fortress Head) comes into view. On the crest at the far end is the tall monument to the Duke of Wellington which is shaped like a cannon pointing to the sky. At the top there was to have been a bronze equestrian statue of the Duke,

Crossing Park Avenue, c.1954. *H. F. Wheeller*

Along the gravelly flat, No. 9 passes the gas works in July 1961.

but money and enthusiasm ran out before it was completed. Below lies a caravan site, deplored by many because it can be seen, but naturally those staying there enjoy a magnificent view right up the valley.

Close by to the north comes the modern Plascrug English-language Primary School built over the site of an 18th century house designed more as a folly than anything else, and known as the House on the Hillock. 'Plas' as a term for a home is a bit more pretentious than the usual expression 'Ty'. Behind lies the suburb of Llain-y-gawsai (The Narrow Field by the Causeway) a reminder that this area was once a gravelly delta, much water-logged, and passable only via the raised road along its northern edge. Several river courses wound their separate ways across it until, centuries ago, engineers diverted them into one course, taking the Rheidol into the Ystwyth to the south of Castle Head, whereas formerly a stream reached the sea over by Constitution Hill. Aberystwyth is held to be At the Mouth of the Winding River. Welsh place names are practical and factual. Derived in the main from the most ancient forms of Welsh, they describe clearly what a place looks like, where it is situated, or with whom or what it was associated. The name Rheidol itself does pose a few problems in arriving at a satisfactory equivalent in English. First of all, some old maps and a number of the older folk now passed away called it the Rheidiol. There is an old word Rheiddio which could be used in reference to the way the valley thrusts its way directly into the mountains. Then, too, there is a lovely word Rheiddiol which is Radiant. The Radiant Vale? What a splendid and suitable name for it.

Now the railway runs along its own causeway, raised and fettled by the gangs as a result of the Borough Surveyor's insisting all those years ago, and raised again by the GWR after the 1922 floods. To the north, beyond the old Cambrian main line, are the playing fields of the Aberystwyth Athletic Association and the Rugby Club. Half a mile to the south lie the commuter suburbs of Caeffynnon (Spring Field) and Penparcau (Field Head) under Pendinas, and further to the east, past the low saddle where A487(T) heads south for Carmarthen, is Southgate. The intervening land is mainly grazing. Halfway along the straight, on the north side, are the gas storage tanks which were once a complete generating works with a standard gauge railway siding. Then, right next to the track, is a little red-brick building housing the pumps which supply well water to the overhead tank by the shed, and then comes the old commuter station of Llanbadarn (St. Padarn's Church).

The first ecclesiastic buildings were in turn priory and bishopric, and the present church is early 13th century with a 15th century chancel at an angle to the rest and termed the 'Weeping Chancel'. There are two important Celtic crosses. Here Dafydd ap Gwilym wrote the poem 'The Ladies of Llanbadarn' in the 14th century.

The first mile of the journey is past and the engine is whistling insistently before crossing a well-used road, the B4581. To the south are the fine Blaendolau (Meadow Head) playing fields belonging to Coleg Prifysgol Cymru, and above Llanbadarn to the north we can see the modern buildings which mark the southern limit of the University campus. These buildings are The College of Librarianship, Wales, The Welsh Agricultural College, and the Aberystwyth College of Further Education. A brief straight run brings the train to the trestle bridge across Afon Rheidol. To the south was once a broad bed of shingle

No. 8 passing Llanbadarn in June 1959.

Crossing the Rheidol Bridge on No. 9 in September 1959.

Optical illusion — the Rheidol Bridge in April 1957.

Rheidol Bridge, track and deck, looking towards Aberystwyth in 1957.

No. 8 crossing the Rheidol Bridge in June 1959.

where the gangs collected stones for ballast, but now the river has been re-aligned to run a straighter course. The little building is the Hydromatic Station where instruments record graphs of water flows and levels.

A gentle bend allows us to look back on the north side of the train to see the length of Pendinas and Aberystwyth with Constitution Hill sealing off the end of the Vale like a pair of enclosing horns. It is this lower part which is Dyffryn Rheidol, the true Vale of Rheidol extending for the first seven miles up to Aberffrwd. After passing a few houses and small fields and along a row of majestic trees by the 2 mile post, the engine is whistling like mad before crawling across a broad road leading into Stad Glanrafon (River Bank Estate), a highly successful modern industrial development managed by Datblygu'r Canolbarth (Mid Wales Development) and Cyngor Sir Dyfed (Dyfed County Council). This is the last trace of urban development we shall pass.

At the far end is a disused lane crossing and a sign board bearing witness that the bramble-choked hollow was once Glanrafon Halt; here the line is bending to the north so as to clear Rhiw-las-crug (The Stone-crowned Green Hill), which thrusts northwards from the southern ridges. The next stretch from here to the hill the author once described as where the river played touch with the line, but several diversions of the course to help the farmers have changed several former stretches of fast-flowing water into sluggish backwaters. At the east end of that same bend the rails had once to be slewed over 6 feet away from the river to prevent serious erosion, and the bend now over-runs before deflecting back to the next piece of straight. The gorse is still lovely in early summer and kingcups and water crowfoot are establishing themselves in the stiller water. Ecology, like the river, is always on the move. Further on, Lascrug Ballast Siding trailed back to the water's edge, but little trace of this short-lived work can be found today. Then comes an entrancing glimpse of the river and the track rises on a curve back to the south into a shallow cutting, to emerge onto flat farmland at a

The site of Glanrafon Halt from the crossing, looking towards Devil's Bridge, in 1949. *R. K. Cope*

Curve beyond Glanrafon, looking towards Devil's Bridge in 1957.

No. 9 brings a train back along the bulging retaining wall in June 1956, past what was then the main course of the river, now a weed-choked backwater where the track has had to be set back 6 ft for stability.

THE JOURNEY UP THE VALLEY

From the crossing in the foreground to the next one down was the extent of Lovesgrove station, looking towards Aberystwyth in 1983.

higher level. This is a higher flood plain with better soil, better grazing and dairy farming in evidence.

Past the 3 mile post was Lovesgrove Station, put in specially to serve Territorial Army camps across the river to the north. To the south is a stand of Douglas fir which is our first sighting of forestry managed by Comiswn Coedwigaeth Gwarchodfa Gogledd Cymru (The North Wales Conservancy of the Forestry Commission). It is called Coe Cwm-lletty (Lodging Valley Wood). The Lodgement would have been that of tree-fellers and sawpit carpenters, a very rough affair indeed. The train is now advancing along a great rarity in narrow gauge, $1\frac{1}{4}$ miles of dead straight track, which corrects the diversion towards the north created by Rhiw-las-crug, by aiming diagonally back towards the southern ridge to a place convenient for getting away from the flat. The first farm to the south is Tre'r'ing (The Place of Sorrow). Under Welsh law of succession, land was divided equally between sons. Here, it is told, Prince Arthen of the south side of the Vale fought with his brother Iorowerth of the north side and many men were slain. Next, the straight traverses the lands of Pwllcenawon (Fox Cubs Pool). 'Pwll' is a name given to a calmer stretch or bend in the river, and once the river swept past the door of the farm. Traces of the old course can be picked out first by a long pool raking westwards on the north side, and then by a series of hollows sweeping back from the farm, curving in towards the line and discernible as an S curve to the northeast back on the other side of the rails. The large modern milking parlour is built over what was, up to 1984, another long stretch of water. The ancient river course has imposed its mark upon the railway in the form of a 2 foot lift in about 60 feet where the trackbed goes from a cutting, which is a merest scrape in the

Rheidol driver — a study of Les Morgan taken in 1967 with the fireman steadying the photographer.

The mile-long straight, looking towards Aberystwyth in 1957.

field up to field level. Pwllcenawon is the birth place of Dr Lewis Edwards. He was born here in 1809 and went to school across the river on stilts bearing his younger brother on his back. He went on to become the most famous of the Principals of Bala College. Near here, too, was born John Roberts known as 'Ieuan Gwyllt' the originator of the Welsh Singing Festivals.

To the north are low hills broken by the Lovesgrove Gap where A4159 runs north to Machynlleth, and the higher hill to the right of the gap is Banc-y-Gymryn (Gymryn's Hill). A slight bend southwards marks the end of the long straight and we come back to the river once again. The reach flowing away to the north has scoured its own width further to the west since the line was surveyed. The ridge to the south is Rhiw-Arthen (Arthen's Hillside). The Prince's name may have been derived from arth (bear). The farm lying back at the foot of the ridge is Rhiwarthen-isaf (Lowest Rhiwarthen) to distinguish it from the next house barely half a mile further on which is Rhiwarthen-uchaf (Highest Rhiwarthen).

Then a pretty little stretch of river is past and an old buffer stump, a line of silver birch trees showing where the old shed, in which spare carriages were stored during the winter, once stood. The black corrugated iron shed was the waiting room and ticket office of Capel Bangor (The Wattle-walled Chapel), a proof of the long history of the impressive little church standing half a mile away to the north. The goods yard is now a ballast tip and a retired railwayman cultivates the rest as a garden. We are still only 75 feet above sea level, but the engine is whistling for the road crossing, and once across the road will be starting to puff

'Old' Capel Bangor, as of the 1940s. The low building on the right was once stabling and a smithy. *Landscape View Publishers*

harder to lift the train up a bank curving gently towards the hillside. To the north we can see right up the Melindwr (Watermill) Valley to the Plynlimon range beyond, and we get our last close-up view of the river. At the top of the incline we cross Lovers' Lane by the 5 mile post into a little tree-lined cutting, to come out along higher farmland at yet another farm called Melin Rhiwarthen (Mill Rhiwarthen). Nestling amid the trees to the south is the caravan site. Rhiwarthen had a water mill fed by half a mile of leat cut from the next higher bend in the river, and traces still exist at the bottom of the adjacent fields.

THE JOURNEY UP THE VALLEY

67

Capel Bangor station from across the river in 1955.

Lovers Lane crossing in 1957 before the installation of cattle grids.

THE VALE OF RHEIDOL LIGHT RAILWAY

Tanyrallt between 5¼ and 5½ miles, in 1957.

Above is the start of another forestry plantation, first a small stand of Sitka spruce and then nearly half a mile of Japanese larch. To the north comes a box hedge, behind which is a small group of pines, all that remains of the garden of a corrugated iron bungalow which is now finally rusting away as a tractor shed. We have now reached the farm of Tan-yr-allt (Underhill) which lies very close to the 100 foot contour. Now the engine is beginning to pound and the train is speeding up to get a run at the first real incline and, just past the farm, the 1 in 50 starts so abruptly that if you are alert for it you can feel the fore end of the coach lift as the climb is commenced. From here on there will be no more gentle toddling across level farmland and all will be proper mountain climbing; with everything depending on the teamwork up front.

A field below displays a remarkable set of overgrown ant hills and then we are in broad-leaved woodlands on both sides of the line. The major wood on the right is Coed Troed-rhiw-seire. 'Coed' is Wood and the rest derives from a vanished homestead (At the foot of Carpenter's Hillside) which was the home of saer bach (The Little Carpenter), who was still at work there for a year or so after the line was cut and opened. Of him, another bach, Jack Bach Davies (he who had to stand on a box to drive a Duke class standard gauge engine) used to tell a yarn. The saer and his helper (the man at the bottom of the vertical saw with his eyes full of sawdust) used to walk to Aberystwyth for a good drink or two, or more, and then they would walk back along the track and allegedly would finish, crawling along on their hands and knees. The one is supposed to have said to the other 'I don't think much of the silly B who designed these stairs' as they went from sleeper to sleeper. 'Neither do I, all go and no rise they are.' Whether the story be true or just a straight-faced legpull, the two men must have been used to hard work for the principal tree of the valley is the Durmast or Sessile Oak, whose leaves are more deeply indented than those of the English oaks. Besides the oaks, there are many beech and ash trees, as well as birches, sycamores, hazels and rowans.

The wood ends at the pretty little combe of Nant-y-ronen and the train comes out into the open before the 6 mile post. A

After hand-sanding from the front platform to get the train re-started above Tan-yr-allt on a wet day in 1958, fireman Dewi Williams takes a flying leap down to rejoin his driver as the cab passes him.

Below Nantyronen, looking towards Aberystwyth in 1957.

Where the line crosses Nant-y-ronen (proper), looking towards Aberystwyth in 1957.

quarter of a mile of straight takes us to Troed-rhiw-felen (At the Foot of Yellow Hill). 'Felen' may also be anything from yellowish green to pale brown indicative of relatively poor pasture, and 'las' is the better kind, being green or blue-green. The shimmer of water some way below is Glan-rhyd-ty-noeth (The Bare House on the Bank by the Ford). Now your 'tin' is what you are sitting on, so if a straight-faced Welshman with a twinkle in his eye tells you it is 'tin-noeth', the deep ford of the bare bottoms, he is having you well and truly on. Here extraction of gravel has left a range of beautiful lakes, which are scheduled for landscaping into a fish hatchery and a marina. Behind the upper fields of Troed-rhiw-felen is a long plantation of Norway spruce and Japanese larch with some oaks, and where the woods come down to the line are Japanese larch and a few beech. Here, too, is the first short length of true rock face.

A bit more climbing along a tree-lined and winding way brings us to another little open area above Tyllwyd-isaf (Lowest Grey House), where the line levels off before crossing a minor

GWR style sleeper-on-end hut in Nant-y-ronen cwm below the 6 mile post. This was the upper hut for Gang 61 whose length ended at the 5¾ mile post. Photographed in 1983.

THE JOURNEY UP THE VALLEY

A last look down at the river in June 1962.

The quarter-mile straight leading to Troed-rhiw-felen in September 1959.

The GWR 6¼ mile post by Troed-rhiw-felen, the scene of the 1986 derailment, looking towards Devil's Bridge on 28th March 1983.

A Sunday evening walk for the Burton family of Aberdauddwr by the utility pattern 6¼ mile post, looking towards Aberystwyth in June 1956. Putting these two pictures together shows that not even mileposts are totally static.

Up through sun-dappled woods to Nantyronen in August 1958.

At the 6½ mile post, looking towards Aberystwyth in 1958.

THE JOURNEY UP THE VALLEY

The site of Nantyronen station, looking towards Devil's Bridge with Cnwch-yr-arian beyond in 1957.

road into Nantyronen (Ashbrook). Here the site of the former station is now a stop for refilling the water tanks of the engine and for telephoning to announce the position of the train while passengers enjoy a fine view away to the north across the Vale.

The train is accelerated sharply away from Nantyronen because the succeeding incline is one of the steepest on the line. We traverse more open country past the 7 mile post above Troed-rhiw-ceir (At the Foot of Car Hill), referring to an old sledge road now extinguished by ploughing the upper pasture. Just as we enter Coed Lluest (Shepherd's Bothy Wood) the first noticeable trace of lead mining is to be seen. In the bank to the south is the fenced-off adit, and below to the north are the spoil tips, and 150 yds beyond another mine is crossed; both are now much hidden amid native oak woodland. A sharp curve takes us round and above Abernant (Brook's Mouth) and there is another change to forestry plantations of Japanese larch and

Curve at 7 miles above Nantyronen, looking towards Devil's Bridge in 1954.

Adit of Coed Lluest mine below 7¼ miles, looking towards Aberystwyth in 1954.

Great Western gate and notice near the 7¼ mile post in 1954.

THE JOURNEY UP THE VALLEY

Away on to Aberffrwd in June 1959.

Bend approaching Aberffrwd at 7½ miles. Note the closest rock face on the line and the 50 level post. Photographed in 1954.

Aberffrwd, looking towards Devil's Bridge in 1935.
H. F. Wheeller

some European larch, followed by dark Western Hemlock, which imparts a sombre aspect to the level space occupied by a water tank at the site of the once popular Aberffrwd (Stream's Mouth) station with a fine open view across the eastern end of the Vale. We are now at 280 feet above sea level, with a further 400 feet to be climbed in the next and final 4 miles. The Calvinistic Methodist Chapel is one of the landmarks of this highly-cherished faith. First the followers had to meet in secret at pre-arranged and varied places to avoid being stoned on the way. When matters had improved, meetings were held at Ty Cwrdd (Meeting House) which is now renamed Llyn-onn, and the first chapel proper was erected in 1770.

The engine whistles for a lane crossing for the last time and we pass along a miniscule cutting and on round a steeply-embanked curve across Cwmdauddwr (Valley of Two Streams). Above the bend across Cwmdauddwr is Grand fir followed by an admixture of Sitka spruce, Japanese larch and Red oak. Emerging from a long narrow cutting, the train curves round into the open where we may look back to see Aberffrwd and the Vale for the last time, for we are now entering Cwmrheidol, the narrow upper part which is the Rheidol Valley. The hillside is that of the Cnwch-yr arian (Pointed Silver Hill) and the Pant Mawr Mine hidden at the top of the cwm was the focal point for more fraudulent prospectuses than almost any other in the whole of Wales. Pant Mawr (Great Hollow) has given its name to the entire hillside and wood the line is now following, and the succeeding two miles of plantation are a lesson in forestry in

Aberffrwd crossing, looking towards Devil's Bridge, from the top of the Down Home signal in 1954. Note that the ungated level crossing was not in any way protected by the signals.

The first revival of chocolate and cream, No. 7 on Cwmdauddwr embankment in 1958 before the trees were allowed to grow over.

Leaving the Cwmdauddwr bend, June 1956.

A Stephenson Locomotive Society special in 1955 rounding the Cnwch-yr-arian, W. A. Camwell, then editor of the SLS Journal, filming from the rear coach.

themselves could we be quick enough to recognise all that we will see. About half way round that outer bend, hidden behind the oaks, there is a small stand of the great dawn redwood, *Sequoia sempervirens*, and we will have passed the 8 mile post. Still glancing upwards to the south there is a long parade of Japanese larch, Douglas fir, Lodgepole and Corsican pines, and Sitka spruce. All the while to the north below are the mixed deciduous woods belonging to the Central Electricity Generating Board which, unfortunately, hide the spectacle of the reservoir itself. Here is an auxiliary lower-output generating station working off the outfall from the main station higher up the valley, and a salmon ladder, all most attractively landscaped. A glimpse can be caught by looking back when the train has got higher up.

Just by a high rock bluff is a footpath running downhill back to the road which led via a wooden footbridge to Miss Trotter's Meithrinfa (Nursery) School. All along this steep slope of Pant Mawr the trackbed has been cut as a ledge from the solid rock, and through several rock ribs which show clearly the vertical fall of the strata caused by folding aeons ago. Distant below and beyond the main lake of the reservoir, is the well-laid-out and interesting Display Centre maintained by the Generating Board. At lake level through the woods below the line the Board has laid out an attractive nature trail documented in a leaflet issued from the Centre. Soon we will be passing the 9 mile post just above the 400 foot contour.

The long plantations of Coed Dol-fawr (Great Meadow Wood) extend for more than a mile along the facing hillside to the north. In the centre lies the sterile detritus of the Gelli Mine (The Mine in the Wood). Known as 'The Stag' because of its shape, it was formed first by the tipping of the then useless blende and spoil from the original lead mine about the animal's head. When the invention of the galvanising process to coat sheet iron created a demand for zinc, the now valuable spoil was shovelled downhill to a lower processing floor and so the configuration

THE JOURNEY UP THE VALLEY

Going away round the Cnwch-yr-arian in August 1958.

Above the reservoir in September 1961.

Passing Llwgn-y-groes and the power station in September 1961.

Curves below 9¼ miles, looking towards Aberystwyth in 1956.

was completed. The spine is the line of the old tramway from which the spoil was tipped. The trees are, in the main, those we have already noted on the way up but around The Stag is a fresh variety, Grand fir.

On the valley floor below, and a little east of The Stag, is the hamlet of Llwyn-y-groes (Aldergrove), we have crossed the 400 foot contour and the 9 mile post is coming up. The modern building in the middle of Llwyn-y-groes is the main Generating Station, taking water via a near-vertical tunnel coming down the hillside behind from the great Nant-y-moch (Rushing Stream) Reservoir below Plynlumon. When there is a flow of water from the large culvert beneath the station, we could be watching an outfall of 19 million gallons per hour. Just to the right is a red brick chapel and a faint trace going up the slope behind. This was the line of the massive timber double drive-rod system which transmitted power from a water wheel on the edge of the Rheidol to the Bwa-drain (Thornbow) Mine hidden over the crest in a tiny hanging valley.

A concrete slab at the outer edge and a notice mark the site of Rheidol Falls Halt and very quickly there is a high rock face to the south. Affixed to it is a tablet to Oliver Veltom, a senior railwayman who loved this valley, and whose ashes were scattered here in 1980. The Douglas firs below are hiding the view of Rheidol Falls, the salmon ladder, and the footbridge of Ffrwd-ddu (Black Water), a reminder of the poisoned nature of the river during active years of lead mining, and for many years afterwards, though it was actually named much earlier from the deep stillness of the rocky reach below the falls. Just past Oliver's Rock we can look down into the mouth of a mine adit below rail level in the bank to the south. The next feature is the long open space where the line crosses the vast screes of the Gwaith-coch (Red Workings) Mine. All around, above and below, are old shafts and adits going back in time to the middle of the 18th century. Opposite is the beautiful waterfall of Cwm Colomen-ddu (The Combe of the Black Dove). The stream is Nant Bwa-

Road, river and rail near Rheidol Falls in August 1958.

The outer curve below 9¼ miles, looking down from the cab of No. 8, looking towards Aberystwyth. Note the chopped-down telephone pole and the cable replacement between the rails. Photographed in 1956.

drain, which falls from the hanging valley, flowing from west to east in the hills above. The hill to the left is topped by Castell Bwa-drain, which was a defensible settlement from the Iron Age.

A sharp curve southwards against a rock wall turns the line inwards towards a steep-sided little valley known variously as Cwm-yr-gos, Cwm-yr-ogos and Cwm Rhiw-gos for which no certain English equivalent has yet been found. It is surrounded by later shafts and adits of the Gwaith-coch and Rhiw-rugos lodes and shelters the remains of a much later venture, the Erwtomau (Hummocky Acre) Mine which sent lead ore down to Aberystwyth by rail. The power to work the crushers came from a large single-cylindered engine running on producer gas obtained by felling and roasting trees from the surrounding woods. The second and sharper bend, which turns the line back to its easterly course, has long been publicised as The Horseshoe Bend. Immediately past the bend was a platelayers hut which had been a guard hut from Lovesgrove, being not far short of the 10 mile post, and where decisions were taken on wet days whether to go out and work or not; it was always termed 10 Downing Street. Just beyond, the adit and spoil tip of another

'10 Downing Street', the old hut from Lovesgrove, in 1956.

Taking the Cwm-yr-ogos Horseshoe Bend in 1953.   *G. D. Braithwaite*

On towards Rhiwfron in August 1963.

Looking back along Allt-ddu and Pant-mawr in August 1962.

mine are crossed. This adit reached the upper end of a lode which, to add to the confusion, received the corrupted name of Rath-du.

Now we shall continue our journey along another ledge, cut this time from the face of Yr Allt Ddu (The Black Height), so called because from the valley below it is always seen with the sun behind it and is mostly in shadow. Shortly we are at the 10 mile post and around 500 feet above sea level, going through beautiful deciduous woodland which arches to meet overhead. In the 18th century the original oak woods along Allt-ddu were felled for shipbuilding and one 90 ton schooner named *Rheidol Valley* was launched down across The Gap into the harbour at Aberystwyth. During the 1914/18 war acres of sapling oak and beech were felled for pit-props and the trees we see here now are a third generation. On the north side below there were several viewing bays cut by the gang to allow passengers to see across the valley. These were pleasant little spots with low bushes, some wild flowers and frequented by small birds and butterflies. Now they are growing over and will revert to barren forest floor once again. This entire stretch of woodland on both sides has been designated as an SSSI, a site of special scientific interest.

Three-quarters of a mile on we will be coming level with the extensive ochrous scar of the Cwmrheidol Mine and, looking back, the smaller lower remains of the Caegynon (Cynan's Field) Mine. Presently the site and notice Rhiwfron (Hillbrow) are to be seen and this is where the aerial ropeway brought lead ore up to a siding at the outer edge of the rails. A stout gantry took the pull of the cables above the railway and down to a pair of anchor blocks in the bank uphill. Gates above and below mark the crossing of an extremely ancient way. Then there is a rock

The site of Rhiwfron Halt, looking towards Aberystwyth, in 1957. The figures picnicking on the right are Mrs. Diana Green and our two daughters.

Through the Rhiwfron cutting in June 1957.

The lost view from the Rhiwfron curve in June 1956.

Against a backdrop of mountains in September 1959.

Almost 'Look! No Rails!' across Nant-ar-fynwg in August 1960.

Pulling hard up to Quarry Cutting in August 1960.

cutting, the 11 mile post, and hereabouts we are at the 600 foot mark. Through the cutting was once unfolded the most magnificent view towards Draws Drum (Outfacing Ridge) and the Plynlumon range, but we must wait until the Lodgepole, Scots pines and the Lawson's cypress are mature enough for felling before that view can be restored to us. The line is now taking the train southward along the flank of Castell Faen-grach. Faen-grach (Scarred Peak) is the true old name, but has been mistakenly credited with having been a form of fortification, and so the Castell is a more recent addition. Above are some lovely old native oaks. At the end of this traverse to the south comes the attractive little dingle of Nant-ar-fynwg (The Stream on the Precipice) put down by the Ordnance Survey as Nant-y-fawnog or Peaty Stream. Precipitous is certainly the right description of its headlong plunge to the Rheidol 380 feet below.

The route is turned eastwards again along delightful natural woodland which is Coed Derwen (Oak Tree Wood), cared for on behalf of the people by Cyngor Gwarchod Natur Rhanbarth Dyfed-Powys (The Dyfed-Powys Region of the Nature Conservancy Council). At the end the line rises on an isolated embankment into a very deep rock cutting blasted through the back of a small quarry which faces Devil's Bridge. To the north-east are the ruined walls of an old woollen mill, and to the south-west lie traces of the old lead-smelt. A slight indent in the bank is the last sign of the furnace, from which the chimney was laid as a vaulted flue, running up the hillside at ground level, to finish at a tall chimney proper at the top. The smartly-painted bungalow was the contractor's navvy barracks brought over from the Elan Valley in 1901. The second of the two white houses is Smelting Cottage and is the last part of the original buildings left standing.

The rails turn east again across Nant Llettys and two explanations are given for this name, Lodge Brook from an encampment of shepherds or tree-fellers, and Letitia's from a lady who is reputed to have kept a grog-shop hard by. On the outside of

Quarry Cutting, looking towards Aberystwyth in 1956. Note the more open appearance as compared with the photograph on page 13.

Looking down to Quarry Cutting in 1956.

The woollen mill (below), the Pethick 'navvy barracks' and the quarry face below Devil's Bridge in 1960.

the curve the dam and pound, which supplied water to the woollen mill, are to be seen. At last the engine is pulling the train up the final slope where there are more folds in the rock cutting by the water tank, under the old Dorman Long bridge and into the level yard of Devil's Bridge, now restored to its ancient name of Pontarfynach. This could be Monk's Bridge, but one writer and schoolmaster who lived there has set it down as being possibly the Bridge on the Precipice.

In the hour since leaving Aberystwyth we have travelled a shade over $11\frac{3}{4}$ miles, climbed 665 feet to 680 feet above sea level, and, of this, 565 feet have been climbed in the last $6\frac{1}{2}$ miles. We are now 380 feet above the river.

Into Devil's Bridge past the woollen mill and the site of the old smelting works, on 29th August 1983.

Restoring the signal arms at Aberffrwd while the passengers on the first up train of the season wait patiently in the train half-way out on the lower up and down main line in 1954.

CHAPTER SEVEN

STATIONS, HALTS AND SIDINGS
Incorporating notes on Signalling

From the Accountant's Journal and Ledger and from the Minutes a large number of purchases can be identified and priced and between them these records present an interesting but often frustrating study; the minutes especially can be brief to the point of annoyance. Still, and because of them, a fair idea of what was needed to run a small railway can be pieced together.

First of all they had overspent as against the revised estimates as follows.

	£	s	d
Capital Authorised	68,000	0	0
Less Interest paid out of Capital	100	0	0
Capital Available	67,900	0	0
Capital Expended – Fixed Assets, Land, Track and Installations	62,095	4	0
– Mobile Assets, Locomotives and Rolling Stock	8,148	17	2
	70,244	1	2

The increase was caused by inflation arising from the Boer War and the total expended is still nominally around £2,500,000 of 1986 money. This does not imply by any means that the line could be built and equipped for anything like this sum today. Money may have shrunk by some forty-two times since 1897 in face value in the shops, but wages in terms of hour per hour are anything from 200 to 300 more than they were. It is not easy to equate a ganger at 17 shillings for a 70 hour week to a trainee trackman on a 38 hour average rota system getting between £80 and £90 per week in plain time.

The contract for supplying most of the buildings went to A. & J. Main & Co Ltd of London for good-quality timber-framed structures sheathed with corrugated iron. These comprised the long locomotive shed, three larger buildings for the General Manager's office, and the stations at Aberystwyth and Devil's Bridge; three medium-sized station huts for Llanbadarn, Capel Bangor and Nantyronen; and two down shelters for Aberystwyth and Capel Bangor. Traceable only was 'Additional Building' £90, which might have been the goods warehouse. Also there were five little hutches for the acetylene gas generators. Station lighting was installed by the Imperial Acetylene Gas Co Ltd at a cost of £224. Afterwards, when buying the calcium carbide needed to generate the gas, James Rees shopped around a bit and got it more cheaply from both Forbes Acetylene Gas Co Ltd and from C. C. Wakefield & Co Ltd.

Among all the oddments the Traffic Superintendent obtained for his office for directing the line and its thirty employees, was one of those typewriter repairer's nightmares, the Yost, with its purple ink-pads and somersaulting type-arms. For communication he had wished upon him the Phonopore system as used by the Cambrian. It was put in by J. B. Saunders & Co and it proved unworkable very soon after installation and had to be re-inforced by a load of extra batteries, relays and trembler bells, and so he was lumbered with the stocking of anodes and sal ammoniac for the wet Leclanché cells which were the norm in those days.

Fencing, gates, garden plants and shrubs were bought from varied local sources out of revenue because of that overspending of capital and a further manipulation of resources was effected by having most of the erection and labouring carried out as additions to the duties of the permanent way gangs. The seats had a link with the locomotives built by Davies & Metcalfe as they were supplied by the local foundry of Williams & Metcalfe.

Coal for the engines came from the Ocean Colliery owned by Lord Davies, so providing another link, at 20 shillings and 9 pence a ton for Best Welsh Steam Coal. The blacksmith was supplied with Welsh Smithy Coal from Ebbw Vale. The 18 to 20 tons burnt annually in the stations and in the Traffic Superintendent's office came mostly from the loco stack, but when demand was overtaking speed of contract delivery, odd lots were had from C. Meehan in the main station goods yard, from the Cambrian Railways, and there was one bargain truck-load from the Hafod Colliery near Ruabon at 11/6d plus 3/6d cartage.

Cylinder oil came from C. C. Wakefield & Co Ltd and there was one delightful item in the petty cash 'Candles for Boiler Inspection' 1/6d. There was one absolutely mind-boggling item in 1905. 'Purchased from Mr. C. D. Szlumper, the Engineer 1 truck: 1 barrow: 1 set pigeon holes: 1 × 3-colour handlamp: Lamps &c £2–14–6d'. The explanation simply must have been that he brought his needs on appointment and got the company to pay for them afterwards. Uniforms were bought from the well-known suppliers of firemen's, police and railwaymen's natty menswear, Huggins & Co Ltd. Another purchase was a screwing machine in 1904 from the sale of the equipment at the Frongoch Mine. This was a screw-cutting lathe with the old-style loose change wheels for setting pitch and cost £13 10s 0d.

The signalling and point system for each site will be explained under each place but it is thought that a preliminary overall review would be helpful.

The signalling system was installed by J. B. Saunders & Co who supplied most of it, all for the sum of £1167 8s 4d. The tablet lock apparatus was bought separately from Saxby & Farmer at a total cost of £117 2s 6d. Such apparatus made by Saxby & Farmer would appear to be a bit of a rarity. Saunders went to Worcester for the equipment where Dutton & Co Ltd had sold out to J. F. Pease & Co Ltd in 1899, who in turn sold out to McKenzie & Holland Ltd in 1901, so whatever the label, it seems likely that it was mostly a Worcester set of gear.

The signal arms and posts are McKenzie & Holland in style and the ground frames bore the legend J. F. Pease & Co Ltd, Engineers, Worcester. As we have already learned, preliminary trips up the line had been made by young Mr. Dutton.

Facing points to loops were operated by Pease 'Economic Facing-Point Lock' apparatus. The motion needed long-travel rodding and when setting for the left-hand or facing road the first half of the stroke moved the point blades. During the second half of the stroke the blades were held against the right-hand stock-rails while the locks were pushed home. At the same time another piece of rodding unlocked a slide through which the motion of the relative signal passed and so it could be lowered. If it became necessary for a train to traverse the right-hand side of the loop, the signalman spoke to the driver, and signal and system were ignored. The WR Signalling Foreman who oversaw its demolition has described it as 'The weirdest contraption I ever saw in all my days'.

The line was divided into three tablet sections and instruments were installed at Aberystwyth, Capel Bangor, Nantyronen and Devil's Bridge. All siding points off the main line were releasable only by the tablet for that section.

When Aberffrwd was opened as a passing loop, all the installation was put in by Tyer & Co Ltd, and Saunders moved the tablet instruments up from Nantyronen.

In 1912 Aberffrwd was closed as a tablet station to save manning and the line was run in two sections only. On 25th March 1917 Capel Bangor was closed as well and the line was worked 'one engine (or train) in steam' until 1919. During the winter of 1920/21 working reverted for some time to 'one engine in steam'. Aberffrwd remained clipped and padlocked until the post 1923 period when the GWR restored all sections with Tyer No. 6 instruments made redundant from the Cambrian after the GWR key token system had been installed along the main lines. Signalmen porters attended at Capel Bangor and Aberffrwd as needed. After the withdrawal of winter services as from 31st December 1930, Capel Bangor and Aberffrwd had their signal arms taken down each winter and these were left locked away in the ticket offices, and the loops were clipped and padlocked for right-hand road (looking up) until the first train of the following season. On such an occasion the one compartment of the brake-third was full of railwaymen who descended at each station and swarmed up the signal posts and refixed the arms to the interest and wonder of the passengers. The point-rodding was freed and all movements checked and last of all the man-in-charge lugged all the buckets, brooms, return-pads and tickets needed to run the station into his little office. Then, the train went on to Aberffrwd for a repeat performance. At Devil's Bridge there was the putting off of the station 'gubbins', plus the one refinement that the others did not get. Suddenly there sounded

Detail of McKenzie and Holland signal arm, taken in 1955 with the kind assistance of Crosville who loaned the author a double-decker bus and driver for a moment.

Everything needed to run Devil's Bridge station being offloaded from the first passenger train of the season in 1954.

STATIONS, HALTS AND SIDINGS

As from 1963 the two loops were kept clipped and padlocked and, during the next two years or so, as labour was available, were stripped down to single line.

With the opening of the new LMR terminus at Aberystwyth in 1968, the GW staffs with Annett's key became redundant and a new system was devised using a train staff of polished aluminium with the necessary keys attached and two numbered train tickets with copies of the same keys.

If there is only one train in service, the driver is given the train staff. In the afternoon or at any other time when two trains will be away up the line, the first driver is shown the staff and is given Ticket No. 1. The second is given the staff and the process is repeated at Devil's Bridge for the return journey. On Gala days when all three engines are in service and will be away in sequence, the second driver gets Ticket No. 2 and the last driver to move gets the staff. Always it is the last driver away who carries the staff from either end. At the mid point, formerly Aberffrwd and subsequently Nantyronen, since the watering point has been changed, drivers unlock a telephone and report arrival to Aberystwyth and to Devil's Bridge when travelling in either direction. When an up train has been reported another up train is allowed to leave Aberystwyth. When a down train has been reported, another down train may leave Devil's Bridge. Thus it is just possible to work three trains up to Devil's Bridge, and when they are all 'stacked' working back can be started. To enable this method to work train No. 1 must be watered up and marshalled for departure before the arrival of train No. 2 and there are several permutations of placing the first train to be sent back either in the ballast siding or in the down loop. The former move enables the watering and marshalling of train No. 2 before the arrival of train No. 3.

Observe too that on the Vale of Rheidol, up is uphill to Devil's Bridge and never 'back to the principal terminus' as on most standard gauge lines. In the winter when the Permanent Way Supervisor is in occupation of the line, he takes full charge of the staff and only one engine is permitted in steam. He shows the driver the staff, and the tickets remain locked away.

Guard Joe Rowe with the Aberystwyth-Aberffrwd staff in 1959.

the bump, thud and swoosh as the plumber tested all the lavatories so that the summer could start.

For the 1951 season Capel Bangor was shut down, clipped and padlocked, and the signal arms were taken down so that once again there were only two tablet sections. Aberffrwd was rostered with Bow Street and a signalman cycled across as required. One of the ex-Cambrian Tyer tablet carriers had 'Bow Street' scratched into the leather.

In 1956 when the telegraph poles started falling from the combined effects of age, rot and insects, connection with Devil's Bridge and Aberffrwd was restored by fastening a cable of HSOS sun-resistant grade to the sleepers. This was only slightly tampered with at the Aberystwyth end by vandals, but when a herd of ponies broke through the fencing and spent half a winter trotting up and down the upper ledges, they did not leave it in very good shape, and communication was transferred to the public telephone system for the 1959 season.

Also c.1952 tablet working ceased when the original point systems at Aberystwyth and at the Transfer Siding were altered. Two GWR pattern train staffs with Annett's key came into use with Aberffrwd as the intermediate telephone and staff exchange station, train crews being responsible.

The London Midland Region staff, tickets and keys, in 1985.

Rheidol with top loading of four vehicles including one of the newly converted timber trucks. Note the station nameboard facing the street, the roof of the Traffic Superintendent's office next to it, and the flowerbeds, c.1908.

Courtesy J. I. C. Boyd

Aberystwyth station c.1903.　　　　　　　　　　　　　　　　　　　　　　　　　　　　　　　　*Courtesy E. Griffiths*

Aberystwyth Original Terminus
14 feet above Sea Level

A cattle market, an abattoir, a tannery and a foundry do not make ideal neighbours for a tourist passenger station, and it says much for the enthusiasm of the Edwardian holidaymakers that they flocked along Smithfield Street in their hundreds. The Szlumpers had designed quite a sound and workable layout and once Pethicks had removed their offices from behind the buffer stops James Rees could get his offices turned 90 degrees and see mostly everything that went on. The goods gates and passenger entrances were right next to the offices and were the only way in or out other than the gate of the Harbour Branch which was supposed to be locked except for the passage of a train.

Other buildings were the ticket office and waiting room with a verandah, a down side shelter, the acetylene generator shed and the goods warehouse with a Pooley weighbridge, also there was a carbide store. The Cambrian moved the acetylene generator shed away from the waiting room because of complaints about the smell and later there were five oil-gas connections down the centre of the loop.

The goods yard lost its loop in 1910 when the points were 'borrowed' to make Lovesgrove and, with the diminution of goods traffic, they were never restored, nor were the two spur sidings ever extended the full length of the yard as had been planned. They were removed and a longer spur reaching nearly to the Up Starter was put in instead for holding carriages.

The ground frame was an eight-lever J. F. Pease & Co Ltd frame with seven levers in use, which controlled the station points and the signals. Movement from and to the shed and the Harbour Branch was controlled by a lever released by a Saxby & Farmer tablet lock, and there was a second lever interlocked with the first which worked a trap point. The only signals were an Up Starter and a Down Home, both worked from the Pease frame, and a fixed Down Distant. The curve leading from the junction to the down side of the loop was also used for storing carriages for extra trains which were usually needed at weekends and particularly on Bank holidays.

The sheds were entirely on built-up ground and the pits had water welling up during floods. The long shed was one of the A. & J. Main contract buildings and the short one was built up using second-hand girders bought off Pethicks, possibly from their building at Nantyronen. The water supply was from the town mains into one 1,500 gallon tank. When it started to leak the Cambrian hastily replaced it by two odd-sized tanks holding about 1,000 gallons between them on a timber frame which may have carried the first tank, thought to have been of timber like that at Nantyronen. Then a drawing of one at Borth was copied for Aberystwyth and a 1,500 gallon tank built up from standard Cambrian castings was erected on mass concrete piers like those at Aberffrwd. This was short-lived as the GWR replaced it as inadequate, probably by 1924, by one of 3,000 gallons capacity and also made up of Cambrian castings. It might have come from somewhere on the Cambrian but all four of the standard castings required to make a Cambrian tank were at Oswestry

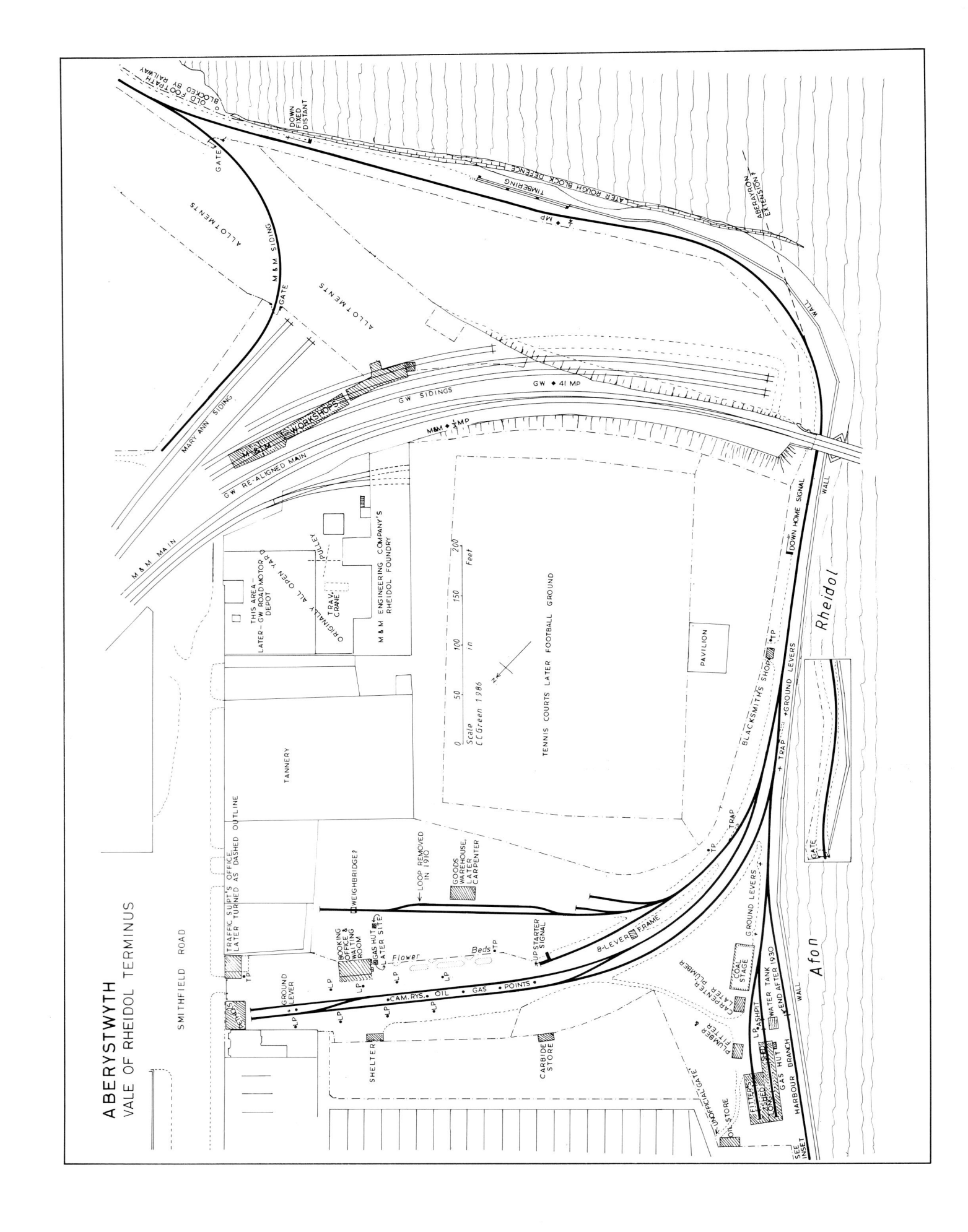

ABERYSTWYTH
VALE OF RHEIDOL TERMINUS

Rheidol about to leave Aberystwyth in a version of the LB & SCR livery c.1904. The original spark-arresting chimney is sagging a bit and the single coach carries a telegraph pole on the foot board. Much can be seen of the down shelter.
Author's collection

and there were probably spares lying about as well, including that one panel dated 1872.

The two workshops look substantial enough to be parts of that first A. & J. Main batch and the coal stage was 'home-made'. The blacksmith's shop up the line was a locally produced shanty. After the Harbour Branch was lifted, a spur was left in as a general utility siding.

The entrance to the station was under a deep signboard on tall posts spaced to allow for one wide gate and one smaller one. Later it was extended and there were several smaller gates. Here on rush occasions most of the staff, including train crews, would be issuing tickets as hard as they could go from rolls slung from string round their necks instead of the usual Edmondson card tickets. Only the guard was exempt and he was busy ushering

Coach No. 11 when first altered. Mr. Evans, an inspector on the Midland Railway, is standing in front with Mrs. Evans. *Courtesy J. G. Rees*

The old terminus c.1928. Only the down shelter seems to have been removed. Just to the left of the pavilion is one of the cattle vans lettered 'GW'. In the foreground is that immensely expensive river defence wall that the GWR was forced to build. *Courtesy J. I. C. Boyd*

Shed scene in Cambrian days in 1921, showing original water tanks with Cambrian replacement under construction behind. The two boards affixed to the van read CAMBRIAN and RAILWAYS. *W. L. Good*

A six-vehicle train traversing the site of the old station after crossing Park Avenue c.1927. Note the addition of steam-heating connection and the replacement of screw-coupling by lever-latch.
G. H. W. Clifford

the crowds into the carriages, filling them from rear forwards so that they could easily shunt another coach in from the loop if needed. Schedules were thrown to the four winds and the three locos were moving every bit of rolling stock, both passing loops at Capel Bangor and at Aberffrwd being used to work trains onwards as rapidly as possible.

In less hurried moments there were the well-cultivated flower beds to be admired, with their bright geraniums and heliotropes edged with lobelia. All the buildings were painted a bright leaf green until 1922. The *Aberystwyth Observer* was most impressed with the station which was 'provided with all the conveniences', and had special comment about the novelty of lighting by gas, considering that its example might well be followed 'in the homes of the gentry'. This was well before the line was running, as to create a good impression, Pethicks had already completed Aberystwyth as a non-working showpiece.

Early in 1905 Mr. Kenrick, a Director, suggested the idea of moving the terminus into the Cambrian main station. In May 1906 Mr. Rees was authorised to expend £10 on hospitality to 'a Railway Official'. Later in 1906, a concession at £3 per annum was granted for the siting of sweetmeat machines. By 1909 moving to a new terminus was strongly to the fore, and the Board held a three day meeting of inspection and discussion, all of which was abortive because of that lapse of powers to buy land already mentioned. Mr. Rees, as we know, had been promoted and the office on Smithfield Street was now the General Manager's office. In 1912 Herbert Jones sought authority to construct a carriage maintenance and repair pit, and was refused. He did get oil-gas connections (uncovered in 1955) installed but only three carriages may have been converted.

Once they had received all the old company papers and documents, the Secretary's office found that as yet they did not own the site of Aberystwyth station; the company had never owned it, they had no title deed and there was £400 at 4% interest still owing and piling up. The Solicitor to the Rheidol Company had been Mr. A. J. Hughes, the Town Clerk. It took another 5 years to get it settled.

By 1914 the river defences from the sheds up to the M & MR bridge were slipping. The Cambrian's first move was not to make one by merely declining to make any contribution towards the cost of the repairs. Subsequently the Secretary met the Surveyor and Alderman Samuel and the latter suggested that if the Cambrian did nothing then neither would the Corporation and so, by risking the tidal wall, the Cambrian would be forced to take action to save the line. The Secretary reported 'I consider Mr. Samuel's remark in the nature of a bluff. Try offering them two or three wagon loads of stone from Devil's Bridge' (more from Quarry Cutting). This makeshift sufficed but the 144 tons so used were not brought down until 1916. By 1921 the trouble had returned and in lieu of stone from Quarry, Cutting stone from the Cambrian's own quarry at Pant Rock could be delivered on site for 16/0½d per ton. But a rider was added that probably the Corporation could obtain local stone more cheaply. So the problem was deferred into the GWR régime.

ABERYSTWITH. — THE HARBOUR.

The Stone Quay c.1920. One Hafan wagon stands on the rails. The steamer against the quay wall is thought to be *Countess of Lisburne*.

National Library of Wales

The Harbour Branch

After leaving the junction the branch went between the sheds and the river and traversed a narrow strip of company land to a gate about 600 ft from the junction. It then curved westwards along the river bank on well-formed public ways to pass under the north arch of the Trefechan Bridge. After a brief curve north on a fall of 1 in 40 it swung round The Gap. This was a soft-bedded relic of shipbuilding days where boatmen hauled their craft out of the water for repairs and repainting. Here the line levelled for a bit, still curving round to nearly due south, to finish on the Stone Quay up a short run of 1 in 30.

The original course was to have been more level, along an embankment, across The Gap, with a culvert in the middle; hence the opposition and that Enquiry which forced the railway to build on the longer route, just above the high-water mark.

Once up on the Stone Quay, the line ran straight and parallel to the edge, about 15 ft in, and ended 20 ft from the end without any form of stop. There is no record of anything taking a dive into the harbour. The rails were let into the surface roughly without any of the usual sett finish applied to lines in public roads. There was a marker post against the warehouse wall, and harbour facilities consisted of a small crane and a capstan at the end of the quay. The wooden jetty extended past the Stone Quay and both were built upon the Rôfawr, the Great Shingle.

For a train to go along the Harbour Branch the signalman had to be in attendance to release the Saxby & Farmer tablet lock leading to the shed and to hand the driver the Harbour Branch staff. In between times rolling stock and particularly

Constructing the Harbour Branch round The Gap, November 1901.
A. J. Lewis

wagons were parked down the branch but never beyond the gate at the end of company land.

Construction began from the quay about December 1901 as soon as the first consignment of rail had been unloaded. All came by sea from Plymouth and one load of 250 tons off the S.S. *Abottsford* of Glasgow is recorded as arriving on Sunday, 16th

The Harbour Branch onto the Stone Quay, 1902.
A. J. Lewis

The Harbour Branch round the Gap, 1902. *A. J. Lewis*

THE HARBOUR BRANCH

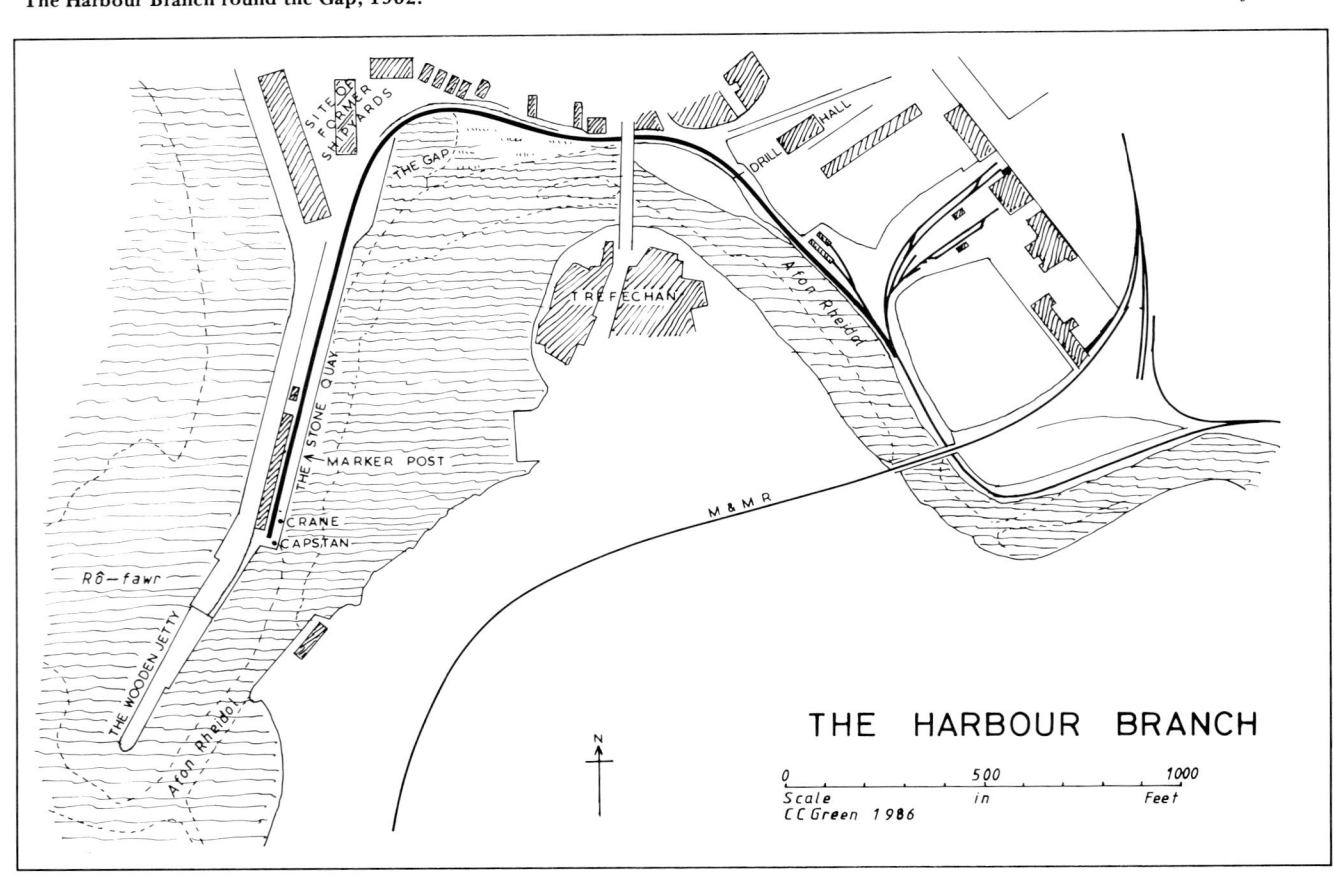

Scale in Feet
C C Green 1986

February 1902. The work was scamped because the whole project was starting behind schedule. Hence *Rheidol* was the only engine light enough to be risked along the branch and she acquired a special warning hooter. The guard was supposed to walk in front with a red flag to warn boatmen and bystanders and pick up obstructions. The driver's authorisation was a single staff and wagons were propelled up onto the quay. Occasionally, when loaded and empties had to be sorted, everything on the quay was coupled up and taken back to be shunted at the junction.

By 1904 the embankment rising onto the quay was subsiding and the Corporation charged £22 6s 7d for putting it to rights. At the end of 1904 the Traffic Superintendent suggested a passenger service. Quotations were obtained for fencing, a loop, a station, a motor and the probable cost of refettling the line to Board of Trade standards. It is an unlikely fantasy by today's standards but few Edwardians owned personal transport and had a great enthusiasm for unusual journeys, and so it just might have come off. When the unrecorded cost and details were reported to the Board, Mr. Rees got a cold semi-reprimand and the Secretary was to 'urge him to do everything possible by advertising &c. to bring the beauties of the line to Devil's Bridge before the Visitors'.

In March 1908 the Town Clerk wrote that the line was in poor condition and needed building up and paving with setts. The cost would be £35 and the Engineer was instructed to see if the Council would pay half. The Town Clerk's reply was the equivalent of the modern expression 'Not on your Nellie'. At the Board inspection on 6th July it was decided that the company could not lay setts outside the rails until the quay wall had been made level with the roadway, which was a gravelly sort of finish on a slight slope for run-off of rainwater. The Council would not budge and then the abashed Secretary had to own up to having lost all his correspondence with the Council. In 1910 he was in a worse mess over it because someone in the Council offices had just woken up to the fact that they should have been levying a Right of Way charge of £1 1s. 0d. per annum and he still had not found the missing file which held also the copy of the agreement. By 1912 the Board had to give in and pay the charge and £50 for laying of fair surfacing.

The right of way had to be kept open by traversing it once a year at least. After goods traffic had failed, it was kept open by *Rheidol* chuffing to the end of the quay and back in a bad year when nothing had been consigned along the branch. After *Rheidol* had been scrapped in 1924, the odd wagonload was drawn onto the quay by hired horses, and, in default of this, two platelayers solemnly pushed a trolley onto the quay, most likely to the accompaniment of cheers and jeers as they negotiated the 1 in 30 both ways if there happened to be a crowd of boatmen. The rails were lifted about 1930 and the sleepers were left in to rot around The Gap. A few still had not been grubbed up for firewood by the 1960s.

The rails, still visible, in the Stone Quay. Note there is no buffer stop and the original small fixed swivelling crane used for unloading sailing ships has gone, c.1913.
A. J. Lewis

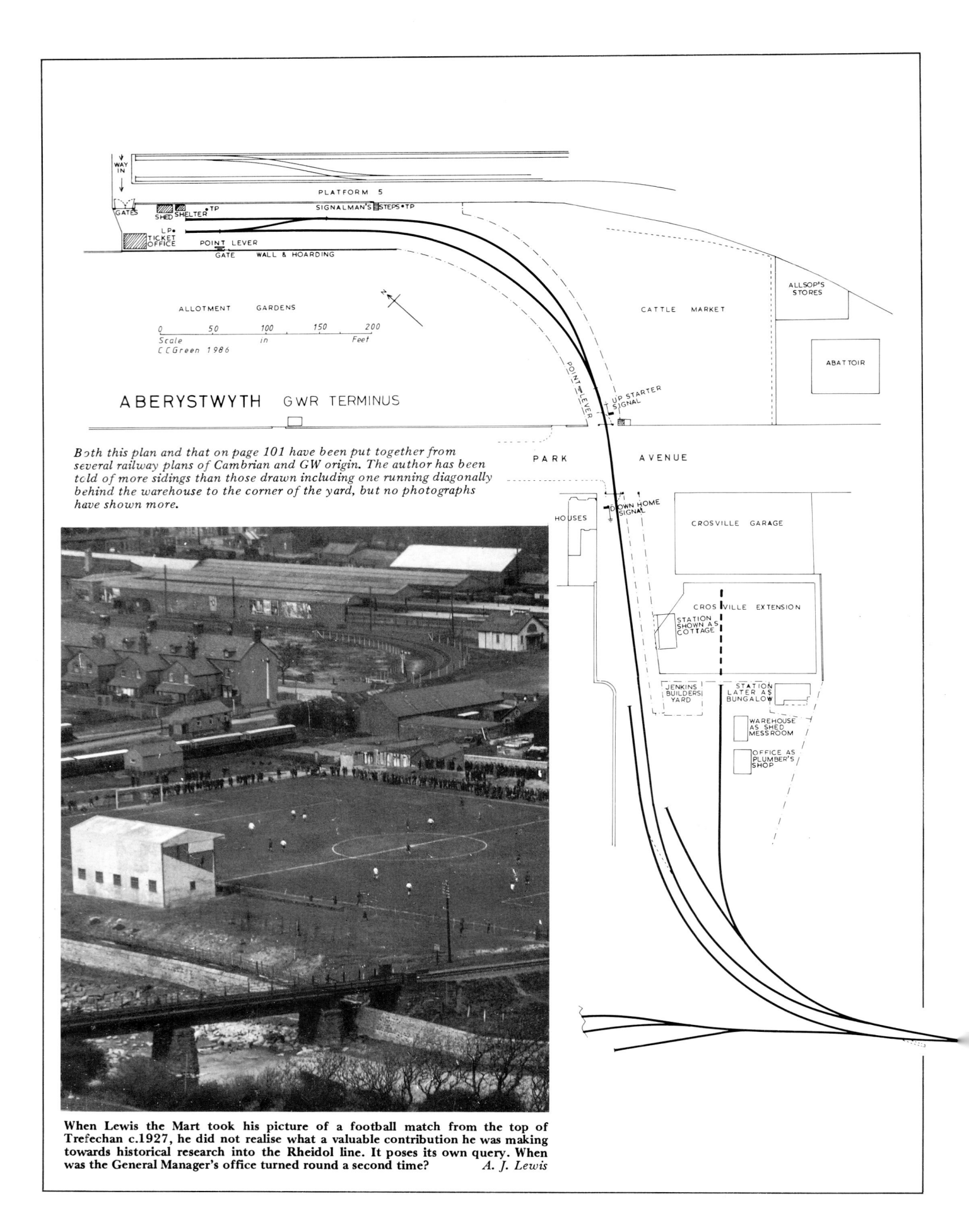

ABERYSTWYTH GWR TERMINUS

Labels on plan:
- WAY IN
- PLATFORM 5
- SHED, SHELTER •TP
- SIGNALMAN'S STEPS •TP
- GATES
- LP•
- TICKET OFFICE
- POINT LEVER
- GATE   WALL & HOARDING
- ALLOTMENT GARDENS
- Scale 0 50 100 150 200 Feet
- C C Green 1986
- ALLSOP'S STORES
- CATTLE MARKET
- ABATTOIR
- POINT LEVER
- UP STARTER SIGNAL
- PARK AVENUE
- HOUSES
- DOWN HOME SIGNAL
- CROSVILLE GARAGE
- CROSVILLE EXTENSION
- STATION SHOWN AS COTTAGE
- JENKINS BUILDERS YARD
- STATION LATER AS BUNGALOW
- WAREHOUSE AS SHED MESSROOM
- OFFICE AS PLUMBER'S SHOP

Both this plan and that on page 101 have been put together from several railway plans of Cambrian and GW origin. The author has been told of more sidings than those drawn including one running diagonally behind the warehouse to the corner of the yard, but no photographs have shown more.

When Lewis the Mart took his picture of a football match from the top of Trefechan c.1927, he did not realise what a valuable contribution he was making towards historical research into the Rheidol line. It poses its own query. When was the General Manager's office turned round a second time?   *A. J. Lewis*

Aberystwyth Great Western Terminus
14 feet above Sea Level

In 1925, and 20 years after Director Kenrick had first suggested it, the up line was extended across Park Avenue (which was the new name for Smithfield Street) and curved westwards to run parallel to platform 5 of the main station. A new loop and loco-shunt ended level with the beginning of platform 5, and the new way to the little trains was along platform 3, turning right behind the bay. Tickets were obtained from the main ticket office and the fact was advertised from the front of the fine new building which was formally opened in 1926. The old down side shelter was moved up and sited with its back to the allotments, but when it fell into disrepair it was not replaced.

Subsequently the whole area was improved by replacing most of the ash and gravel with asphalt. The signalman had a flight of stairs down from the end of the back wall of platform 5 so that he could come across from the main box to open the little Rheidol box by the gates as needed. The tablets, and later the staff, were kept in the small box which housed the two levers which worked the Up Starter and Down Home signals. To despatch a train he had to give the driver the tablet, open the gates, pull off the starter and go and stop the traffic along Park Avenue with a red flag. When he was seen to be in place, the driver would start the train and cautiously whistle his way over the level crossing. The gates which swung inwards onto railway land, were not locked with the signals. The signalman had to be on the alert for returning trains to have the gates swung, the Home off and himself ready to go out to flag the traffic to a halt. Mostly he would have heard the whistle in the distance for Plascrug crossing, again from close to the Fixed Distant beyond the M & MR bridge, and if he was not in sight when the driver could see down the straight, he would get a right fanfare to wake him up.

The returning down trains had to be brought in on the left side of the station loop. The engine would uncouple and run around the train via the crossover points at the far end. These were worked by the crew from a single lever set against the wall and had to be returned to straight after the passage of the engine. At the up end of the loop was one single set of points worked by a ground lever, on which the only bit of 'locking' was a detector to the Down Home signal (not quite as per the Board of Trade requirements).

Down at the old station a carriage siding was formed by removing both the loop crossovers and halving the down road of the old loop. On the other side of the running line the old short spur siding remained, together with the single line up the goods yard which got shorter as land was sold off; this too was a carriage siding for several years. The General Manager's office was placed end on to the warehouse as the plumber's shop and

The new terminus in 1926, with No. 7 receiving right of way. Note the abruptly cut-off vegetable crops.   *A. J. Lewis*

Passengers leaving and No. 7 running round, in 1960.

the warehouse was used as the staff room. The station was twice moved as a bungalow and for a third time to become the messroom in the Crosville yard where it is still. The Harbour Branch was truncated to a short siding behind the loco sheds. Movement control was effected by a hotch-potch of old gear made available by the dismantling of the original system.

For any movement from and to sheds and sidings, the signalman had to go down with a tablet and operate the ground levers. About 1952 this collection of museum pieces was replaced by a three-lever GWR tappet-lock frame with Annett's key. If the signalman was not in sight and perhaps an additional coach had to be fetched, and the small box had not been locked, it was not unknown for crew and guard to go down with the tablet. Now from the position of the one lever it was not easy to judge exactly when the engine was clear of the junction points, and more than one unauthorised signalman has derailed the pony by moving the lever too soon.

The last VIP train to be run into this terminus was on 1st July 1967 when the Minister of Transport, Mrs. Barbara Castle was to be convinced that the line should neither close nor be sold. The last ordinary train crossed Park Avenue at the end of Easter service on 6th April 1968.

One guard missed the start of his train and chased it without success right down to the level crossing. Not giving up, he tore past the markets and along the allotment paths to Plascrug crossing. His magnificent effort went unrewarded for the engine passed the end of the path before he got there and the fireman was looking ahead. The engine crew did not find that they were without him until they reached the gasworks.

Right: The GWR terminus in 1956. Note the single lever against the wall which worked the crossover points. The lower picture shows a close-up of one of the double-post buffer stops in 1956.

STATIONS, HALTS AND SIDINGS

Vale of Rheidol No. 1213 ready to leave with the afternoon train on 21st August 1946. *Selwyn Higgins*

The Park Avenue crossing and box in 1949. The loop facing points were worked by the ground lever on the left and rod bolted from the crossing cabin in connection with the Down Home signal. The departing train is signalled out of the 'arrival' side of the loop. *R. K. Cope*

Flagging a down train across Park Avenue in 1960. *Ann C. Carter*

Joe Rowe flagging No. 9 across Park Avenue in 1959.

The Park Avenue crossing in 1955, looking down to the terminus, showing the two McKenzie and Holland signals taken from the old terminus.

No. 7 on a morning train to Devil's Bridge passing the Crosville bus depot on 29th July 1953. *G. D. Braithwaite*

Shed and Harbour Branch. *J. I. C. Boyd*

STATIONS, HALTS AND SIDINGS

Sheds and site of the old station.

J. I. C. Boyd

No. 7 being prepared for an afternoon train. Note bucket being filled by 'tickling' the valve of the water tank.

H. F. Wheeller

Shed scene c.1948.

F. Hewitt

One of the several versions of LOCO COAL lettering on ex-Hafan No. 34136, outside the carpenters' (later fitters') shop on 13th August 1939.

J. I. C. Boyd

STATIONS, HALTS AND SIDINGS 117

Shed scene. From left to right: GWR water tank, long shed from A & J Main, fitters' shed using ex-Pethick materials, fitters' and plumbers' shop, carpenters' (later plumbers') shop, and coal stage, in 1946.
Selwyn Higgins

The third (Great Western) water tank, in 1957.

By 1957 both disused workshops had been carted away. Note all of the minor details essential when reproducing the atmosphere of an old steam shed in model form, the ash pit and the 'loo'. It was with the modeller in mind that the decision was taken to include views from many angles.

STATIONS, HALTS AND SIDINGS

No. 8 taking water at the shed in 1965. *Paul Karau*

Cleaning while steam pressure builds up, in 1965. *Paul Karau*

Top: No. 9 at the back of the long shed in 1956 and showing the ankle-ricking division between the two sheds. Above: No. 7 in the fitters' shed in 1956.

STATIONS, HALTS AND SIDINGS

The sheds from the north-east, in 1957.

From the south-west.

The fitters' shed showing its age.

The Western Region levers and rodding controlling the carriage siding and shed neck, with the bonus of a train under and one over the M & M bridge in 1956.

The ground frame made of GWR pattern levers controlling the shed points in 1955. The levers were released by the tablet (later Annett's key on the train staff). Note the channel section point rodding.

STATIONS, HALTS AND SIDINGS

The old route along the river wall, No. 7 in 1961.

Detail of that ingeniously devised route along the river bank and under the end span of the Manchester & Milford Railway Company's bridge in 1955.

Left: The fixed distant at the approach to the M & M bridge in 1955. Note the complete absence of a signal lamp.

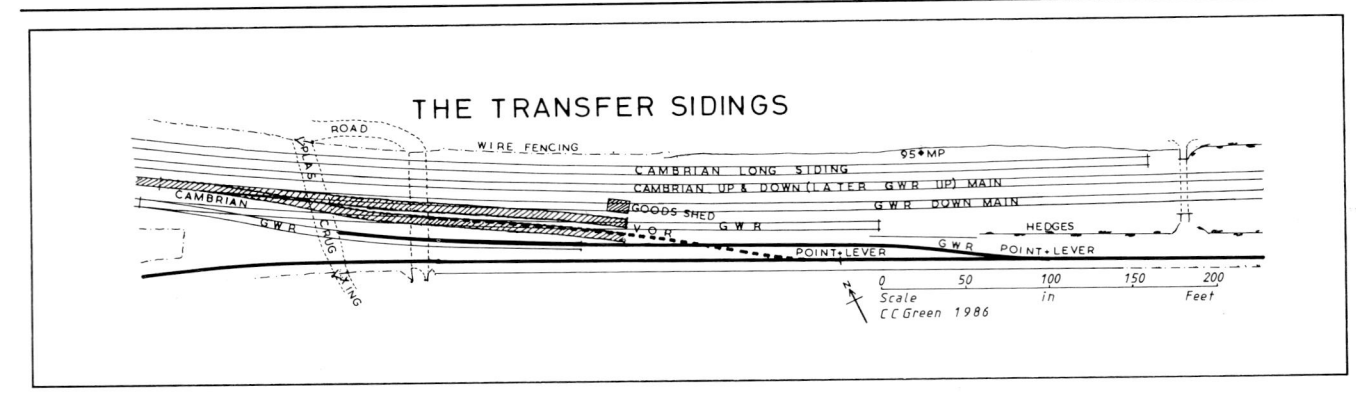

The Manchester and Milford Siding

About 300 yds past GWR ¼ milepost, & circa 20 ft above Sea Level

Passed for use on 26th August 1903, the siding faced down trains and curved in a northerly direction to run alongside the M & M Railway's Mary Ann Siding. This may have got its name from a sailing ship from which imported grain was offloaded onto the railways for maize once grew wild along the siding. When the GWR rebuilt Aberystwyth main station, the name was borrowed for another siding by Plascrug Avenue. The siding was released by Saxby & Farmer tablet lock.

As soon as the Cambrian-influenced Board assumed power, the siding was ripped out without warning during July 1910. The GWR goods agent protested that there was an undertaking in force and that the connection ought to be maintained. The Secretary was instructed to 'peruse any document and to report whether the Company has any such obligation' and he duly reported that he was unable to find any such document. The GWR was informed that 'This Company is unaware of the existence of any such obligation'. As the goods traffic had fallen to practically zero, the GWR did not pursue the matter any further.

Across the river was the Brick, Tile and Terra Cotta Works and the Rheidol line had severed the accustomed route of the employees to and from Aberystwyth. There was some small rumpus over their climbing fences and gates and trespassing along the railway and siding. During 1906 a siding to the south by Plascrug was proposed for loading the products of the works but nothing came of it.

The Cambrian Transfer Siding

About 90 yds short of GWR ¾ mp & c. 20 ft above Sea Level

Passed for use on 26th August 1903, the siding faced down trains and was released by Saxby and Farmer tablet lock. Initially it went off at a slight angle to run for about 100 ft alongside a similar slanting siding from the Cambrian. Both were laid erratically using the poorest of Pethick material on the Rheidol side and old worn rails etc on the Cambrian side.

The transfer siding in Cambrian days, looking towards Devil's Bridge in 1921. One wonders how the travelling crane was used, and the purchase of the 5-ton Ransome & Rapier crane from Birmingham Corporation Waterworks on 18th January 1905 may be significant.

STATIONS, HALTS AND SIDINGS

Collecting a trackload of coal for the shed in August 1952. *J. I. C. Boyd*

The Exchange Siding from the down train in 1954.

The Traffic Superintendent asked for a transhipping shed to be provided because he felt that the poor initial traffic was caused by the exposed situation under which goods had to be handled. Mr. Gough, for the Cambrian did not see the need for spending money on this scale, but agreed to improve facilities for transhipping timber. This was probably when an additional siding was run from the Cambrian to gauntlet the narrow gauge to allow end loading and unloading. A crane was provided by the Cambrian from 1906 for timber working but this is most likely to have been a standard gauge travelling crane. There was also a small shed at the end of the Cambrian siding.

This siding was taken up in 1925 during the GWR's doubling of the main line between Llanbadarn and Aberystwyth.

The Great Western Exchange Siding

About 50 yds short of the GWR ¾mp & c. 20 ft above Sea Level

Built in 1925 to replace the old Cambrian siding, it had half as much again of total accommodation but, with the withdrawal of goods services as from 1st January 1927, it passed the remainder of its days as a loco coal siding for the supply to the Rheidol engines and as a loading and re-railing point for locomotives and rolling stock sent away to Swindon for heavy repairs.

Initially, the old Saxby & Farmer lever and tablet lock were moved along but later (c.1952?) a GWR lever and standard Annett's key lock were fitted. Closure and removal came in 1968 when the new transfer siding east of the ex-GWR engine shed came into operation.

The transfer siding in Great Western style, looking towards Devil's Bridge in 1955.

Transfer siding, looking towards Aberystwyth in 1957. The Economic Facing-Point Lock mechanism lay between the switch blades just below and behind the stretcher bar. The single lever ground frame, incorporating the tablet lock in the flat portion in front of the lever, worked the running line point together with its lock, and also the single-bladed trap point.

Past Llanbadarn and the gas works (now mainly demolished) c.1925.

A. J. Lewis

Llanbadarn Station
About 140 yds short of GWR 1¼ mp c. 25 feet above Sea Level

Llanbadarn station, looking towards Devil's Bridge in 1949. *R. K. Cope*

Although never manned, Llanbadarn was always given the dignity of being a station; it is said that the guard of the last train before dusk lit the four gas-lamps. The engine crew and guard worked the crossing gates for a short period until this practice was dropped by arrangement, because of the delay to the trains. The 240 ft siding faced up trains and was released by Saxby & Farmer tablet lock. This was mostly worked by *Rheidol* propelling wagons from Aberystwyth but both goods and passenger trains did propel and shunt. If empties were to go back to Aberystwyth an ordinary train would leave them in the siding to be collected on the down journey. If they were needed at Devil's Bridge, they would be propelled to Capel Bangor where the train would be re-marshalled so that all wagons were at the rear of the train and with the brake van last, which was the rule for all goods and mixed trains beyond Capel Bangor. It was not always strictly observed.

Although there was a ticket office and waiting room, the guard had to issue tickets and most of the passengers had season tickets, a number of them being first-class. Llanbadarn was fast developing into a high-class dormitory suburb. The gas generator was removed in 1910 and fitted into one of the brake vans so that the trains could become gas-lit.

Llanbadarn's moment of greatness came in 1957 when the Royal Welsh Agricultural Show was held on the Blaendolau fields. The tablet instrument and a telephone were moved into the ticket office and Aberystwyth station limits were extended to Llanbadarn. A long train with a loco at each end shuttled out and back as hard as it could go. Business ran to 50,520 sixpenny returns. The third loco ran an abbreviated service to Devil's Bridge and a down train halted at the 1¼ mile post while the guard went forward for instructions. As soon as the shuttle was safely inside the loop at Aberystwyth, the train was allowed to go on. Driver Gwilym Davies established another record. He did most of the time on the shuttle and figured that he might get a bit extra if he was paid on mileage. He got an additional 1/6d and the distinction of being the only British Rail driver to earn a mileage payment on the narrow gauge.

The station was painted mid-green up to 1922, salmon brown and stone until after 1948, and chocolate and cream until it was deleted from the timetable, when it was later on painted black. Llanbadarn remained for many years the only intermediate stop listed in timetables and was not deleted until after the end of the 1969 season.

STATIONS, HALTS AND SIDINGS

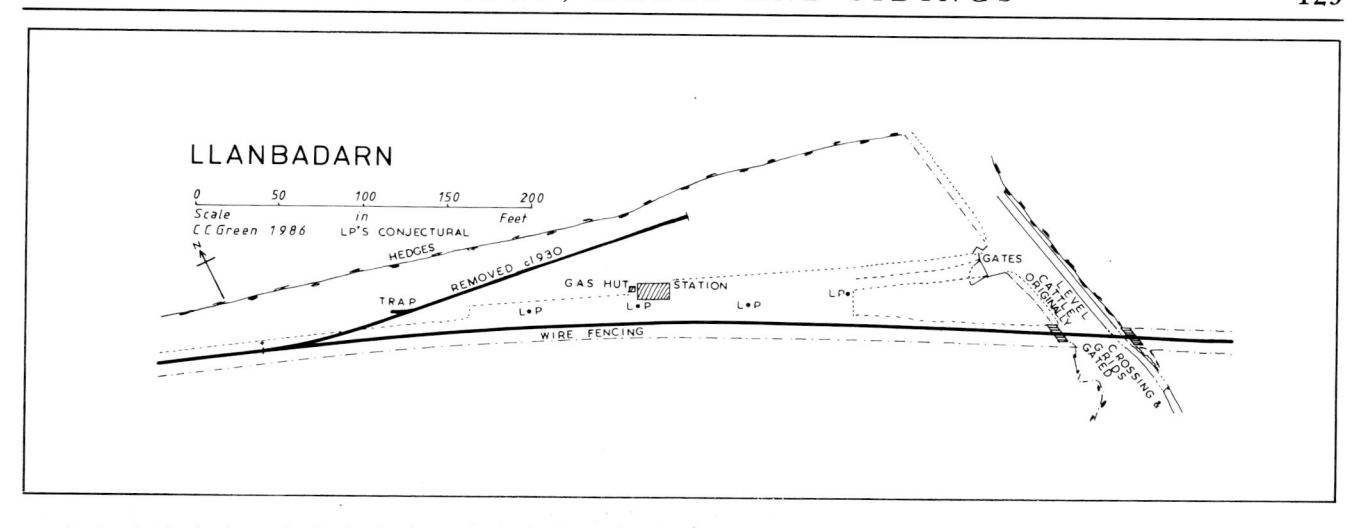

Llanbadarn station, looking towards Aberystwyth in 1949.
R. K. Cope

Llanbadarn crossing and station, looking towards Aberystwyth in 1957.

In the foreground is the magnificent spread of shingle which was reached by running the siding under the bridge and so trespassing to the annoyance of Mrs. Ann Morgan. Visible around the west abutment is the timber palisade protection against river erosion which seemed inadequate to Major Druitt.
Railway Magazine

Geufron Ballast Siding
By GWR 1½ mp, c 30 ft above Sea Level

Here, by the kind permission of Mr. Powell of Nanteos, the company got all its original unstable ballast. The rails were at a lower level than they are now and a steep drop to the shingle bed was just negotiable by *Rheidol*. Wagons were manhandled to the turntable which had to be steadied while they were pushed off in any direction in which the rails were at any particular time. The rails were more of the dregs of the Pethick lot.

Major Druitt criticised the unlocked siding off the running line and it was removed for his official inspection and then put back again with a padlock. Working practice was that *Rheidol* followed an up train and slipped down the siding. When all was shovelled on, the wagons were drawn up onto the main and were then propelled back to Aberystwyth before the down train came by. Not always was the timing quite right and Jack Bach (driver J. E. Davies) has recalled catching a glimpse of the down train at the end of the Llanbadarn straight as *Rheidol* shot over the Plascrug Crossing and round the curve onto the river bank, on at least two occasions.

Then there was the trouble with Mrs. Anne Morgan, who was the tenant of Geufron; the company had refused her request for additional drainage and was disputing the claim she was making for her tenant's rights, so she had not been paid. When she noticed that the gang had abstracted shingle from a small area under the bridge and beyond the abutments, she threatened a claim for trespass. Besides this, whenever she saw *Rheidol* stop and go down the siding she went across and vented her extreme displeasure on the unfortunate gang. Having already angered her with an offer of £48 to settle her principal claim with a 14 day ultimatum attached to it, the company made things worse by offering £1 for her £5 claim for trespass, upon which she took out a summons in the sum of £8. After a Board inspection of the site, they ordered a settlement of her claim. Mrs. Morgan agreed to a settlement over the land under the bridge but refused to give an undertaking 'to refrain from interfering with the removal of ballast'. Until she had got every penny that she felt was due to her the gang were going to get a piece of her mind whenever she felt like giving it. It dragged on until 1910 when she settled for £6 6s 0d for the bit of land under the bridge and by arbitration she got £80 for her main claim. By then all use of the siding had ceased and as she had only a life interest in the leasehold she started to harass the administration instead until she had actually received payment; she must have been a remarkable lady.

Being extremely heavy, the turntable was abandoned. During the drought and consequent low water in 1959 the author saw the edge of it and dug it clear for measurement. Since then the course of the river has been re-directed and all trace has been lost. The dotted line marked 'possible' on the plan is a concession to a suggestion that it could have worked downstream a bit in 49 years.

The turntable used at Geufron ballast siding in 1959, after an hour or so of gardening with wet feet. Probably it is now about six feet under after re-alignment of the course of the river.

GEUFRON BALLAST SIDING

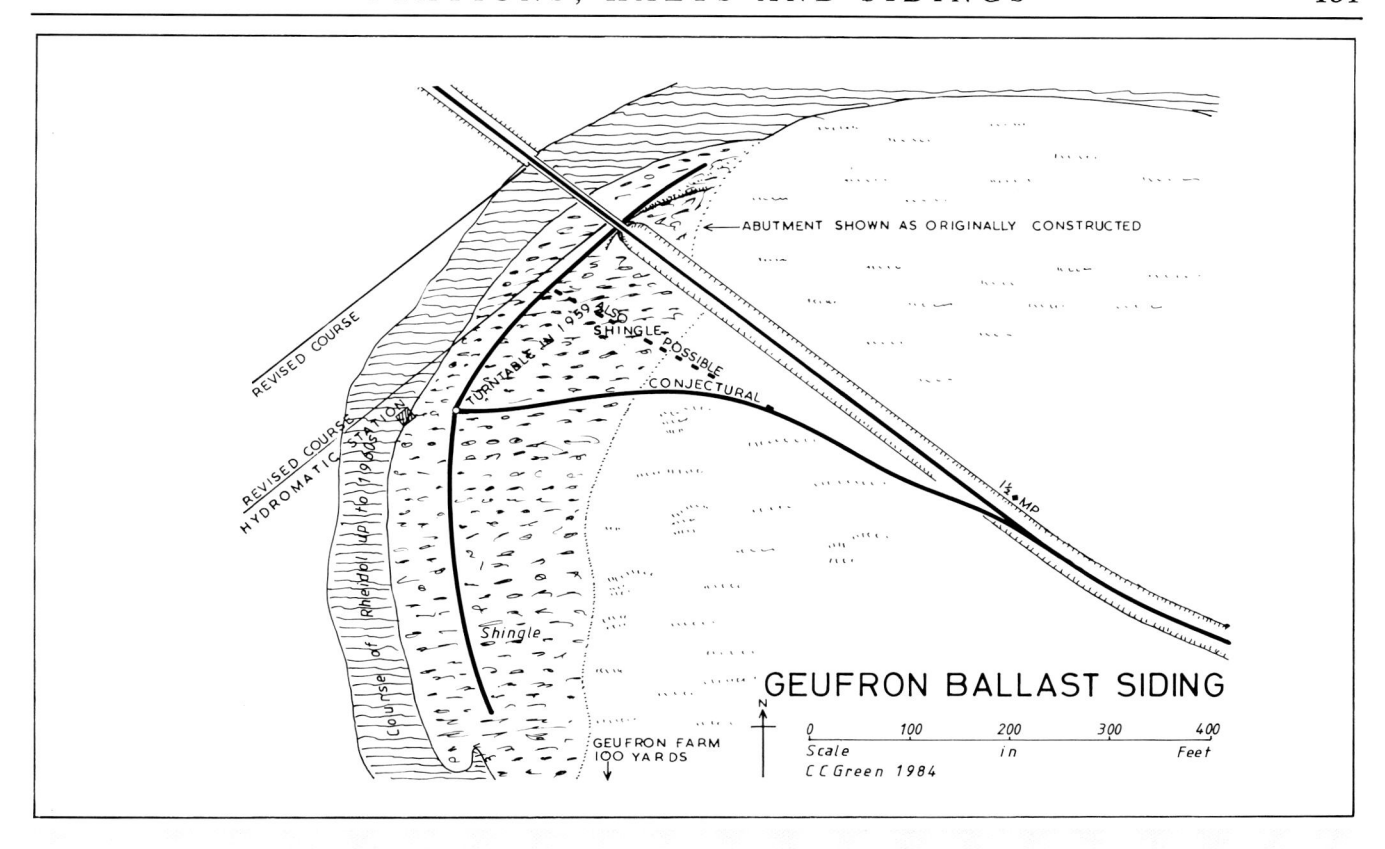

Rheidol on the bridge c.1905.
Courtesy E. Griffiths

Glanrafon crossing, looking towards Aberystwyth in 1957.

Glanrafon Halt
About 150 yds past GWR 2¼ mp, c. 33 ft above Sea Level

The *Aberystwyth Observer* had stated even before the line had been opened that there would be a station here. It would be useful to Mr. Powell of Nanteos who had written in support of the railway and to his tenants. The Board approved that the halt should be provided at a cost of £5 for a gate and a nameboard. It was opened on 7th May 1904 with the naive proviso that 'the principal quick trains from Aberystwyth to Devil's Bridge should not stop there'. This was soon forgotten. A shelter was shown on the 25 inch O.S. map but not on the 6 inch and none could be remembered.

Brambles hide the extent of the little quarry which formed the site and Williams & White (candlemakers who probably occupied Y Ffatws in Smithfield Street) did consider in 1905 that they might remove their manufactory to the quarry. The company were not unwilling and even offered Capel Bangor as a better alternative, then the issue was dropped.

Lascrug Ballast Siding
About 200 yds past GWR 2¾ mp, c 35′ above Sea Level

No details are known about this apart from a documentary reference, but it is a possible and practicable place for collection of river stones, and may have been used only by Pethicks. A note suggested that it faced up trains and there was in 1901 a fair-sized bed of shingle. The river course has since been re-aligned.

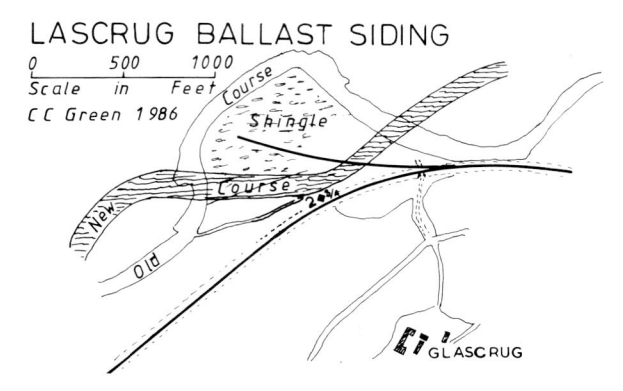

The turning-down point of Lascrug ballast siding, looking to Aberystwyth in 1986.

Lovesgrove Station
About 60 yds past GWR 3¼ mp, c 40 ft above Sea Level

In time for the first camp of the Cardiganshire Territorials from 23rd July 1910 to 6th August 1910, a temporary loop about 200 ft long was put in on the north side of the line. The points and rails were borrowed from the goods yard which had failed to attract the expected traffic, and the goods yard loop was never restored. As part of their exercises the Royal Engineers floated three pontoon bridges across the three arms of the Rheidol so that the station was connected by footpaths to the camps. During the daytime the bridges were demounted and used for assault crossings of the river and could be seen almost anywhere but in their proper places; they had to be back by evening, there being no leave on major exercise days until after teatime.

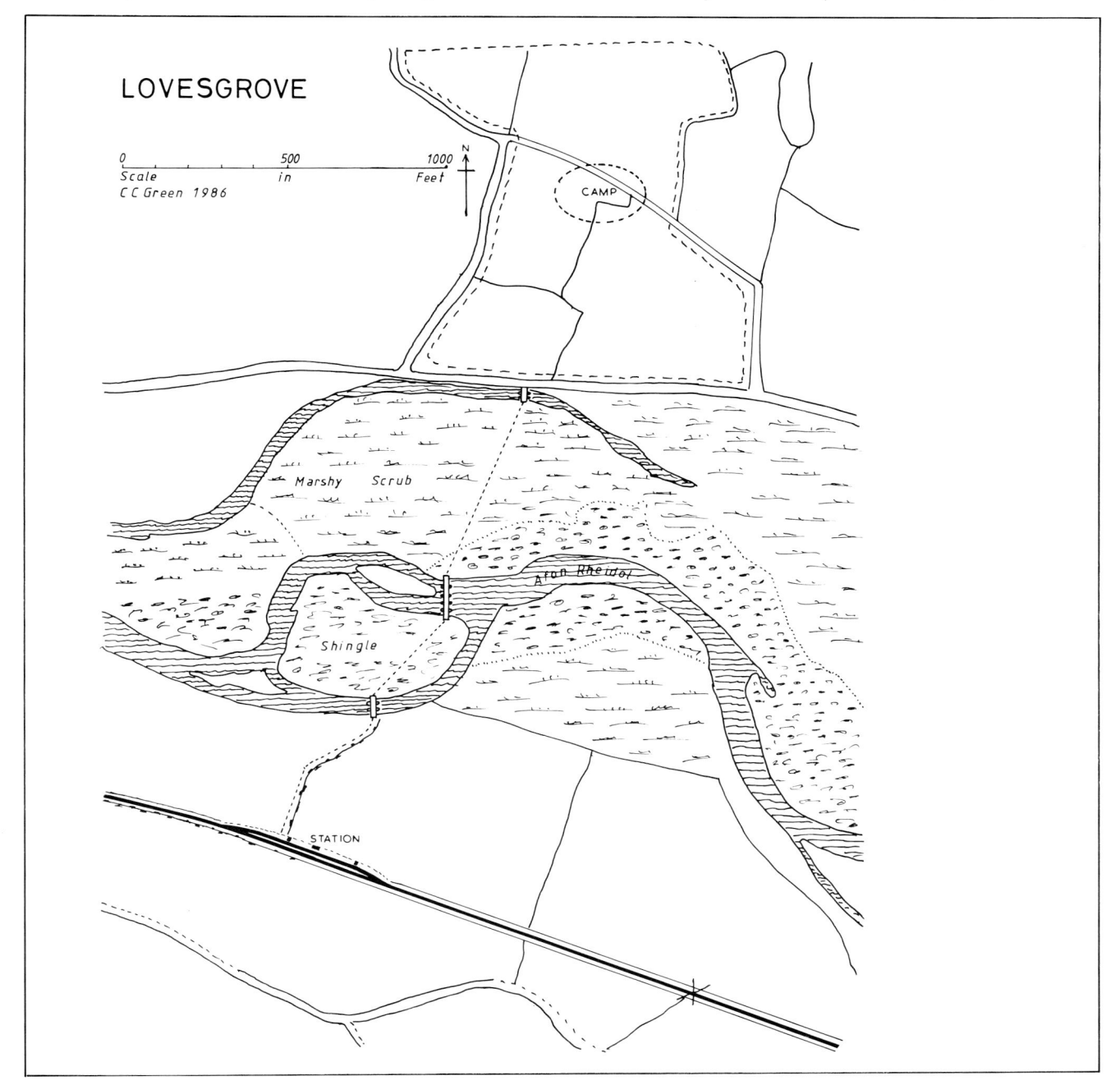

The station consisted of a few huts, probably all provided by the army, and the one which looked like a narrow gauge van, with its rounded roof, ended its days as the gang hut beyond the Horseshoe Bend. The highly successful operation brought the company £375 14s 11d for a total outlay of only £103 10s 1d, out of which the landowner got £2 and the tenant farmer £1 10s 0d for the use of a strip of field to accommodate the loop and station. Mr Rees got a pat on the back from the military and an honorarium of £12 12s 0d from the company. It is not recalled whether the point levers were tablet-locked but in the interests of safety they should have been. The layout functioned each summer thereafter until 1914 when the soldiers marched away on urgent recall and the loop and buildings were removed.

Lovesgrove station, looking towards Devil's Bridge in 1910.
A. J. Lewis

Capel Bangor Station
About 180 yds past GWR 4½ mp, c 75 ft above Sea Level

Only the down road of the loop is on firm ground, being laid along the old river bank. The rest is entirely built on top of a bed of shingle made level by collecting more shingle from up and down the site. Consequently, it is the only Rheidol station which has no recorded dispute or litigation to mar its inception. Indeed the nearest complaint came from Farmer James of Pwllcenawon who had claimed £8 19s 0d for loss of crops because the contractors had severed his access before he could harvest them; he settled for £7 10s 0d.

It was a very nice example of a narrow gauge station intended to serve a country and farming community. Capel Bangor with its church-sized chapel was the largest of the four hamlets, Penllwyn, Capel Bangor, Dol-y-pandy and Maes-bangor and so it was given its name to convince folk that it was their station. It had been, at first, referred to as Rhiwarthen from the nearby farm, and even as Rhiwarthenissa from another farm of similar name further to the west. Rhiwarthen (Arthen's Hill) is the ridge to the south and there are three farms bearing that name, viz Rhiwarthen-isaf (lowest), Rhiwarthen-uchaf (highest) where the station is, and Melin Rhiwarthen further up the line.

The buildings consisted of the standard A. & J. Main ticket office and waiting room, a down side shelter and the acetylene generator shed. The four-coach 150 ft long carriage shed was erected by a local contractor. Access was by footbridge, from the far end of which ran a footpath to Blaengeuffordd as well as to the lane along the bank to the Capel Bangor road. The gas lamps must have looked very pretty shimmering by reflection in the water and one of the journalists wrote of the place as one of 'many opportunities of gazing upon the clear shallow waters'.

Signalling was worked from a Pease nine-lever ground frame with seven levers in use. The Up Home and Down Home signals were detected through the Pease Economic Facing Point Locks. Major Druitt had the Down Home moved to well beyond the road crossing. As happened frequently elsewhere, the Postmaster General took full advantage of the erection of a convenient new set of telegraph poles. For a wayleave of £100 per annum Devil's Bridge Post Office was linked to Penllwyn via additional wires attached to the railway telephone poles between Capel Bangor and Devil's Bridge stations.

It prospered only moderately well and just enough to tempt one station master into some irregularities for which he was dismissed.

By 1907 there was difficulty in getting enough water stored to supply three locomotives in rapid succession, although there

Capel Bangor station, looking towards Devil's Bridge c.1905.

A. J. Lewis

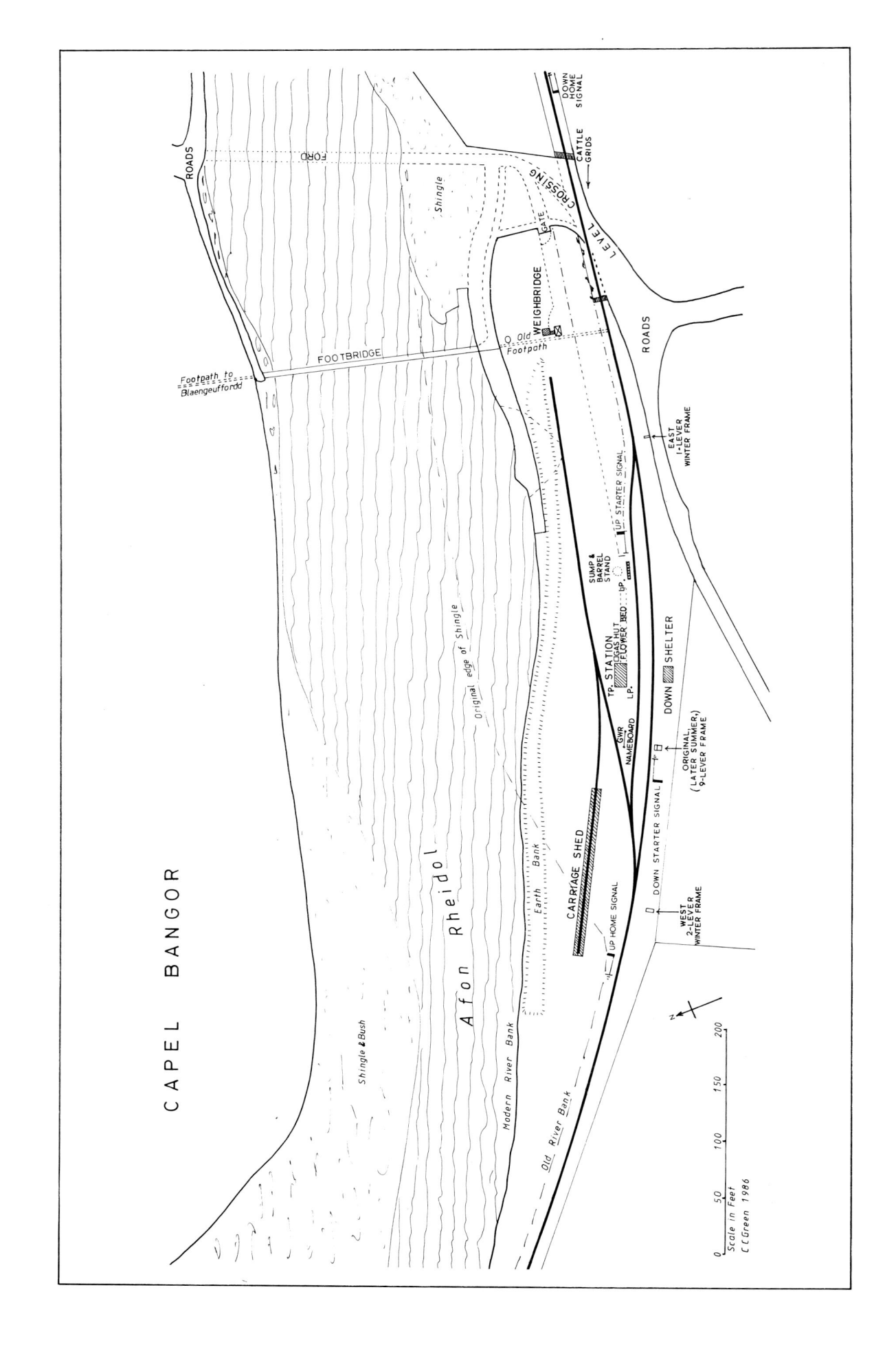

CAPEL BANGOR

STATIONS, HALTS AND SIDINGS

Capel Bangor station and carriage shed, looking towards Aberystwyth in 1948. *Selwyn Higgins*

were tanks at both Nantyronen and Aberffrwd and something had to be done very quickly. The problem was solved at Capel Bangor and as usual the permanent way gangs got the job, as ganger Isaac Jenkins related one evening at his fireside. 'We set up 6 wooden paraffin casks and we dug down about 10 feet into the river bed where there was ample supply of water. We had to fix a handpump, and I tell you I would rather be at Dartmoor Prison than be pumping there with the barrels leaking badly'. Corroboration came from the ledger: 'Payment 14s 8d to National Boiler & General Insurance Co. Ltd. for hire of pump'.

In 1906 the County Council proposed the construction of a bridge across the site of the ford; the company contributed £15 6s 3d to the funds of the Rhiwarthen Bridge Committee and agreed to give free cartage for all materials. The Council reformed the ramp from the goods yard for the duration of the work and refashioned all when the work was done.

In 1908 a weighbridge was bought from the sale at the Wemyss Mine for £8 8s 0d. The gang trudged over, dismantled it and dug it out. Then with a strong cart and horses hired from a farmer they moved the pieces over the hills, dug for and set all up at the back of the yard. The gas plant was removed for fitting into one of the vans in 1910.

By 1917 so many men had been released to join the forces that the Cambrian was finding it difficult to keep up with the day to day running of the system, and from 25th March Capel Bangor was left unattended, the station master and staff (of one) being withdrawn to work elsewhere. The tablet instruments were taken out of circuit and the lines connected through. The signalling layout received a most interesting modification. The loop points at both ends and the siding points were disconnected from the ground frame at the actuating cranks. At the west end there was erected a 2-lever frame to Tyer's Patent by J. Tweedy & Co of Carlisle, connected to the cranks of the down end points and to the siding points. At the east end a single Saxby & Farmer lever worked the up end loop points via another connection direct onto the crank. The signal arms were taken down while the main frame was out of use. During the winters when the rule was 'one

The Pease nine lever frame at Capel Bangor in 1955.

Capel Bangor carriage shed and Great Western station nameboard, looking towards Aberystwyth in 1954. The train is on the original river bank footpath, all the spacious remainder is on scraped-up river shingle.

The Tweedy 2-lever frame to Tyer's patent serving as west winter frame at Capel Bangor in 1955.

STATIONS, HALTS AND SIDINGS

Capel Bangor, end of shunt and the weighbridge hut in 1954.

Capel Bangor station from the rear in 1955.

Capel Bangor station from the front in 1955.

The up starter at Capel Bangor in 1949, a McKenzie & Holland signal with a long arm fitted. *R. K. Cope*

engine in steam', the levers were padlocked to leave through running in either direction via the down side loop road. If goods wagons had to be shunted the necessary points were unlocked and re-padlocked as required. For summer working the Pease frame was re-connected and a signalman was in attendance. The system received the names Summer Ground Frame and West and East Winter Ground Frames.

The GWR continued the system with the removal of the signal arms during the winter. After withdrawal of winter services from 1st January 1931 they were never put back again. The tablet instrument was taken away and the West and East Winter Frames were left connected and padlocked to give running through in either direction via the down side loop road.

The carriage shed was last used to house four of the open bogie cars during the war. It got very rickety, flood water reached it and the doors blew in during a storm. It was sold to a farmer in 1962 for its material, having been shored up on both sides for several years.

By 1955 the Rheidol was bidding fair to reclaim its own, it had managed to scour away the outer edge of the defences and had burrowed under the head of the carriage siding. The points had been cannibalised for the repair of others and the whole layout was lifted after 1963, leaving only the smooth curve of a through running line along the top of the original river bank. The best of the ground is cultivated as an allotment by Mr. W. Goodson of Penllwyn, a retired guard, and the old weighbridge hut serves him as his shed. The remainder of the yard is used as a ballast dump.

Now only the black-painted station and the stump of a buffer stop at the end of a line of silver birches evidences what was once a neat little station with white fencing and colourful flower beds and gas lamps. The station building followed that at Llanbadarn in livery but Capel Bangor had one item the others never attained – a full-size GWR nameboard on tubular posts and with the name in cast-iron raised lettering.

Always the river seeks to reclaim its own. 1955.

STATIONS, HALTS AND SIDINGS

Capel Bangor in 1955, looking towards Aberystwyth, showing on the right the Pease locking mechanism. Note the removal of signal arms.

Capel Bangor cattle grid from the top of the Down Home signal in 1955.

Left: The Saxby & Farmer lever serving as east winter frame at Capel Bangor in 1955, showing connection to Pease Economic Facing Point Lock.

Edward VII taking water at Nantyronen in 1909 just before the tank was moved to the down end at Aberffrwd, with driver Evan Lloyd Jones and fireman J. E. Davies. Note the W. H. Smith's newsboy going up to Devil's Bridge.
A. J. Lewis

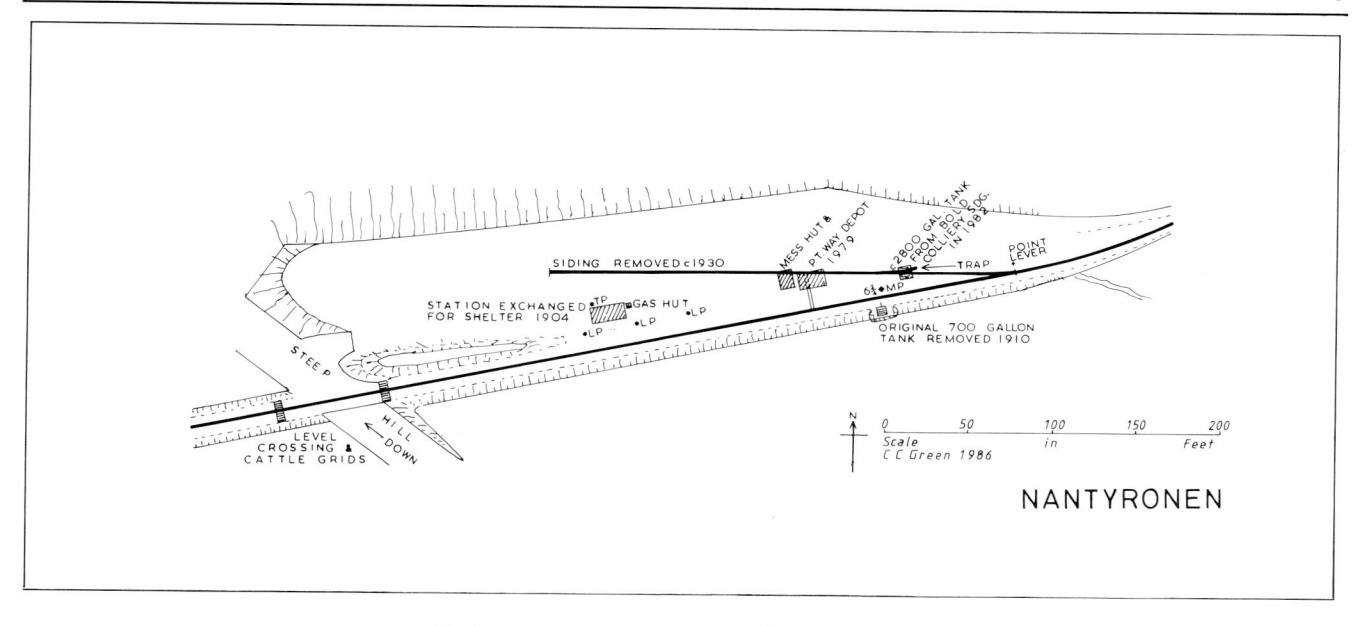

Nantyronen Station
About 50 yds short of GWR 6¾ mp, c 200 ft above Sea Level

Here Pethick had a depot with a shed for *Rheidol*. The station was the third of the medium-sized A. & J. Main buildings with a generator hutch and three gas lamps. The tablet-locked siding faced down trains and was serviced by up trains. First known as Ty-llwyd and then as Rhydyronen, it was settled as being Nantyronen from the nearest farm on the top road to give people in the hamlets up there the idea that the station was intended for them. The stream properly called Nant-y-ronen comes down below Troed-rhiw-felen.

It proved a useful little goods yard for farmers on the South side of the river and there was a bit of coal traffic to the folk of Aberffrwd, but passenger traffic rarely amounted to much and the Stationmaster was soon withdrawn; probably when the tablet instruments were moved up to the newly-opened Aberffrwd on 27th April 1904. The station was loaded entire on two flat wagons and, with the gang walking with it hauling from behind on steadying ropes, the unstable ensemble crawled its faltering way, a bit at a time, up to Aberffrwd. Replacing it with the Down shelter from Capel Bangor was a longer haul but much less risky; both moves were carried out without mishap, and both upset normal schedules.

Aberffrwd was supposed to receive gas lighting as required by Major Druitt when he passed the new loop, but there is no record of the removal of any from Nantyronen where the lamps remained five years later; and in any case they would have been removed when the generator was required for one of the guards vans in 1910. The wooden water tank held about 700 gallons and was left at Nantyronen for emergencies when the similarly unreliable supply up at Aberffrwd was running short.

W. H. Smith & Sons sent a newsboy with a tray on the morning up train and while the engine was taking water he would take the opportunity of selling his wares through the carriage windows either at Nantyronen or Aberffrwd.

After goods services had ceased the siding was taken up and the shelter had been boarded in for use as a ganger's hut. Later a purpose-made one was put in its place to house the man-rider trolley and later still the Wickham. This was used by Ganger Arthur Jenkins for returning home after working down on the main line and one could hear the roar of that J.A.P. twin-cylindered air-cooled engine from a mile or more away and see the rooks fly up as he neared Tyllwyd; Arthur would soon be home for his tea.

In 1979 a much larger shed was put up for the Permanent Way Supervisor and the Trackmen and for housing the Wickham and gear in better circumstances, in fact there are two sheds just by the 6¾ mp. In 1982 Nantyronen gained a unique new landmark. It had been decided that henceforth all water used by the engines must, as much as possible come from mains water supplies. A new pipe was laid in and the tank which was first used at the Bold Colliery Siding for replenishing the historical locomotives which paraded before the fascinated crowds at the 150 years celebrations at Rainhill was put up to replenish the three historical locomotives of the Rheidol line.

The rate of delivery is much better than that of the old tanks at Aberffrwd giving the crews a few minutes in hand. On balance they prefer full tanks at Aberffrwd higher up, but as Driver Gwilym Davies showed on 4th December 1982 full tanks at Nantyronen will do. The sanding gear had clogged up and with a heavy train on a damp day on rails coated with a light film of rust he had his engine slipping unavoidably for well over an hour without running out of water; but it was a bit close. The only disadvantage has been to PW trains in winter; the Aberffrwd supply never freezes because it is ground water and protected by trees; and pure mains water in an exposed position freezes much more readily.

144 THE VALE OF RHEIDOL LIGHT RAILWAY

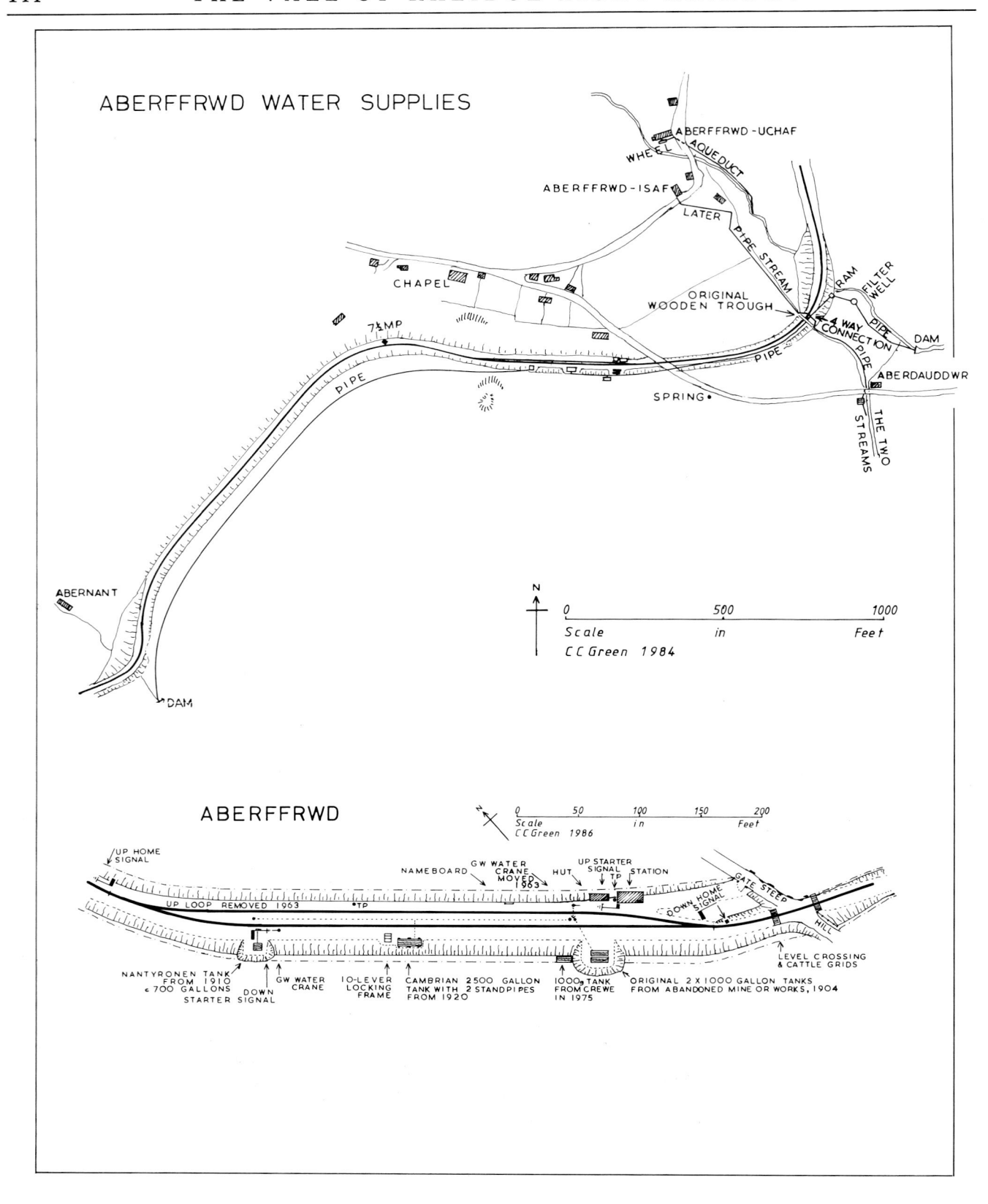

Aberffrwd Station
About 270 yds past the GWR 7½ mp, c 280 ft above Sea Level

Aberffrwd c.1907. *Rheidol* has just taken water from the twin metal tanks out of sight on the left. *A. J. Lewis*

On 29th May 1902 the *Aberystwyth Observer* forecast that there would be a station here, but two months later termed it 'a stopping place'. In December trains were to stop by signals. Reality was a dignified gentleman with a long beard, Mr. Thomas Hughes, who sold tickets and waved trains down as required. The *Railway Magazine* of 1903 refers to 'a nameboard and a ticket collector whose salary, we understand, is partly defrayed by the R.D.C. who asked for the station to be provided'. In similar ponderous style the writer described the novelty of the cattle grids, 'the foot that slips merely plunges into space for about 1 foot in depth, but is just sufficient to roll the intrepid wayfarer on his back and render his approach to the neighbouring station lacking in grace'. Because of the fine view, and to impress the passengers, the nameboard included the height as 200 ft, which was odd because it has always been 280 ft above sea level.

It was obviously the proper place for the local station, and a supplementary water supply was needed and could be laid on here. James Rees reported to his Board that the construction of a crossing place at Aberffrwd would enable more passengers to be carried within the existing rolling stock because holiday trains could be worked round each other more quickly with two passing loops instead of one. Some bright member of the Board wanted to know if there were any old Pethick rails lying about which could be utilised, and probably there were. The first approach had been to the Board of Trade and, whilst the Inspector considered that the sighting of the approach across the lane from the bend and the cutting was poor, the whole station could be seen well in advance by descending train crews from the bend over ¼ of a mile away. He gave his consent and his requirement that the station should be lit was complied with (by oil?).

The new station opened on 27th April 1904 in advance of the scheduled Whitsuntide opening and is the only one for which a complete and accurate cost is recorded, £255 17s 2d, which might be around £9,000 of 1986 money. T. Summerson & Co made the points for £22 the pair. Wages for moving the station up from Nantyronen came to £4 15s 6d and they used £18 14s 5d worth of timber and other materials. The station is outrigged a bit on timber trestling down the bank. J. B. Saunders moved the Saxby & Farmer tablet instruments from Nantyronen for £5 1s 0d. The major item was the complete Tyer & Co signalling system costing £184 12s 5d. Signalling was controlled from a 10-lever locking ground frame halfway along the loop. Four levers worked the points and their facing-point locks and four worked the signals, leaving two spare. The up signals were normal Home and Starter, the Down Starter was similar, but the Down Home

The Western Region steel arm and tubular post sited at Aberffrwd as the replacement Up Home. Photograph taken in 1956.

STATIONS, HALTS AND SIDINGS 147

Light engine held in loop for the down train to pass and showing Cambrian water tank and Tyer's locking lever frame, 2nd August 1935.
H. F. Wheeller

Aberffrwd, the Cambrian water tank and Tyer's lever frame in 1956.

Aberffrwd, looking towards Aberystwyth, in 1935. Note the angle of the Down Home turned for maximum visibility from the distant curve.
H. F. Wheeller

The Tyer Down Starter at Aberffrwd in 1956.

was sited clear at the end of the loop and was turned some 30 degrees to face that point by the 8 mile post from which the driver would first see the station.

Two long narrow 1,000 gallon water tanks were sited in a recess dug out of the hillside at the up end and the water came from the Abernant by arrangement with Major J.J. Bonsall at a cost of £3 per annum. The tanks seem to have been recovered from a nearby but unspecified mine. There were the usual land disputes including one with Farmer Richards who obtained a judgment against the company for £116 15s 5d. The place settled down as a useful adjunct to the service, its neatness and flowerbeds were much admired and the extra crossing place more than justified its cost.

Only the water supply was inadequate, and after the temporary expedient down at Capel Bangor an improvement was sought. A ram from Warner & Co at a cost of £22 1s 4d was installed in the dingle above the Cwmdauddwr bend to lift water directly from the stream. In a small sump at stream level they used some filters confiscated with other items from the Lugo Goldfields Co as part recovery of a debt. The supply was rented from Mr. John Morgan for £5 per annum. Mr. Evan Morgan claimed £2 and £1 1s 0d costs for trespass and taking land for placing the ram to which the company had no right. He also sought a cessation of trespass, but the ram was there and the company had to buy the bit of land from him. It started working in December 1908.

In 1910 the old wooden tank was brought up from Nantyronen and set up at the down end. Now there were nearly 3,000 gallons in store. From 1912 to c.1923 the tablet instruments were taken out of circuit and the line set locked for through running along the down loop road. By 1919 the old tanks were leaking so the Cambrian built a new one holding around 2,500 gallons at the down end and put two standpipes, one at each end, between the loop lines. The GWR took out the standpipes and put their standard pattern of water crane at each end but outside the loop lines. The next change was that of the installation of Tyer No.

STATIONS, HALTS AND SIDINGS

Aberffrwd in 1949, the nameboard and the gangers' hut and station.

R. K. Cope

6 tablet instruments in place of those originally supplied to Nantyronen by J. B. Saunders & Co. The bay where the long tanks were, was made into a flower bed, but, being in the shade, this did not do well. Instead the signalman smoothed the bank and set white stones reading WELCOME TO THE VALE OF RHEIDOL and the year with ABERFFRWD underneath between a pair of Prince of Wales emblems. After 31st December 1930 when the winter service ceased, the signal arms were taken down each winter and the loop points were clipped and padlocked for running through on the down loop road. In the summer a volunteer from Four Crosses filled the post of duty signalman for many years, and finally a man used to cycle over each day from Bow Street. One of the tablet carriers was marked Bow Street.

Around 1948 the Up Home was replaced by a steel arm on a steel post, and later the Down Home received an earlier GWR pattern of arm with the built-up spectacle framing. In 1948, too, the water supply was revised yet again. A ram lifts only 10% or less of its intake of water and there was a steady flow from a small stream above Aberdauddwr Cottage which was piped down to the cowshed at Aberffrwd-isaf, crossing the railway along a wooden trough at the edge of the dingle. The Works Supervisor from Oswestry, Frank Roberts, came down and was shown the situation by Isaac Jenkins who put a bucket down and proved the flow to be nearly 3 gallons per minute. A 1600 gallon tank was set up above the lane to give a pressure head and this auxiliary supply was piped direct into the station tank over the top of the supply from the ram. A branch pipe was laid under the rails to maintain the supply to the cowshed.

The ram stopped of its own accord some time in 1968 and the entire supply was again in doubt by 1974 because the tank by the lane was rusting through. The choked filtering sump was cleaned out as a preliminary and, to everyone's amazement,

from the tiny shed came the old familiar 'ka-thump ka-thump'. The minute it had water the old machine had re-started itself. On making enquiries for spare sealing rings, it was found that Green & Carter of Winchester were still making the Vulcan ram and a new one was installed. An additional 1,000 gallon tank taken out of Crewe Works was placed up the bank level with the water crane so that about 3,500 gallons was in store at any one time and the slow replenishment from the ram became adequate once more.

After 1963 all trains ran through on the down side of the loop and the up side and signalling were demolished later on in easy

Because the railway company had put it there, everybody believed it. The board that should have read 280.

Aberffrwd, looking towards Aberystwyth, on 12th September 1949.
R. K. Cope

Aberffrwd, gangers' hut and station, signal arms removed, looking towards Devil's Bridge, in 1954.

Down train, No. 7, entering Aberffrwd in 1956.

stages. The water crane at the up end was moved over to be close to the running line and was used until 1982 when the Nantyronen installation came into service. So this once-popular station became a deserted stretch of straight line attended only by unwanted water tanks and cranes. In colours Aberffrwd followed Llanbadarn until 1963 when tank and station were painted a drab green. The station was removed in 1986.

Looking back over the histories of Nantyronen and Aberffrwd emphasizes the importance of a good supply half way-through the journey and there was only one occasion on which the use of water from the streams caused any trouble. On one day in spring the fireman could not get either of the injectors to work properly and the driver had to nurse the engine gently all the way up to Devil's Bridge. On examination it was found that both injectors were bunged up with tadpoles.

Mr. Dennis Benjamin has recalled two events which delighted children going to and from Aberystwyth Grammar School by the lein fach in the heyday of Aberffrwd. In early summer before school had broken up, the train on which he was travelling up to Rheidol Falls would get held in the loop when timing had gone adrift. It was always hoped that the down train would be one of the very long ones that almost looked as if it was wrapped round the little school train. On the down journey the train would be held for an up train to pass, and frequently the man in charge would forget to lower the Up Home signal. Now one of the drivers was nearing his pension and a bit slow with it, but he was accompanied by a younger and more alert fireman. Seeing the signal at danger, the fireman would get the brake on before his driver had reacted and shut off the regulator, and the train would lurch to a sudden halt with no diminution of the exhaust beat from the chimney. It just got slower and died with a final half-strangled chuff.

Right: Aberffrwd, east face of Cwmdauddwr embankment in 1957, showing upstream portal and three layers of successive widening.

The unofficial halting place for small children going down to Miss Trotter's school, photographed in 1984.

Meithrinfa Halt
About 300 yds past GWR 8¼ mp, c 330 ft above Sea Level

This halt was quite unofficial and was something done out of kindness by the train crews for children going to Miss Trotter's Meithrinfa (Nursery) School which was held in the end room of the house by the bridge below the dam. Then the falls cascaded over steep rocks and were traversed by a footbridge with handrails; the falls became known as Trotter's Falls instead of their proper name Felin-newydd. It was used also by a few grammar school children from nearby farms and houses.

Rheidol Falls Halt
About 40 yds past GWR 9¼ mp, c 425 ft above Sea Level

The Traffic Superintendent had advised the Board to authorise the creation of a halt here in 1902 but he was refused by 'deferred until it can be done without expense'. Mr. Rees tried again in 1904 and he was met initially with one of those cheap management ploys intended to make the man on the spot look an idiot. Someone on the Board asked whether a train had actually been stopped and restarted successfully at that spot. The Secretary did not know and was instructed to write to Rees and tell him to hold trials in fine and in wet weather.

Of course it was possible anywhere and trains halted there from 7th March 1904. Descending passengers had to ask the guard to have the train stopped and passengers wishing to join the train just waved. Popularity led to the provision of a corrugated iron shelter with a bench seat and windows in both ends about 7 ft × 10 ft. The Rheidol Mining Co gave permission for the site to be widened a little, provided that a similar shelter was erected at Rhiwfron. The shelter stood there until it rusted through and the remains seem to have disappeared by the end of the war.

STATIONS, HALTS AND SIDINGS 153

Rheidol Falls Halt with a short mixed train c.1925. *Courtesy Dennis Benjamin*

Mixed train at Rheidol Falls Halt c.1926. *Photomatic*

Train passing Erwtomau Mine in 1912, with the newly erected buildings showing behind the train drawn by *Edward VII* in the later form of two-tone green livery.
Courtesy J. G. Rees

The Erwtomau Mine
About 25 yds past GWR 9¾ mp, c 480 ft above Sea Level

Lead ore was first mined here from 1785 onwards and it was named the Nant Rhiwrugos Mine. In 1855 it was revised as the Rhuroggos Mine and in 1912 mining was commenced once again under the name Erwtomau, which was taken from the farm on the main road where it traverses the top of the cwm. Latterly the hollow has been known as Cwm-yr-ogos but as yet no satisfactory equivalent name in English has been found. Tourism added the term of The Horseshoe Bend.

A siding was requested, but the mine traffic was loaded directly into wagons on the running line. Two short tracks of possibly 15″ gauge tramways served the mines. The first ran just above roof level and tiny trucks tipped the ore into wagons filling one at a time, whilst goods inwards were winched up a sloping way from the dropside wagons. Ironwork, cement and other materials were delivered by up trains and ore was loaded out into down trains. If the transhipment would take longer than 20 minutes, it would be worked by goods, or special trains propelling up.

The mine was operated by a rare source of power, a producer gas engine with a 20 ft flywheel, which worked off the product given off by roasting timber from the adjacent woodlands. After a batch had given out all gaseous elements, it went into the stokehole to roast the next lot, and so on. The mine closed down after 1918.

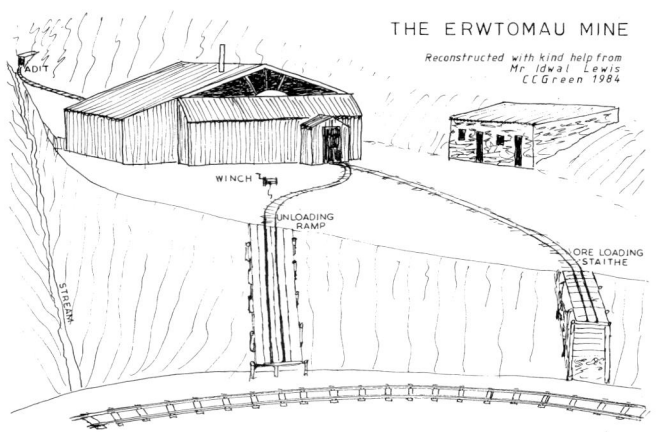

In 1987 there was a considerable landslip here which stopped trains for several days and lost 10,000 passenger journeys.

Rhiwfron Siding and Halt
About 222 yds past GWR 10¾ mp, c 590 ft above Sea Level

Here the line crossed an important way dating back to prehistoric times, which was still much used by miners walking between the Frongoch and Cwmystwyth mines to the south and the Ystumtuen group to the north. The great Cwmrheidol mine tapped the Ystumtuen lode from a level which was driven in from half way up the mountainside. Working commenced in 1705 and continued with a break of only 20 years because of flooding just before efficient pumps were contrived. Output went down the valley by packhorse and cart until the coming of the railway and the wonder of the upper valley, the aerial ropeway.

Trains stopped for passengers semi-officially right from the start and it was a booked stop in 1903. The siding, built at a cost of £51, was passed by Major Druitt on 26th August 1903. It was tablet-locked, faced up trains and was permitted to be worked by down trains only. Shunting had to be worked so that wagons parked on the running line while the engine went into the siding always had the brake van at their lower end.

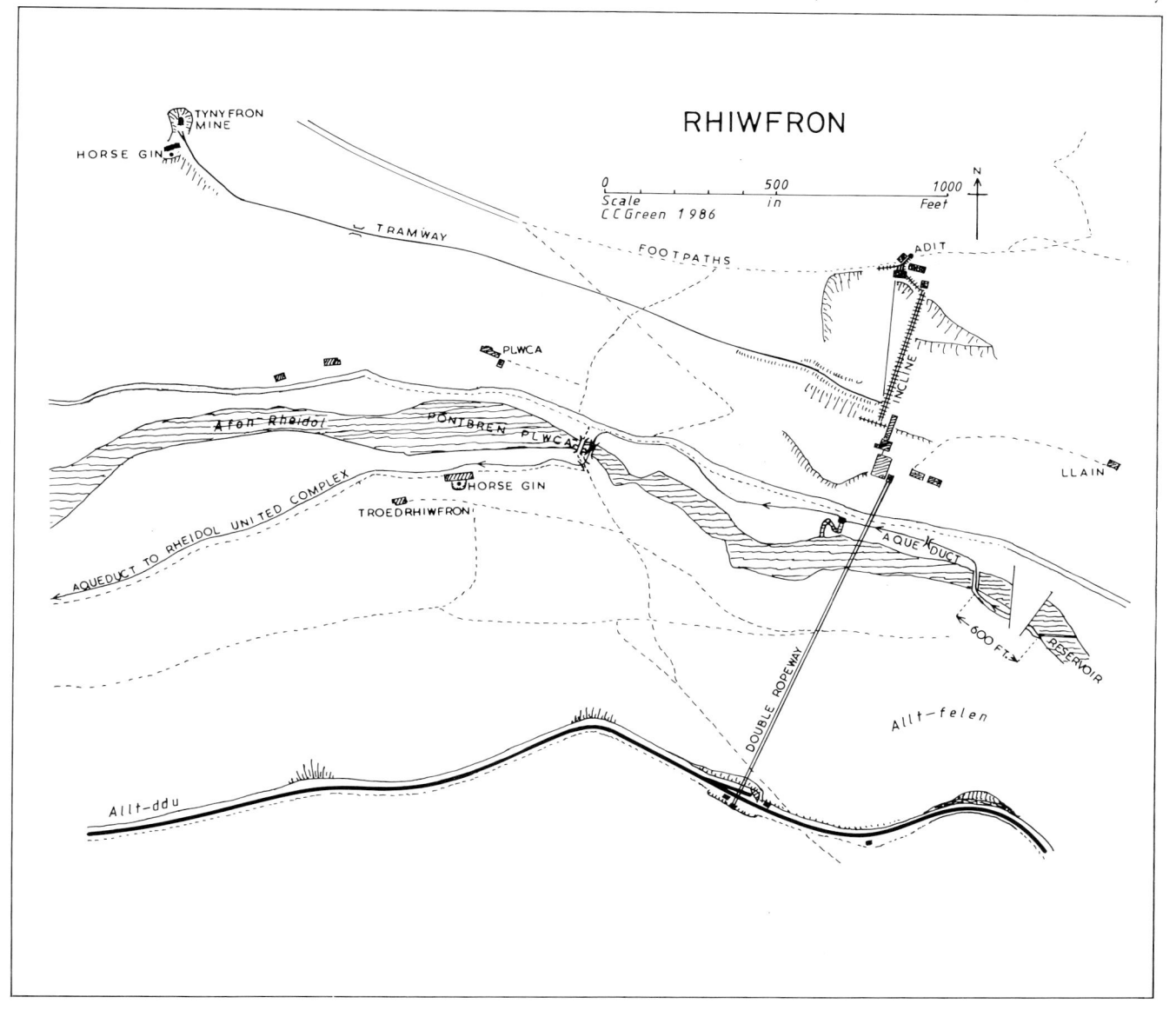

Along the twin ropeways travelled two buckets, which first slid down the carriers when over the hopper and then rolled over to discharge. Two men stood on the gantry to handle them. O.S. maps show a hut close to the stayblock of the ropeway, and the base to be seen today on the north side was the shelter. One reporter of that time referred to 'the busy scene at the rustic station', but in those days rustic meant rural and not necessarily of logs and the measurements of the base is similar to that at Rheidol Falls; so it was probably of the same sort.

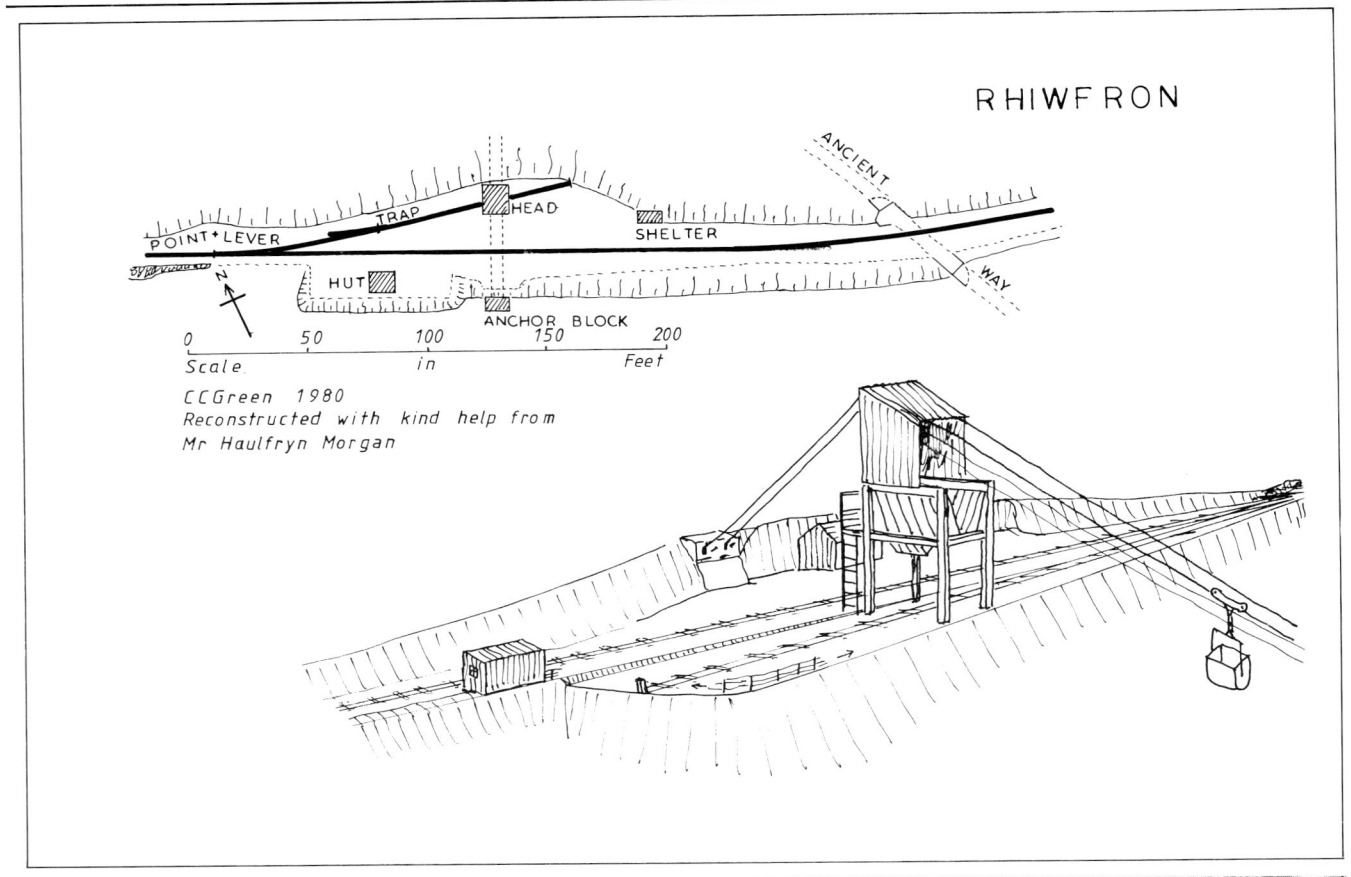

By 1910 the output from the mine had fallen off badly and the company was left with an irrecoverable debt for cartage. The siding was lifted about 1914. In 1918 a Mr. Hodgkinson-Carrington had re-opened the mine and he paid £21 to have the siding put back. He was the provider of the most unusual mine tractor the writer has ever seen. It was a Renault 8 CV 2, minus its road wheels, strapped down intact onto a heavy baulk timber frame. Outside the rear brake-drums were a pair of heavy sprocket chainwheels which drove the 2 ft gauge rear axle. It lay on its side in a ditch until 1954.

The ropeway stopped work around 1925 and the traffic had never been up to expectations. No precise demolition date for the ropeway is known so far, but buckets and ropes were still down on the valley floor in 1954 when they were carted away for scrap. The siding was finally lifted around 1955. Like the one at Rheidol Falls, the passenger shelter stood until it was in danger of collapse.

The men were forbidden to travel in the buckets, but, one day, the woman who lived at Llain Cottage above the mine, got out of the train with a piglet she had bought from the market. After a bit of joking about the hard time she was going to have getting the piglet down the long hill and over the wooden bridge at the bottom, the men gave way. They put sacking in the bucket and, with her knees close to her chin and clutching the protesting little squealer, she sank gently away across the 500 yard abyss to a safe landing.

Rhiwfron siding, showing trap in 1954.

The Cwmrheidol mine from Rhiwfron. Note the continuous roofing to the leet to avoid evaporation loss, c.1905. *A. J. Lewis*

Devil's Bridge c.1906, the company card which carries a publicity puff (page 21) on the back.

Author's collection

Devil's Bridge Station
11 miles, 71 chains and 87 links by GWR survey, c 178 yds short of 12 miles
680 ft above Sea Level

When Carey drew his map for Campden's *Britannica* in 1704 he showed the bridge as Pont ar Vunach vulg, Devil's Bridge, and because it had become desirable to attract tourists from England, the English form of the name was adopted. After the Aldersons had built the smelting works about 1818 the name adopted was Pentre Smelting. The works had been built so that Rheidol timber could be hewn and burnt to extract the lead from the ores of Cwmystwyth where the valley had been reduced to a desert of tree-stumps. This process ceased by 1826 and some ten families set up their homes in the abandoned buildings. As standards of living improved, most of them moved away and the place became a corn mill. About two years after the construction of the smelting works with its reservoir across Nant Llettwys, Mr. Taylor, the son of the first owner of the original hotel, built the Woollen Mill on the other side of the stream. More dwellings were built and the growing hamlet took its name from the bridge, as the failure of the corn mill had left the old works to go to rack and ruin. Stone for building the works and for the Hafod Arms Hotel (built anew c. 1833 by the Duke of Newcastle) came from a small quarry just to the north of the works. George Borrow had lionised the place in his book *Wild Wales* published in 1854, and made much of the appearance of the two bridges. The first bridge is of 16th century origin and replaced a series of earlier timber bridges. The second was built in 1753 so that a coach service could be run from Aberystwyth to Eisteddfa Gurig. (Then there was no road going east from Ponterwyd.) The third was built in 1901 just in time to be shown on the company's seal. So the scene was set for the railway. Half the approach through the bluff had been cut in getting the stone; a level way over an old ruin led already to Nant Llettwys, and the place had become a tourist attraction thronged with horse-drawn charabancs.

Pethicks formed the station yard first and then carried on cutting rock and making formation downwards. When the first rails were laid, they were of the lightest section carefully hand-picked by the carter, who was paid by the rail and not by weight. Even before connection was made, Mr. T. Oliver Jones had taken his option on a lease of 40 sq yds for a coal yard and the Cwmystwyth Mining Company had leased a site for three ore bins. They took their options in February 1902 and then had to wait until 12th August for the first goods train.

Devil's Bridge station c.1906. Note the new galvanised can for watering the flowerbeds.

A. J. Lewis

'Devil's Bridge from the neck, in 1909, but no trace of those ore bins. Were they ever erected?

H. L. Hopwood

STATIONS, HALTS AND SIDINGS

Rheidol, just arrived, at Devil's Bridge ic. 1905. Note the total burial of sleepers in all these early station views, and that Mr. Rees had been allowed to have lavatories installed.
Courtesy J. I. C. Boyd

The first ordinary service passenger train arrived at the terminus on 22nd December 1902. All was far from complete but there was a station building like the one at Aberystwyth but shorter, and which was lengthened in 1905. Trains entered the station along the left-hand road of a loop and the engines ran round the trains via a crossover, with points moved by bobweight ground levers, which meant they could spring the points on the trail without having to get off, the points being set almost permanently for crossing over. There were two signals, an Up Home on top of the rock bank which was visible as the engine emerged from the Quarry Cutting, and a Down Starter. All was worked by four levers of a Pease five-lever ground frame, with an arrangement of Pease Economic Facing-Point Locks, with variations permitting entry into the goods yard. This lay behind the station and had its own loop, and there was a short siding for spare coaches used when adjusting train lengths so that people returning on the last train could still expect to find seats because the staff had counted heads on the earlier trains and taken empty carriages off. To complete that initial layout there was of course the generator and a good array of gas lamps.

The station neck was in a short narrow cutting through rock and the water tanks were below the cutting. There were two, each of 400 gallons capacity, fed from a private supply provided by T. Oliver Jones of Rheidol House Farm which was formerly a tavern known as the 'King William IV'. In exchange for the water, Mr. Jones had the free grazing of the field between the station and the road. After taking water, the engines had to shunt the van round the train ready for departure from the down side of the loop.

Besides worrying over the state of the track, the gang made a base for a warehouse to be put up by a local contractor early in

Believed to be Mr. Edwin Davies, station master at Devil's Bridge, in the new style double-breasted uniform which replaced the single-breasted one around 1908.
A. J. Lewis

Devil's Bridge c.1920 in Cambrian days. Note the use of a flat wagon with a wagon sheet (dropped on the left) for carriage of grain in sacks.

A. J. Lewis

1903, dug out flowerbeds and made the bedding for and erected the bridge across the neck for which Dorman, Long & Co Ltd had delivered the girders for £70. In 1905 a Pooley weighbridge was set up. It cost £53 but the gang had to dig out the pit. It was hoped that its presence would attract more coal traffic but it did not. Isaac Jenkins in his memoirs has referred to the railway bringing to the countryfolk the benefit of a supply of coal: 'The poor miner who lived on the slopes of Plynlimon was able to have a lump of coal to put with the peat he dug from the land around him to keep himself and his family warm during the snow storm'. And that was the trouble; countryfolk could afford to burn coal only by the lump, and those mostly on Sundays. In 1905 the company bought a 1-ton Henderson derrick crane and after the end of the goods yard loop had been slewed inwards to make room for it the station was basically complete.

Mr. Jones defaulted on his payment for the rent of his coalyard and moved his business to his own farmyard, collecting in bulk from the wagons. Summonsing him would only have resulted in the loss of the water supply. The stream which supplied the hotel was known to run low in summer. James Rees solved the problem by arranging a supply from the same stream as before, but off Smelting Works land for £3 per annum, and he had a taker for the field at £2 per annum. Then the freehold of the smelting factory site came on the market, so the Pethick family bought it and continued to lease the water to the company which had not the power to buy for itself. They rebuilt the end house, now known as Smelting Cottage, and the house next door as holiday homes for the family.

At first there were no lavatories and the Board gave consideration to providing them, ending up with a minute reading 'Resolved to let the matter remain in abeyance for the present'. Later two little hutches appeared at the east end of the station. In midsummer 1903 the Board started to think about providing refreshments on the station and sounded out the agent for Mr. Waddingham's Hafod Estate. He appeared to raise no objection at first and then moved extremely quickly. In 1906 by the time the company had found Mr. Morgan of Aberystwyth who would pay £2 per annum for the lease of a site for his stall, the Hafod Estate had let a site for the Woodlands Tea Rooms which were open. The Hafod Arms Hotel had also opened its own tea-room, and now the agent did object. But in vain, for the company were able to establish that there was no prohibitory clause in the bill of sale of the site for the station. So Mr. Morgan had his stall; sweetmeat machines followed, as well as a W. H. Smith & Son bookstall which continued to be augmented by the boy with the tray, who came up on the first train with the day's newspapers. It was even proposed that there should be a row of lock-up shops,

No. 2 as GWR No. 1213, taking the tablet at Devil's Bridge in 1923, before being allowed to water up and complete the run round.
Mr. James

but this idea fell through. The view of the mountains was not yet obscured by trees, but travellers, when tired of looking at them, could see the pyramids instead, via one of the Stereoscopes for which a concession had been let at 10/- per annum for each machine.

In 1910 the Hafod Estate required access to Coed Cyd to cut the timber there, and reminded the company that the level crossing had not been provided in front of Smelting Cottage as required in the conveyance. Fortunately, the girders of the bridge, which had been put up for sale because nobody was wanting to go across it, were still in place and the decking was renewed instead of making the crossing. For one day each year it was roped off by the ganger to preserve the company's rights.

From 1912 to 1914 was a busy time for the trains in summertime with all the extra traffic from the army training camps which were set up nearby as well as the Territorial camps down at Lovesgrove. After the troops had marched away, the Ministry of Works brought a steam-powered sawmill, and pit-props were cut to size and loaded away down the narrow gauge in thousands of tons. By 1919 there was no more timber traffic and the derrick was removed. The siding lines were straightened back to their

Devil's Bridge in 1955, with the McKenzie & Holland Up Home signal fitted with a long arm.

Water-pound in Nant Llettys for water supply at Devil's Bridge. Photographed in 1984.

Left: Devil's Bridge in 1955. The 1,675 gallon tank installed second-hand in 1924 is only now, at the time of writing, beginning to fail.

Devil's Bridge, cutting and Dorman Long bridge, looking towards Aberystwyth in 1955.

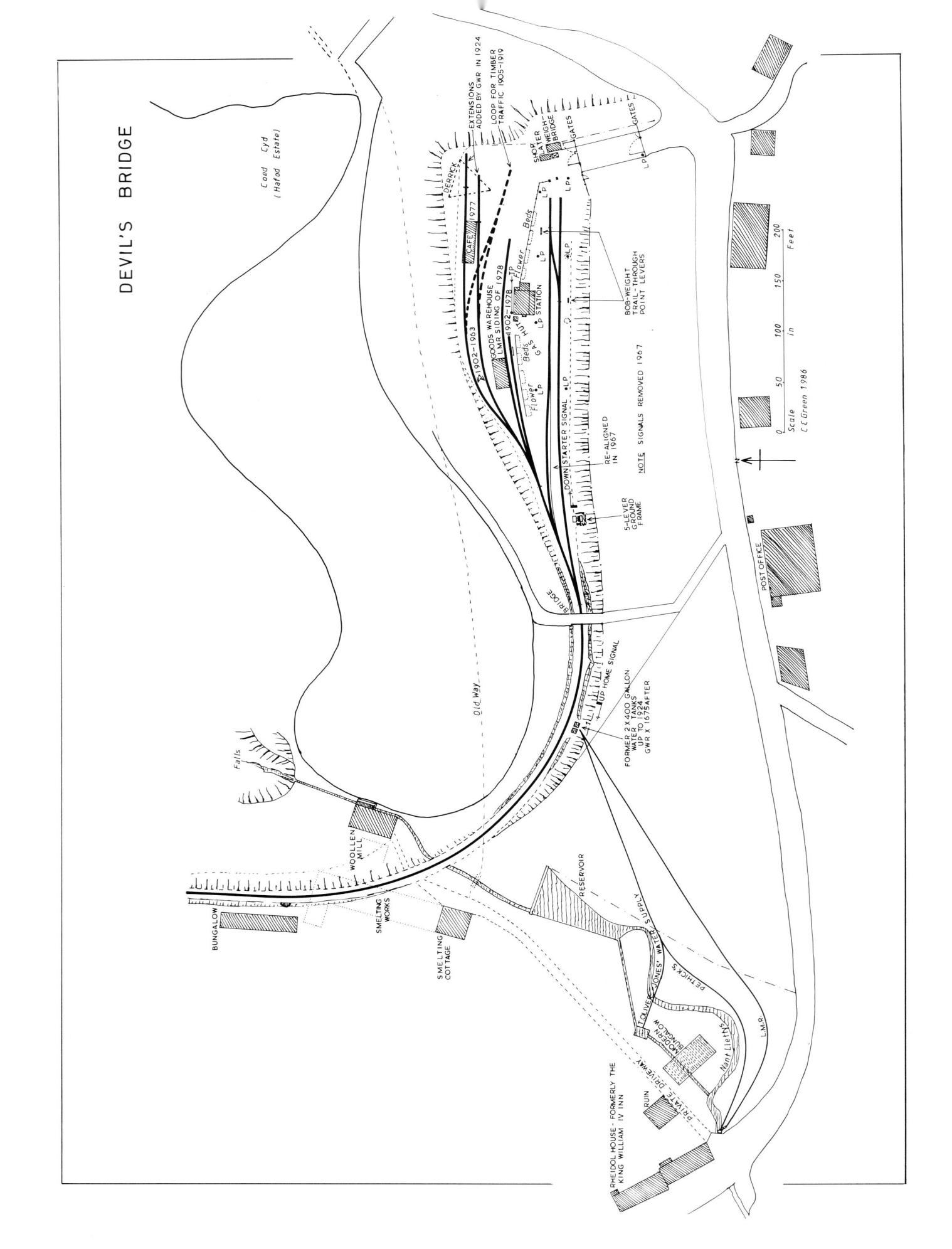

DEVIL'S BRIDGE

Coed Cyd (Hafod Estate)

Falls

Old Way

EXTENSIONS ADDED BY GWR IN 1924
LOOP FOR TIMBER TRAFFIC 1905-1919
SHORT AT WEIGH-BRIDGE
GATES
DERRICK
CAFE 1977
GOODS WAREHOUSE 1902-1978
LMR SIDING OF 1963
Flower Beds
GAS HUT
LP STATION
Flower Beds
LP
LP
BOB-WEIGHT TRAIL-THROUGH POINT LEVERS
RE-ALIGNED IN 1967
DOWN STARTER SIGNAL
5-LEVER GROUND FRAME
NOTE SIGNALS REMOVED 1967
BRIDGE
UP HOME SIGNAL
FORMER 2 x 400 GALLON WATER TANKS UP TO 1924
GWR x 1675 AFTER

WOOLLEN MILL
BUNGALOW
SMELTING WORKS
SMELTING COTTAGE
RESERVOIR
PETHICK'S
OLIVER JONES' WATER SUPPLY
MODERN BUNGALOW
Nant Llethi
RUIN
PRIVATE DRIVEWAY
RHEIDOL HOUSE— FORMERLY THE KING WILLIAM IV INN
L.M.R.

POST OFFICE

Scale in Feet
0 50 100 150 200

N↑

C C Green 1986

Devil's Bridge in 1935 with all three trains shunting. Note the cattle van on the extreme left and gas piping still on roof of nearest carriage. *H. F. Wheeller*

original alignment but the loop points were never restored. The refreshment and other facilities had gone and were not replaced, but all renewals of Hafod leases contained restrictive clauses preserving the monopoly of the Hafod Arms Tearooms. Even the lease granted to the Cambrian re Factory Cottage, as it was then called, stated that the premises were 'not to be used as a hotel, inn, public house, beerhouse, club or other such place for supplying the public with refreshments or beverage whether intoxicating or not'. However, blind eyes were directed upon the antics of a pair of feuding 'barrow boys'. Each had a costermonger style handcart with a canvas awning and sold nettle beer and other dubious home-brews such as sarsaparilla and ginger beer.

The GWR lengthened the two sidings to the end of the yard and erected a second-hand 1,675-gallon water tank to replace the old twins for £265 in 1924. After a derailment in 1967 had damaged the Pease equipment, the whole entrance to the station was subsequently re-equipped with modern BR components worked from the original Pease frame. Then the signal arms and posts were also removed. The two long sidings were lifted and the short one only was left. This was lengthened in 1978 so that three trains could be held in the station at the same time on Gala Days; it also serves as the ballast siding.

In 1968 some refreshments were available once again, served by railway staff, and in 1978 a Portakabin Tea Bar was placed

Right: Devil's Bridge, the yard trap point and Cambrian point lever in 1954.

Devil's Bridge in 1949. Dai Williams (with long-shafted hammer) supervises his summer gang.

R. K. Cope

STATIONS, HALTS AND SIDINGS

The warehouse at Devil's Bridge in 1956.

Devil's Bridge in 1956, the sidings as lengthened by the GWR.

THE VALE OF RHEIDOL LIGHT RAILWAY

Devil's Bridge in 1960, the down outlook towards the throat. Note the lever frame barely showing from the recess in which it was installed.

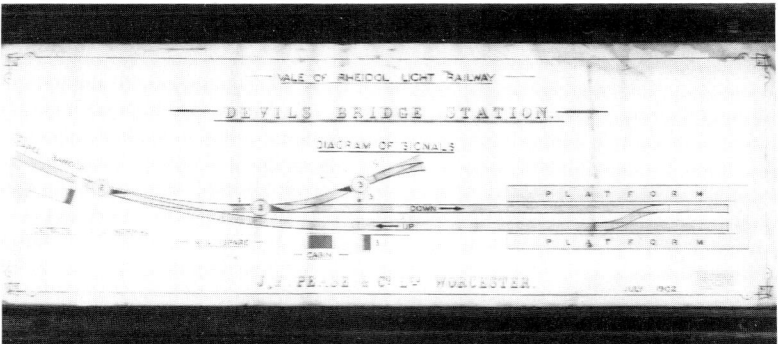

The Pease signalling diagram for Devil's Bridge. No cabin was ever erected around the lever frame.

Devil's Bridge in 1956, the Pease 5-lever frame in the recess large enough to take a small cabin.

STATIONS, HALTS AND SIDINGS

Devil's Bridge on 14th June 1954. After arriving with the first train of the year, the locomotive is shown running round to water up and re-marshall the train so that the brake third will be at the rear on the downward journey.

Devil's Bridge station in Western Region style in 1956.

Devil's Bridge station, Aberystwyth end, in 1955.

Devil's Bridge station, rear and Aberystwyth end, in 1955.

The author at work measuring the track at the end of the loop at Devil's bridge in 1956.   *Hermann Broedelet*

on site along with Portakabin toilets. The tea bar was run by Travellers' Fare until 1982 when it was taken over by Mr. & Mrs. Norman Simkins.

The painting followed the general pattern, i.e. mid green until 1922; stone and salmon brown until 1948; chocolate and cream at the next repaint thereafter. Then in 1978 it was repainted with ivory and dark chocolate, with litter bins etc in rail blue. The tea bar is in ivory and dark chocolate and the toilets were ivory with orange topping until recently when they were repainted in plain ivory.

Generally, the service was never interrupted by bad weather but one train did get snowbound. Driver Owen reported the situation back to Aberystwyth and was asked the rather useless question as to whether there was anything he needed. He could not resist the opening given to him. 'Well if you could send me up some hot water in the morning, I like to start the day with a good shave'.

The weighbridge office at Devil's Bridge in 1956.

The end of the track on 15th August 1985. Note the spare summer car held on the spur of the down loop.

H. F. Wheeller

The Great Western gates at Devil's Bridge in 1956.

Devil's Bridge at Easter 1956.

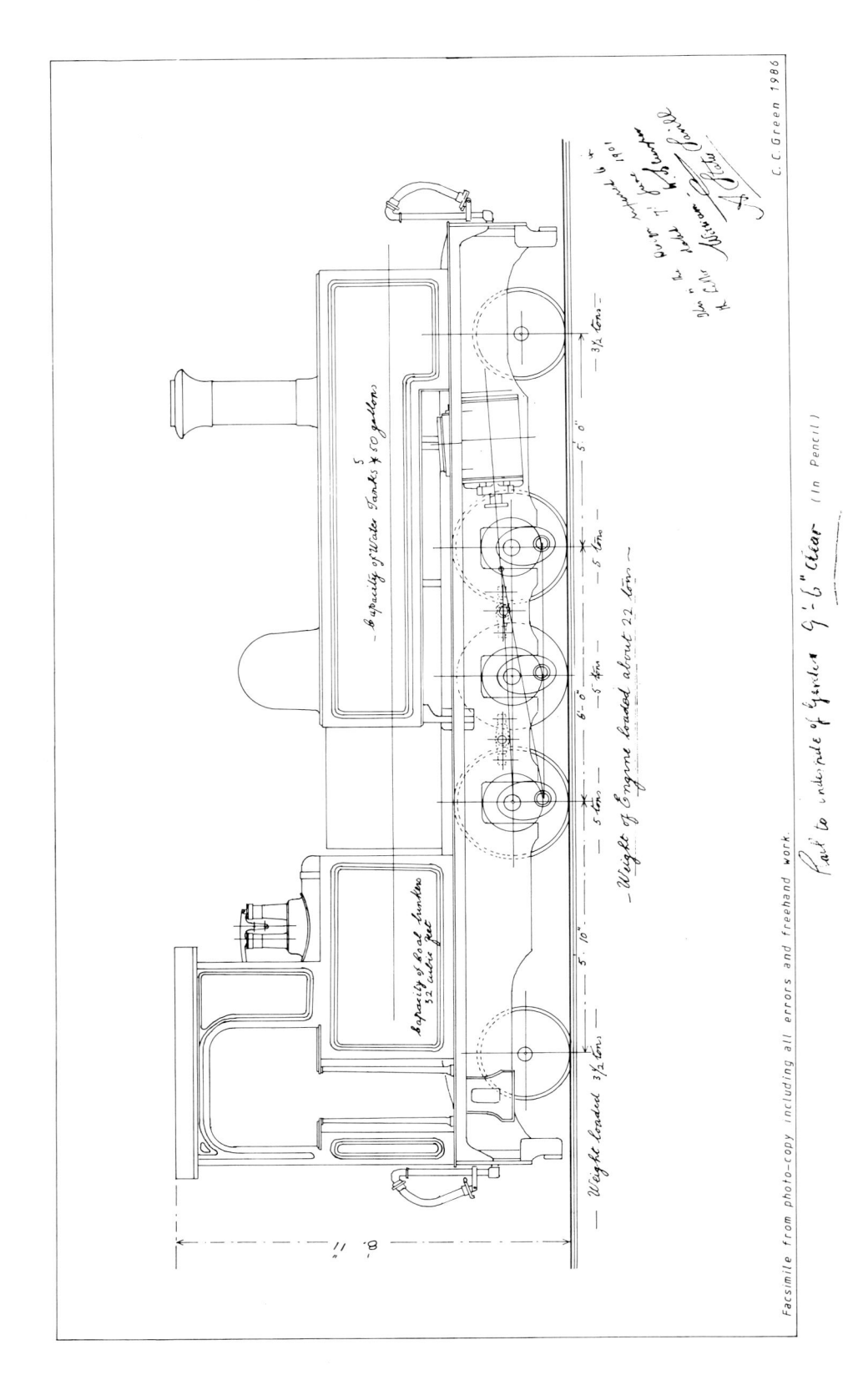

W.W. Szlumper's tender drawing of a Lynton & Barnstaple style engine. The draughtsmanship has all the marks of the haste in which it was most obviously prepared.

CHAPTER EIGHT

THE LOCOMOTIVES

Nos 1 & 2 The Davies & Metcalfe 2-6-2 Tanks

When Sir James Szlumper was Consultant Engineer to the Lynton & Barnstaple Railway his half-brother, William W. Szlumper, was employed under him to do the mechanical designing. The engines designed by the younger Szlumper were extremely good-looking but lacked the necessary power, and once wear had set in a pilot engine was needed on any L & BR trains exceeding four coaches and a van. Also when the wide tanks were three-quarters full or less, the water sloshed about quite a lot and the engines could roll about under these conditions.

William W. Szlumper's design for the Vale of Rheidol was an L&BR 2-6-2 tank with the rigid wheelbase reduced from 6'6" to 6'0" and the total wheelbase reduced from 17'9" to 16'10". With the relatively undetailed drawing went a very sound specification which neither the original L&BR locomotives nor the reduced version could ever have met. Six firms quoted from these two documents.

Avonside Engine Co. Ltd.	£1,325
W. G. Bagnall & Co. Ltd.	£1,350
The Patent Exhaust Steam Injector Co. Ltd.	£1,450
Sharp, Stewart & Co. Ltd.	£1,490
Manning Wardle & Co. Ltd.	£1,625
The Hunslet Engine Co. Ltd.	£1,650

The third tender was only £75 more than the lowest and the firm was about to become Davies & Metcalfe Ltd. Richard Metcalfe had a high reputation in Aberystwyth from his years of partnership in Williams & Metcalfe, Ironfounders, and the tender was awarded to the former local man whose secure backing from Lord Davies must have helped. The quotation of 7th June 1901 was accepted on 8th June 1901 on the company's London letterhead bearing the telegraphic address 'Hallidie', one of the names of Mr. H. H. Montague Smith the Chairman.

Then happened one of the most remarkable episodes in the entire history of the Rheidol. With James Metcalfe was the Manager, Mr. A. Slater Savill, who was another of those Victorian-style instinctive engineers. They went down to the L&BR and to the Festiniog where they must have seen the designs for the Fairlies including that for *Little Wonder*. They must have seen the weaknesses in the L&BR design as against the specification, and noted their behaviour on 5 chains radius bends, whereas they had to produce an engine which could perform well round bends of only 3 chains radius. By the 29th July they were ordering the materials for the totally different design of engine which was built. This was barely seven weeks after acceptance of tender and how much drawing board work was done by gaslight in the small hours we shall never know, but it was an extraordinary effort.

The little variations that were to make all the difference were the reduction in the diameter of the driving wheels from 2'9" to 2'6" and the increase in boiler diameter from 2'6" to 2'9", with a drop in pressure from 160 lbs psi to 150 lbs psi, and lastly the increase in cylinder diameter and stroke from $10\frac{1}{2}'' \times 16''$ to $11'' \times 17''$. The grate area was only a fraction higher but the heating surface had gone up from 383 sq ft to 425 sq ft. This gave a freer steaming engine which really could take an 80-ton train up nearly 4 miles of continuous 1 in 50. Getting the tanks right was another item on the credit side. Szlumper had first specified 450 gallons but had altered that up to 550, and Davies & Metcalfe achieved 584. The tractive effort had gone up from the 7269 of the L & BR engines to 7713.75 lbs; not a great deal but enough to produce a better performance.

Then Richard Metcalfe made another very shrewd move. The materials were to come from the suppliers and all was to be put together at the works at Romily i.e. as far as possible it was a pair of Davies & Metcalfe products which would leave the works. They could machine raw forgings from Nasmyth, Wilson & Co. Ltd., they could fit up the brake mechanisms from the Vacuum Brake Co. Ltd. who, in their turn had their components made by Gresham & Craven and they could take good advice. When offered an improvement to the layout of the brake piping, they accepted it; when the suppliers of metal plate suggested that the backs of the cabs would be easier to handle in two halves instead of in one piece they agreed. The only expertise they did not have at Romiley was that of boilersmith.

That shrewdest of moves was to appeal to the Manchester, Sheffield & Lincolnshire Railway's Gorton Works for the loan of a skilled boilersmith. The man selected was Thomas Kay, chargehand boilersmith, and he went from Gorton for a year to work for Davies & Metcalfe, and followed the engines down to Aberystwyth for their steaming trials and for part of the maintenance period. He regaled his family and friends with stories of the troubles he was having with assistance from men not used to working with boilers, and one story was of the suggestion that when a seam was failing to close he should try driving in a wooden wedge. He acquitted himself well at Romiley and went back to become boilershop foreman under the Great Central.

Delivery had been specified for 20th January 1902, and the one engine was well to time but the second could not be finished at the same time because the one boiler had to be finished before the other could be put in hand. In any case there were no rails they could be run upon and the company had not the ready funds to pay the first instalment on even the first engine. Davies & Metcalfe helped them out by accepting Lloyds 4% Bonds payable in March and July for £500 on each engine.

Then Pethicks were needing another engine to help their own dilatory progress and No. 2 *Prince of Wales* was hired to them by Davies & Metcalfe directly. Logically this was engine No. 1 *Edward VII* but as the coronation had not taken place the two had changed places to avoid a bad example of lèse majesté. In fact No. 1 was to have been nameless to begin with and there would have been a naming ceremony on Coronation Day, and the company did send a letter demanding delivery of the second engine in time for the original date, 26th June. Then Prince Teddy had to have his royal appendix removed and was not crowned until 9th August when the track was still incomplete and the coaches still had not been delivered. So it was all a bit pointless. Thus although records suggest 20th January 1902 as the building dates, No. 2 arrived at Aberystwyth at the very end of May and No. 1 in September.

The deliveries were effected on L & NR bogie flat trolleys and Davies & Metcalfe had to hire a pair of cranes from the L & NWR for the Romiley end and these may have run right through to Aberystwyth for the offloading. Both engines were delivered in works grey, and when No. 1 had arrived, the men, under the direction of James Rees, set to work flatting down and applying the undercoats. The gloss coats and lining were put on by painters borrowed from James Rees' old employer the M & MR. Sir James Szlumper was very fond of the livery of the London, Brighton & South Coast Railway and his friend Mr Marsh obliged him with tins of paint of the colours of the Stroudley-Billinton era.

No. 2 was given a fairly close copy of how the engine would have been painted and lined at Brighton Works but No. 1 was given a claret edging round the tanks where No. 2 was olive green, and the claret was applied also inside the reveals of the tanks and to the wingplates adjacent to the smokebox. On both engines the frames and much of the gear below was all in claret. Looking back the men called the operation 'putting their best suits on them'. Having regard to the King's reputed life style the Royal Flush was singularly apt.

Thomas Kay, chargehand boilersmith at the Gorton Works of the Manchester, Sheffield & Lincolnshire Railway, who went to Romiley to supervise the construction of the two boilers. This photo was taken later when he had become boilershop foreman under the Great Central Railway.
Courtesy Miss Margaret Kay

One of the boilers under construction, presumably that of the intended No. 1 which left the works as No. 2. The cylinder and tank edge on the right show how Davies & Metcalfe were already involved in narrow gauge loco repair. *Courtesy John G. Rees*

THE LOCOMOTIVES

The engine which left the Davies & Metcalfe works as No. 2, seen in works grey in the yard at Romiley. *Courtesy Miss Margaret Kay*

No. 2 c.1903 as repainted at Aberystwyth. *Courtesy A. W. Croughton*

No. 1 at Capel Bangor. The back corner of the down shelter is just visible beyond the back of the van, c.1903.
Courtesy E. W. Hannan

THE LOCOMOTIVES

No. 1 on a short train about to leave Aberystwyth from the down side of the loop. This was probably the last time she was photographed in LB & SCR livery, 28th June 1909. *H. L. Hopwood*

When new the engines worked very well indeed and when the maintenance period had expired, the company bought in a lot of the spares lying at Aberystwyth, and the rest was up to Tom Savage and Harry Millman, the foreman fitter and his assistant. While some repairs were effected by sending parts away, they managed entirely inside the cramped sheds and the engines were never sent away. By August 1905 James Rees had to explain to the Board that the reason for the increase in coal consumption was the normal effect of wear and tear. General performance was still good and both engines could always handle six- or even seven-coach trains. The injectors were Davies & Metcalfe's own patent Non-Lifting, Automatic Re-Starting, Live Steam Injectors and they were standing up to the demands made on them, but the weakness lay in the valve-gear.

William Szlumper had insisted on concealment and, doubtless with the Festiniog's *Little Wonder* in mind, the valve-gear was a

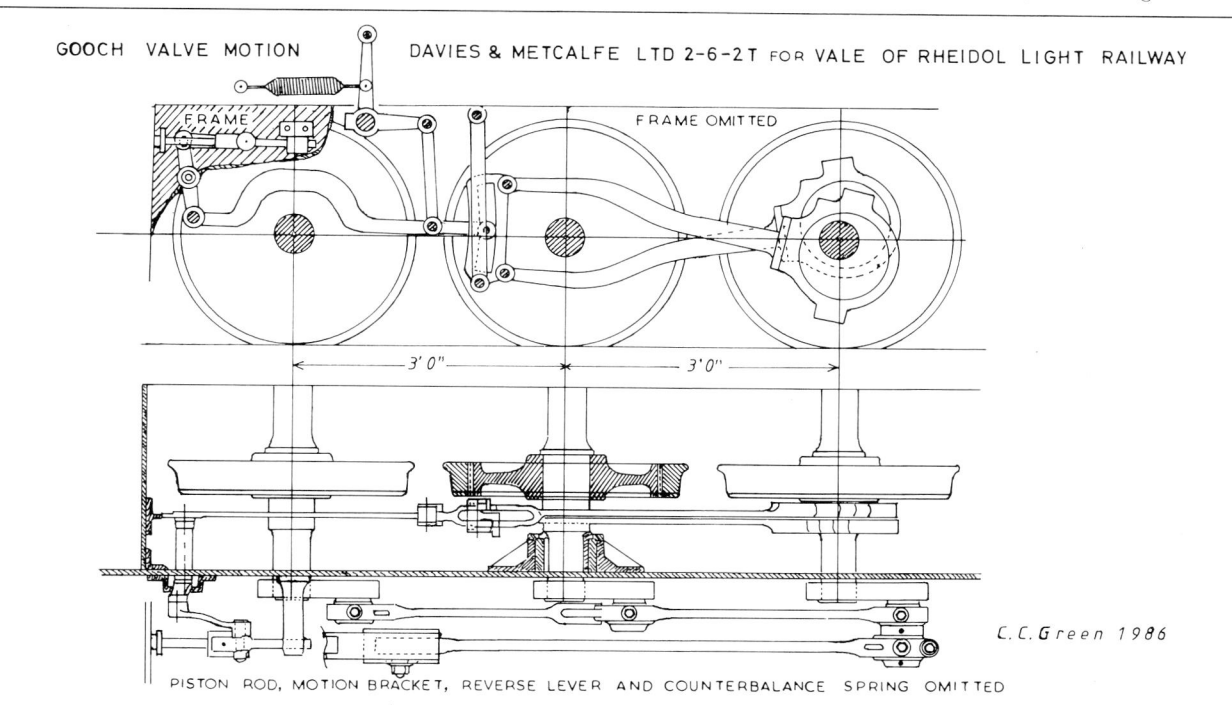

Davies & Metcalfe's solution to W. W. Szlumper's insistence that the valve gear should be concealed. It was a marvel of ingenuity and quite definitely worked very well indeed as new. It is not hard to understand that eventually wear and distortion of the springing on the centre axle, combined with wear in the cross-spindle at the top of the hanger-block, would take up the half-inch clearance between the lower end of the block and the outer face of the wheel-rim.

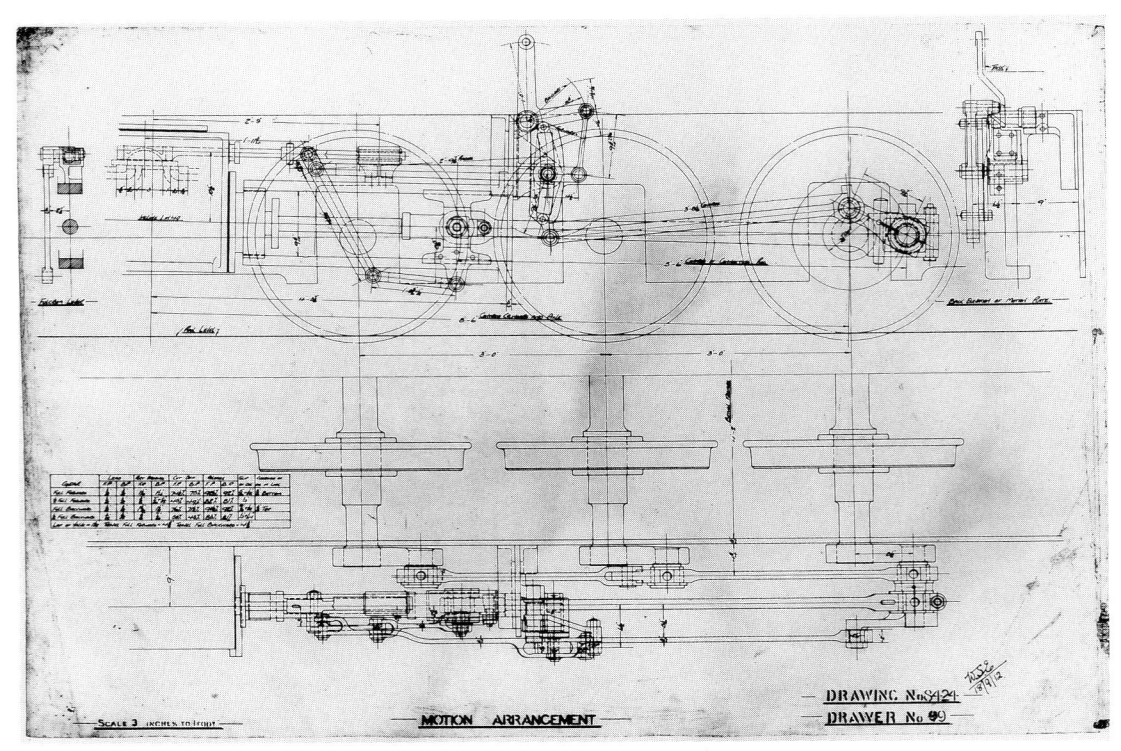

The Bagnall proposal for outside Walschaerts valve gear dated 18th September 1912. *Courtesy Alan C. Baker*

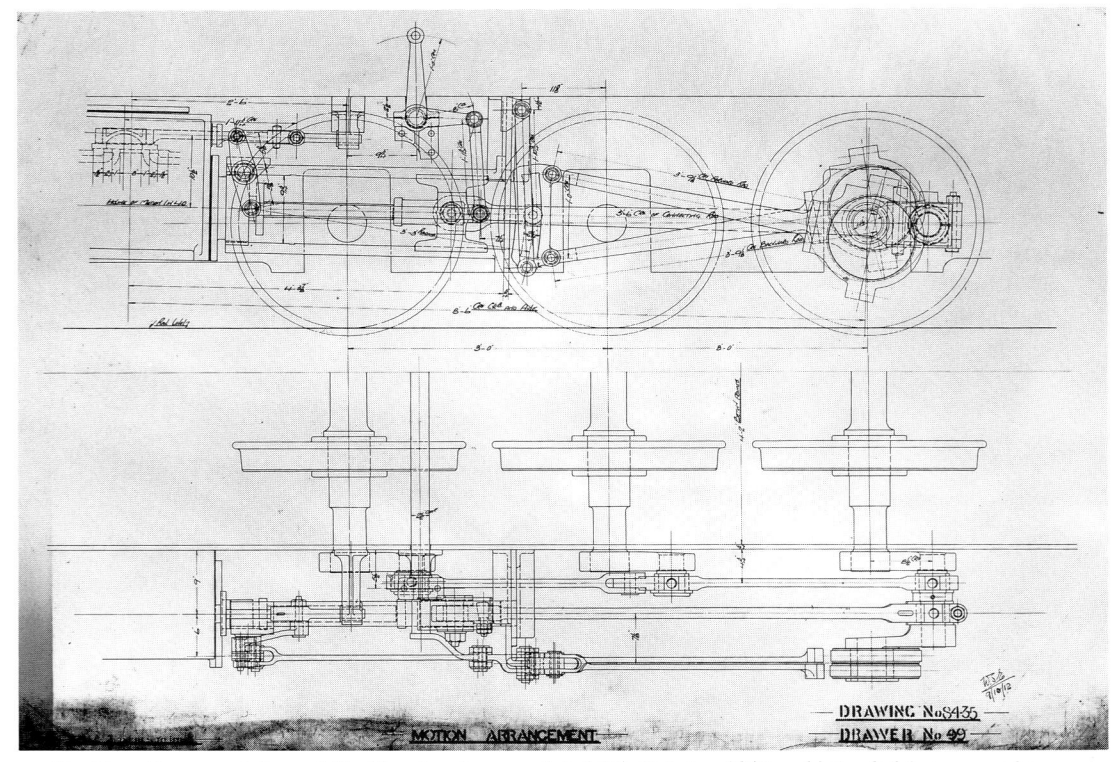

The Bagnall proposal for outside Gooch valve gear dated 9th October 1912 and intended for re-use of some of the original components. *Courtesy Alan C. Baker*

THE LOCOMOTIVES

One of the original Davies & Metcalfe works plates.
W. H. Whitworth

steam-launch link version of Gooch gear. This was quite all right in itself but had been designed fine and slender to get it in between the inside of the frames and the wheels. As soon as wear set in in the top bushings of the suspension link blocks, the lower ends scraped against the wheel faces. Time and time again the drivers heard that first ominous scrape and the engine had to be nursed along slowly for the rest of the trip, or for the rest of the day if all three engines were out and up.

Mr Eddie Savage has recalled the many times the message would come up from the shed that his father would be working very late, and his mother would pack up a supper for him to carry. There, down in the pit, would be Tom Savage and Harry Millman working by the light of spouted oil lamps, augmented by cocoa tins with holes through the lids and pieces of rag for wicks, re-bushing the valve-gear so that the engine could be in service next morning. If the wear was caught in time little or no harm would be done, and the drivers were all very much aware of the damage which could be caused by allowing the link blocks to flail about as they soon would do if the speed was not reduced. It was a sound gear for a steam launch, but the hammering motion of a railway engine stressed it unmercifully.

Sometimes, and because of the spongey nature of some of the bedding of the track, the big-ends got thumped when negotiating points. Another tribulation caused by the track going into hollows was the speedy buckling of the transverse guard irons, and these had to be replaced by something home-made but very much more substantial. *Edward VII* got neatly-shaped timbers and *Prince of Wales* got heavy plain beams so that they could scrape the rails with impunity. They were also invaluable in giving warning when the springs were getting soft, which happens all the time with all forms of transport. When the eccentric bearings got a bit worn they emulated some of the L & BSCR locomotives whose livery they bore; because of the artificial lead produced by the original setting plus the wear, they could, if the brake was not screwed firmly down, toddle quietly off on their own.

Generally, in the hands of competent crews, they did their job well, and it was unfortunate for Davies & Metcalfe that, after all their effort, the engines should be tucked away on the Welsh coast instead of being in a place where they would be noticed. Their square appearance led to comparisons with armoured trains and local humorists, including one of the biggest leg-pullers of them Jack Bach, driver J. E. Davies, fostered the illusion that it was the boilers that were square also.

About 1909/10 they were repainted in a bright green only a shade darker than North Eastern Railway green, with darker green and black banding round the tanks. These bands were separated by very pale cream linings. Frames and all below tank level became black. They were repainted in the same livery with a slight variation in the lining.

Repairs were done locally and as cheaply as possible e.g. T. Williams & Sons of Aberystwyth sent in a bill for £50 in 1911 for repairs to No. 2. In the same year they had to approach Davies & Metcalfe for the right spares and Herbert Jones of the Cambrian had to negotiate a settlement when the cost was disputed. Herbert Jones, on assuming full responsibility for the Rheidol stock, reported that the overall condition including the boilers and fireboxes was 'fair'. On 30th May his drawing office produced a rather inept drawing of the valve gear and Class Diagram 17 (later renumbered 14) of the Rheidol engines with dustbin sandboxes on top of the boilers. There must have been an unadopted proposal drawing amongst the junk sent to Oswestry and the draughtsman cannot ever have seen the engines before he drew it.

While repairs to the 2–4–0 Bagnall tank *Rheidol* were being discussed the question of the valve gear on these other two was raised and Bagnalls turned out two drawings. The first dated 18th September 1912 was for outside Walschaerts gear and the second, dated 9th October 1912, was for an outside version using as much as possible of the existing Gooch gear. Of this, like the idea of a fourth engine, no more was seen and Tom Ryder (who had replaced Tom Savage soon afterwards) and Harry Millman did not get relief from the job of refitting valve gear. By then, of course, the Cambrian were not running as many trains and they no longer had to work past midnight to salvage the timetables.

As soon as the engines became Cambrian property, the nameplates and insignia were removed and the bare patches were dabbed over with the addition of Cambrian Railways on the cabsides. As an extra they were given the large standard Cambrian locomotive jacks as carried since the Welshampton disaster. Something else arrived which was not much help either – Ruabon coal. Szlumper had specified an inadequate 'Cokebox of 32 cu. ft.' which could hold barely 15 cwt of coal. Coke was tried at first but bags of the stuff had to be stacked all over the tank tops and coal could always give out more heat per cubic foot, so good Welsh Steam Coal it had to be. The problem was that to counteract the poorer steaming performance on Ruabon coal, more had to be carried, and Tom Savage had already boarded over the spaces on both sides of the fireboxes to enable more to be carried. And when the even poorer dirty wartime rubbish reached the little sheds matters got even worse.

There was no money to spare for a loss-making line which had depended on holiday traffic, and matters carried on as they were, but c 1916? or 1918? both engines were given larger bunkerage and became the widest on the 2 ft gauge. The fireman's lot was improved by moving the handbrake back by affixing a half-drum on the backsheet to take the circle of the handle. That was all the Cambrian could afford to do for them and they just carried on wearing out as before. Unlike the slate railways where the engines had only empties to haul uphill, the Rheidol engines are fully loaded uphill as well as down; now that the principal slate railways are preserved passenger-carrying lines, their engines probably consistently work harder than they did when new.

No. 1 at the coal stage on 13th August 1913 in two-tone green livery, with driver Bob Morris (standing). Note inside the fitters' shed is converted open No. 11, which was given windows in both ends.
K. A. C. R. Nunn

No. 2 at Devil's Bridge c.1914 in two-tone green livery, lettered CAMBRIAN RAILWAYS and minus nameplate and device.
Courtesy E. R. Mountford

No. 2 in grey about to cross the road at Llanbadarn in 1921.

W. L. *Good*

No. 1 in unlined Cambrian livery, with *Rheidol* completing a run round at Devil's Bridge in 1921. Note that *Rheidol*, which always piloted, has also run round the train engine by both engines making a shunt at the neck.
W. L. Good

No. 1 on Llanbadarn crossing in 1921, giving a good rear view of structural doctoring by the Cambrian. The driver is Bob Morris.
W. L. Good

The livery became the usual black all over with CAMBRIAN in French grey 7 inch letters shaded red along the tanks. It is not certain whether No. 2 was lettered before the end of the Cambrian Railways era, but seemingly it was not.

When the GWR took them over, No. 1 had just had an overhaul only 1,959 miles ago but was taken to Swindon where another £876 2s 8d was spent on her. She returned in plain GWR green with Great Western along the tanks. Work was completed by May 1923.

Both received new number plates of the standard GWR pattern in cast brass, No. 1 becoming 1212 and No. 2 1213. Both numbers had become vacant in April 1920 by the scrapping of two of the last batch of Standard Goods or 388 Class' 0–6–0s. Built to standard gauge in 1876, both had been converted to broad gauge and back again.

No. 2 was all right but more worn than No. 1, so she was left running and went into Swindon in 1924 and was never seen again.

By 1925 No. 1212 had run another 15,298 miles and she went back to Swindon where another £334 6s 3d was spent in putting her into good order as a spare engine. Now she looked very different with new tanks and standard GWR top fittings. She lay virtually unused at the back of the long shed because the three new engines were quite capable of moving every bit of rolling stock on the line without any assistance from a fourth. In 1932 she was sent back to Swindon to be put on the sales list. There was no buyer and, sad to relate, an engine of considerable historical interest was cut up while in extremely good working order. The official withdrawal date was 9th March 1935.

No. 1 as GWR No. 1212 parked at Swindon when on the sales list. Note that Swindon features included new tanks with raised edges to stop tools being lost over the side.

Courtesy F. E. Hemming

The Swindon-Built 2–6–2 Tanks

In 1922 the newly-arrived régime found one small badly-worn out engine and two of sound enough design but both needing a lot of attention. No. 1 had only run 1,959 miles since the last overhaul to Cambrian standards which were not considered good enough so, as already mentioned, she went into Swindon for a further £876 2s 8d worth to make sure. No. 2 had not had any repairs at all for the previous 18,000 miles. This does not sound much by standard gauge standards but in terms of motion wear it compares with 44,000 miles for a 4-6-0 'Castle'. Also the time under stress would be around 1,000 hours for the larger locomotive, whereas the narrow gauge example would be under pressure while in steam for up to 3,500 hours with all the extra waiting about. Notice, too, that the nomenclature has changed. The old company had engines, the Cambrian had a Locomotive Superintendent, but often referred to engines. Mr. C. B. Collett was the Chief Mechanical Engineer and he had thousands of locomotives on his books, many of which still referred to them as engines.

He would have received reports from his Locomotive Examiner and had the general opinions of the folk at Oswestry, and probably that of C. M. Colclough whom he promoted from Oswestry into Swindon Works. He would be aware of the difficulties of access and maintenance of the valve gear. It is known that even the drivers were listened to before the final decision was made. And there was that Bagnall drawing of outside Walschaerts valve gear. By hiring Palmerston, services could be kept going while better things were put in hand. So authority was obtained for Lot 227, two new locos which followed the original Davies & Metcalfe design, but with all the improvements of hindsight that a great locomotive works could devise.

It was a work that was much enjoyed by all concerned, something totally different and quite non-standard. Only the safety valves, the whistles and the backplate fittings came off the shelf. Also possibly the cylinder castings were derived from those of the steam rail motors. They were given miniature Belpaire fireboxes, a much heavier set of valve motion than Bagnalls had designed and with broader bearing surfaces, and a higher coal capacity. As a result, they were three tons heavier than their forebears. An increase of the bore of the cylinders from 11" to 11½" and the raising of the boiler pressure from 150 lbs psi to 165 lbs psi produced a 20% increase in the tractive effort. The official completion date was 19th October 1923 and the cost was £2,737 each.

They were finished in plain unlined loco green which at that time was a shade darker than most of us will be able to remember. The tanks were lettered GREAT WESTERN in the newly-

The kindness of a great man. When young Frank Hemming wrote in 1935 to C. B. Collett asking for details from which he might make a model, he was sent a ferro-prussiate process 'blueprint' of both the diagram and of this photograph, from which this reproduction has been made. No. 8 in works grey in 1923.

Courtesy F. E. Hemming

THE LOCOMOTIVES

introduced style of 1922 with yellow letters shaded red and black. On the small tanks it was bold and enhancing, especially when combined with a copper-capped chimney, a brass safety-valve bonnet and highly-polished motion. The shape of the bonnets was rare for the GWR; instead of being compounded entirely of curves they had a straight central section.

The numbers had been borne by some interesting and illustrious predecessors. No. 7 was first carried by an ex-Shrewsbury & Chester Jones & Potts long-boilered 2–4–0 of 1846 which was withdrawn in 1859. From 1859 to 1876 it was an Armstrong 2–2–2. A rather inept Dean 2–4–0 Tandem Compound took the number in 1886 and somehow, while withdrawn in 1887 and 'dismantled' in 1894, was made over in some devious way into the brilliant Dean 7 ft 4–4–0 'Armstrong'. This was renumbered 4171 in February 1923 barely in time for the newcomer to have it. No. 8 had a similar history – Jones & Potts up to 1859, Armstrong 1859 to 1883, a better form of Tandem Compound 1886 to 1894, made over to 4–4–0 *Gooch* which gave its number up to receive 4172 in February 1923.

Their arrival at Aberystwyth was hailed with delight by footplate crews, shedmen and passengers alike. They could punch their way steadily up to Devil's Bridge with nine bogies, a van and a 4w toast-rack without losing a minute. No longer would the tourists be complaining over sight-seeing time lost because of late arrival.

Now we come to one of the strangest pieces of locomotive history the author has ever encountered. On 12th January 1923 the GWR Board had authorised the construction of two locomotives for the Vale of Rheidol at an estimated cost of £2,500 each. These were processed through the works as Lot 227 and were ready for delivery on 19th October 1923 at a final cost of £2,737 each, as already related. While the authorisation was for two only, when the success of Nos. 7 & 8 was known, a third set of parts was put in hand. By July 1924 these parts had become No. 1213.

If the working drawings of the original Davies & Metcalfe engines are compared with those for Lot 227, it becomes quite clear that no part from the one could possibly fit the other, and that the present No. 9 is an entirely different new engine built in 1924 without authority and cloaked up as a heavy repair. It was concealed so effectively that it was to deceive the future owners, British Rail. It does illustrate adequately the power of a great CME in those days and there may be many other cases which we may never know about. The booked cost of that 'heavy repair' was £2,589 5s 4d and the prime records were never altered. Only the internal Works records give the game away.

No. 1213 as nearly new in 1926. Note the summer car with gartered crest, wing and arm livery, standing on the Harbour Branch. Like 7 and 8, she arrived with screw-tightened couplings.

A. W. Croughton

The lower cost is quite correct because administrative, draughtsmanship and pattern-making costs had already been recovered in the booked costs of Nos. 7 & 8.

Nos. 7 & 8 started life as like as two peas in a pod, but 1213 had a few different minor features. She had the sliding roof shown on the Lot 227 drawing but not cut into the roofs of 7 & 8, and toolboxes and grab-rails differed too. Because they were hand-worked, all three copper caps vary slightly, as do the safety-valve bonnets. Mechanically they are identical and only 1213 failed to get a new pattern of regulator about 1945 which has imparted a fractionally different exhaust beat and a slight difference in response to the regulator when compared against 7 & 8.

Once the line and the crews had settled down to life with three splendid matching pullers, the account becomes comparatively dull compared with what has gone before. Other than livery changes there will be nothing to comment about; they merely ran, received general overhauls, boiler inspections (every 7 years), and heavy repairs, and were photographed very frequently.

No. 1213 was repainted to include the circular GWR totem in 1936 but it is not certain that 7 & 8 bore it. Steam-heating pipes were not taken off until after the arrival of the new unheated coaches in 1938. All three were under cover throughout the war but receiving maintenance checks and lubrication. After the war 7 & 8 were painted over in plain unlettered green while 1213's paint of 1936 was still acceptable. In 1948 No. 7 was

No. 8 on 15th August 1935 at Devil's Bridge. Note steam-heating connection minus hose. *H. F. Wheeller*

No. 7 on shed on 15th August 1935, with a bit of 'spot cleaning' of the lettering. *H. F. Wheeller*

THE LOCOMOTIVES

No. 1213 in Swindon on 16th February 1936. *H. F. Wheeller*

No. 1213 at Devil's Bridge with 'shirtbutton' totem, in August 1936. The author's earliest photograph taken on a cycling tour with a 'Brownie' box camera.

No. 8 in unlined green in 1949.
R. K Cope

repainted with G.W.R. in large letters on the tanks and during the winter of 1948/49 No. 1213 was painted plain black and had the number changed to 9.

The previous bearers of the number 9 were more odd than those of 7 & 8, and none could be said to be illustrious. The first was an ex-Shrewsbury & Chester 2–2–2 withdrawn in 1873. Then came William Dean's only total failure, the 7′8″ 4–2–4 tank of 1881 which was said to have spent more time off the rails than on. In 1884 it was rebuilt into 7′8″ 2–2–2 and into a 7′ 2–2–2 in 1890 being withdrawn in 1905. From 1922 it was the number of a Barry Railway 0–4–4 tank No. 69 until that was withdrawn in 1927.

For 1955 No. 7 was repainted in unlined Western Region green with the lion-over-the-wheel logo. The other two received the logo at Aberystwyth without repaints, No. 9 being still black; all were repainted green for the 1956 season with the same lion-

The last appearance of GWR No. 7 with a good full train on 9th July 1953 at Aberffrwd.
G. D. Braithwaite

THE LOCOMOTIVES

Nos. 7 and 8 together in Swindon A shop on 25th April 1954.

E. R. Mountford

Power to move — the motion of No. 9 with 1213 stamped into every part. This picture was taken in September 1957 when shed visitors were allowed to clean and polish.

The first year of the lion-over-wheel logo. Nos. 8, 9 and 7 on the Harbour Branch siding in 1954. *T. P. Dalton*

No. 8 in plain green with lion-over-wheel logo, at Devil's Bridge in 1955. *G. H. W. Clifford*

No. 9 in plain black paint with the lion-over-wheel logo, after taking water at Aberffrwd, on 2nd August 1955. This unusual movement was occasioned by the failure of the train engine. Note the opened sliding hatch in the cab roof.
H. F. Wheeller

No. 7 sorting wagons at the Exchange siding in June 1956, showing the new nameplate and the replacement logo below.

Re-wheeling with the Swindon 50-ton crane at the Exchange siding in April 1956.

Pat Dalton

THE LOCOMOTIVES

When one of the Lein Fach engines was in trouble the whole shed turned out. No. 8 fetched off at the shed points by that over-large sized pony restraining chain, in September 1957.

Joined by track chargeman Arthur Jenkins, still in his Sunday best, in September 1957.

No. 7 in the new Western Region green livery with orange and black lining and the roaring-lion logo, in August 1958, with driver Jacky Jones and fireman Dai Burgess.

THE LOCOMOTIVES

To make this comparison possible, it took two hours hard weeding the afternoon before and seventeen movements of *Lechlade Manor* in August 1958, to give the photographer eleven minutes to shoot off nine frames before No. 7 had to be rushed off to take the 10.30 a.m.

over-the-wheel logo, above which were magnificent polished brass nameplates in the best Great Western style. No. 7 was *Owain Glyndŵr*, No. 8 *Llywelyn* and, having regard to antecedents, No. 9 became *Prince of Wales*. For the following (1957) season they were painted yet again with GWR orange and black lining with the striking new roaring lion logo.

These three names were aptly chosen, all three characters had visited Aberystwyth, and all are mentioned by William Shakespeare. With aid from the King of France, Owain Glyndŵr took Edward I's new castle of Aberystwyth in 1404 and held it for four years, and he is the fiery mystic allied to the Hotspur faction in *King Henry IV Part I*. Llywelyn the Great would have stayed at the old castle of Llanbadarn south of Aberystwyth and in *King Henry V* there is the valiant Welsh captain Fluellen who makes an example of the cowardly Pistol by making him eat a leek. Many Princes of Wales have visited Aberystwyth and there is the youthful playboy Prince of Wales, again in *King Henry IV*, whose roystering companion is the bibulous, Falstaff.

Sad to tell, but after that last checkover and repaint, Nos. 7 & 8 fell under a cloud. No. 7 started getting the front pony off the rails first, and occasionally No. 8, but never No. 9. It was always after going through points and the track chargeman Arthur Jenkins was first to be censured, unjustly as it was to be proved. The trouble was so persistent that the District Mechanical Inspector, Frank Roberts, had hinged sections cut away in the front platforms of both 7 & 8 so that a man could watch the pony while hanging on to the front of the loco. At last No. 7 was caught in the act with the new slightly larger safety chain picking up a lug on the side of the pony truck and holding the one wheel barely half an inch in the air. On the next roll, off she would come and could run as an 0–6–2 tank until the next set of points.

Soliloquy, fireman-passed-driver John Mostyn James waits for the all-clear to take No. 9 off shed in 1958.

A top view of No. 8 drifting down to take water in June 1956 before the unchecked overgrowth made this picture impossible.

THE LOCOMOTIVES

No. 7, now a reformed character with the correct restraining chains on her ponies, goes through Stourbridge Junction en route for Aberystwyth on 1st September 1961. *Michael Hale*

So it was back to Swindon for the pair of them for replacement chains, this time of the correct specification.

In the early 1960s the instruction was given for steam to be given a dirty image so that the public would see grimy steam engines with filthy motion, and receive the new clean diesels and electrics more favourably, but they kept polishing the motion of the little Rheidol locos for a bit longer.

1968 saw the extinction of the green livery and its place was taken by Rail Blue with the double arrow logo in white. The nameplate and numberplate grounds, main cranks, return crank and lifting arm were signal red. When new and clean it looked smart enough, but at a distance it soon began to look dull. At later repaints the red on the motion was not renewed. For the 1976 season No. 7, after an overhaul at Swindon, came back with black and white lining, the number moved up to the top sideplate of the cab, with a handsome brass cut-out of the double arrow on the bunkers, and she looked really good. No. 9 followed suit in 1977 and No. 8 was the last in time for 1978.

Meanwhile fresh trouble had arisen. June, July and August of 1975 had been abnormally dry and several small fires occurred. 1976 was much worse with April to August almost rainless. After taking one photograph the author spent an exhausting quarter of an hour flattening a fire below some pines and later a stand of pines above Gwaith Coch was burnt. Later he got a very tender face after over an hour spent with many others on a large fire which was raging behind the bungalow and above Smelting Cottage. All manner of claims were being cooked up and the Forestry Commission were charging the cost of maintaining fire patrols. All this seemed most unjust because the railway was there first, and it was much later that inflammable pine trees were planted right up to the railway fenceline and other trees took root and grew next to the track totally unrestrained. Many times when the sea was mirror-calm and the still air at the top of the valley was heavy with the scent of pine, no trains were run.

The real cause of the trouble was the LMR supply of Maltby Black coal. The locos were designed to burn Welsh steam coal, a good quality of anthracite, and there was no trouble when

No. 9 in unlined BR blue in April 1967.

Top left: No. 7 in lined BR blue at Aberffrwd, with driver Owen Jenkins and fireman John Hitchcock, on 11th April 1977. Top right: No. 8 leaving Devil's Bridge in Cambrian 'invisible green' livery, with driver Gwilym Morgan on 5th May 1986. Above left: No. 7 at Aberystwyth in the Shell-UK sponsored version of Western Region lined green livery, with driver Gwilym Davies on 15th October 1984. Above right: Three historical liveries: No. 9 in the original LB & SCR Stroudley, No. 8 in the GWR totem on Brunswick green, and No. 7 in the Western Region lined, on 28th August 1983.

they got it. Maltby Black dusted and threw sparks and something had to be done. After consultation with the people running the Festiniog, a conversion system for adapting the locos to burn ordinary 35 secs diesel loco fuel was designed. No. 7 was so converted and ran very well throughout the 1978 season and No. 8 was put onto oil for 1979. No. 9 was kept running on coal and bore the brunt of the 1980 season when the OPEC countries were engineering a shortage of petroleum products; she started running as an oil-burner in 1981. There have been benefits, oil is easier to fill than coal and it is delivered right alongside the shed by road tanker. Firemen can be trained more easily and the tubes and smokeboxes stay cleaner.

Another phase of change was seen on 4th May 1981 during a Gala Day when No. 8 took the first 'Welsh Dragon' (the 14.30) with a nicely-fashioned headboard up to Devil's Bridge in a return to GWR green with the GWR circular totem. The next historical livery to be revived was the LB & SCR style of the first engines. No. 9 was painted in a form as near as possible to that borne by her ancestor in 1902. Mr James Metcalfe paid generously towards the cost and it was a case of 'The Prince is Dead. Long Live the Prince'. After all, the direct descent of the *Prince* can be traced through those impressive records once kept at Swindon and there is sound historical precedence for having a 'Young Pretender'.

Shed glimpse, a close-up of the fuel controls on No. 9, on 15th October 1984.

Oil-fired footplate of No. 9 on 3rd September 1984.

There was an official unveiling ceremony on 10th April 1982 during which *Prince* could only stand and simmer because at anything over 40 lbs psi the loco vented down the steam pipe, and there was a fine blast coming forward from the drain cocks. No. 8 had to stand in and take the special train. Later a hair crack was found in the J casting of the regulator which had found its way across to an air bubble in the 58 year-old metal. It cannot be said that the fault was put right with an exasperated kick at the backplate, but someone did give that casting a right good thump with a heavy spanner; there's know-how for you!

Shell (UK) sponsored the third historical livery which was a return to the Western Region finish with the roaring-lion logo for No. 7 on 18th June 1983. The next engine due for repainting was No. 8 *Llywelyn*. The nameplate has been removed as was the Cambrian practice, and the tank sides bear the railway's name CAMBRIAN in 7 inch letters, extending for 6 feet in all, shaded right and below in red. The overall finish is Cambrian 'invisible green', a green so intense that, while it went well with the bronze-green of the Cambrian carriages, it looks black by itself. However, the greenish cast is just discernible when the engine is seen against the British Rail's bluish-black which, in its turn, goes well with Rail Blue. The letters and numbers are in the Cambrian's French grey, and characters on the buffer beams are shaded white to the right and black below. The numberplates now have red backgrounds. The new livery was seen for the first time on 5th May 1986.

So it does seem that the Vale of Rheidol locomotives have, between them all, established an untouchable record for the number of different liveries carried by narrow gauge specimens; it could be a record not equalled anywhere on the standard gauge either.

No. 3 The Bagnall 2-4-0 Tank *Rheidol*

This engine was built at the Stafford works of W. G. Bagnall & Co. Ltd., Works No. E1497 of 1896. Built to the order of Collier, Antunez & Co., agents for and operators of Usina Treze de Maio, which was a cane plantation and sugar factory near Pernambuco in Brazil, she was designed to run by burning cane-waste. Treze de Maio means 13th May, the date slavery was abolished in Brazil. The order was cancelled because of internal disorder.

In late August 1897 she was bought by Thomas Molyneaux, the Lancashire business man behind the roadway sett and stone quarry to be served by the Plynlimon & Hafan Tramway. The gauge was reduced from 75 mm nominal (for which she had been made 2′5½″, which was 1 mm under) down to 2′3″, and she was named *Talybont*. It is not certain whether she was ever named *Treze de Maio* but it seems a likely possibility.

After the failure of the sett quarry, because, it has been suggested, the stone was not hard enough, Bagnalls bought her back out of the liquidation proceedings. Soon she was sold to Pethicks and regauged, for the second time in her short life, to 1′11½″ for work on the Vale of Rheidol contract. Possibly it was the additional stress brought about by moving the bearing centres that caused the crank axle to shear. She skittered off the rails in the only safe place for miles and fetched up against the outer face of Quarry Cutting.

Driver J. E. Davies, who started his career by firing her, recalls her arrival with the name *Talybont* in green letters and he said that she was black lined somewhat like the L & NWR in cream and red. Pethicks left the lining alone but changed the name to *Rheidol*. They also built a more protective matchboard cab to improve something designed for hotter surroundings. Her subsequent transfer into the Rheidol Company's stud attracted the usual sort of shilly-shally.

In February 1902 Pethicks offered her for £350, with boiler certified by the National Boiler & General Insurance Co. as being fit to be pressed at 150 lbs per sq inch, with a further £97 to be paid to Bagnalls for a thorough overhaul and repair. The Finance Committee, 'whilst recognising the importance of having such an engine of this class for shunting purposes', passed the buck to the next full Board meeting who postponed consideration. By that time the rising of costs caused by the Boer War prompted Pethicks to up the price to £400 which the company had to pay.

The Finance Committee may have thought of her as a shunter, but who could have thought at that time that she would be capable of being driven to Devil's Bridge and back twice and sometimes three times a day for the next 20 years? She was a marvellous buy and her passengers came to know her affectionately as 'Coffee Pot'. With that short rigid wheelbase she

No. 3 *Rheidol* in 1921, as modified by the Cambrian.   W. L. Good

THE LOCOMOTIVES

No. 3 *Rheidol* as running for most of her over-worked invaluable life, seen here in two-tone green livery on 28th June 1909. Note the end of the general manager's office with the legend TO TRAINS FOR DEVIL'S BRIDGE and the useful detail of the lettering on the wagon.
H. L. Hopwood

boxed and corkscrewed abominably at a fearsome periodic rate, which was not surprising when one realises that when she was trying to get up to 20 mph everything was oscillating and vibrating at the same timing as the parts of a GWR 'Castle' Class locomotive doing 60 mph, and wearing out as fast.

Firing had to be to corners only because the motion speedily shook the fire to the middle of the grate; an inexperienced fireman could fail to top up little and often and get most of the fire shaken away through the firebars. This oscillation also did things to the water over the firebox crown, which caused a bit more wastage there than was normal. It speaks volumes for the skill of her crews that an engine designed to chuff happily over level fields burning cane waste should be performing such heavy duties continuously for so long.

By the end of 1904, three quotations were obtained for repairs to the firebox, front tubeplate, retubing and a new chimney. The Yorkshire Engine Co. £105, Bagnalls £48 10s 0d, and Davies & Metcalfe £44 15s 0d. So she was sent off to Romiley where she got that chimney which looked rather like those on her stablemates. Other later repairs were done by Williams & Metcalfe's foundry and on at least one occasion a GWR boilersmith was brought in to rejuvenate that firebox crown once more. She received the two-shades-of-green livery of 1906/7 and then reverted back to black with pale cream lining.

In 1910 a split steam pipe was brazed up locally and estimates had to be obtained for more extensive repairs. From 1912 repairs were carried out at Oswestry but the Cambrian had to order a new set of springs from Bagnalls in 1915. At Oswestry the wooden back was scrapped and a sheet steel back substituted, the front buffer beam was cut away at the lower corners to give better access to the cylinder heads, the inevitable large screw jack was added, the name was subtracted and 'Cambrian Railways' added.

Occasionally, a Cambrian main line driver got rostered to drive her once the Cambrian terminated 'one engine, one driver', which had been the original Vale of Rheidol tenet. One of them asked immediately 'Where's the pressure gauge?'. 'Away for repair.' 'I can't take an engine out like this.' 'Why not? You have the feel of her and the safety valve is working.' In the words of the contemporary *Punch* magazine 'Collapse of main line driver'.

The GWR loco examiner looked No. 3 over and reported back, the official photographer being sent to Aberystwyth to record items which should be replaced. Among his pictures was one of No. 3 nearing Quarry Cutting and pulling only one coach and a van, which could have been for presentation on the basis of 'And this is all this engine will pull'. Thus she came to be the first of the line's original engines to be stopped as on 31st May 1923. Nobody could recall seeing the brass plate bearing the allotted number 1198, which had been another 5 ft Standard Goods cut up in what the Railway Correspondence & Travel Society have termed 'the massacre of 1919–21'.

Final instruction of withdrawal was given on 17th July 1924, and so ended a gallant little engine which was always driven far beyond her designed capacity. Even after the Cambrian blotched the name out she was always 'Rheidol' at Aberystwyth, never plain No. 3, and years after the old gentlemen writing about her invariably wrote about 'Rheidol'.

Palmerston could easily take one coach more than *Rheidol*. Note the general manager's office has been turned round and the street name board is now much larger. Photographed on 13th August 1913.
K. A. C. R. Nunn

Festiniog Railway No. 4 *Palmerston*
George England 0–4–0 Tender Saddle Tank of 1864

The Rheidol line has been chronically short of motive power right from the start. When it became known that there would be Army camps at Devil's Bridge, as well as the Territorials at Lovesgrove, during the summer of 1912, something had to be done. The Chairman (the Cambrian's Alfred Herbert) authorised overtures to be made to the Festiniog. These were successful, and on 16th July *Palmerston* went into the Boston Lodge workshops for couplings to be modified to be compatible with those of the Rheidol stock. *Palmerston* was loaded for the journey south on 31st July and worked between Aberystwyth and Devil's Bridge most successfully until returned to Minffordd on 21st August for transfer back to Festiniog metals. (Both lines were to the same gauge of 1′11½″.)

The hire charge was 40/- a day and the engine was accompanied by her individual driver 'Old Dafydd'. Driver David Davies wore a goatee beard and an extremely greasy bowler hat. He was so fond of his engine, and so determined to keep the Rheidol men away from her, that at night he would sweep out the tender and sleep in it, bowler hat and all. The first time he arrived at Devil's Bridge his first words were 'Ple mae'r inn?' – 'Where's the pub?' and off he went to the Hafod to talk his way round at the back door. Almost as soon as he had left, Mr H. Warwick, the Cambrian Superintendent of the Line, arrived to see how *Palmerston* and Dafydd had got on. 'And where is he?' he demanded to know. 'Oh, he's somewhere about.'

He duly came back, saying that he had been walking in the woods listening to the birds singing. 'I never gave him away', said Driver Edwin Davies, 'and he went to hear the birds singing every time he was there. You see, in those days, I was a bit fond of birds and beer myself.'

The hire arrangement was renewed for the next summer and this time *Palmerston* had a longer stay because *Rheidol* broke down and had to go away to Oswestry for a heavy repair. Now was the Rheidol men's chance when *Palmerston* was regularly on short trains instead of always piloting the longer ones. Dafydd had left his engine for a moment with steam up and driver Jack Davies and his mate changed engines and took *Palmerston* out, when Dafydd was nowhere to be found and it was well past the time of departure. They did very well until, rounding the Erwtomau Horseshoe Bend, they got a wheelspin and *Palmerston* did not seem to run as freely as before. They had bent a side-rod and 'Duw! there was trouble!'

Dafydd himself was in hot water soon afterwards. At short notice he was detailed to pilot an augmented 2 o'clock and he hadn't refilled his tender after the morning run. There was none on shed either so with the train engine they nipped off to the siding to fetch another wagonful. Dafydd's mate was left to carry on firing up *Palmerston* but he muffed it and lost what was left of the fire. When the others got back he was frantically chopping up an old sleeper to get things going again.

THE LOCOMOTIVES

The train left at 2.30 and everyone got a wigging, starting with the foreman who did not hesitate to pass it on down the line. On another occasion, *Palmerston* was piloting *Rheidol* with four coaches and a van, and a steam pipe joint went in the smokebox just before Llanbadarn. She was put off up the siding using the tablet and, after *Rheidol* had drawn the train on, she was released to limp back to Aberystwyth minus the tablet. *Rheidol* struggled on solo and actually got right up to Devil's Bridge, rather late but she was got there by frequent halts on the level bits for a restoke, getting full pressure up and charging on for the next mile or so.

Palmerston once got off the road very badly indeed, tender as well, after a disagreement with the frog of one of the sets of points in Aberystwyth station. Lewis Hamer attended with the breakdown crew and ordered a placing of sleepers so that she could be run up and back on the rails. Something slipped and down she went again in worse case than before. Old Dafydd, his face as black as the ace of spades and with tears in his eyes, pleaded 'Don't do that again, you will smash my little engine before I can take her back to Festiniog. We will lift her back on again for you, there's plenty of us here now.' His letter relating the story ended 'And indeed lever her onto the rails again we did, just to console the old fellow.'

The Festiniog hired *Palmerston* back again in 1914 but this time the period was cut short by the outbreak of the 1914–18 war. By then the hire charge had gone up to £22 per week for the first two weeks and £2 a day if kept on after that. In 1915 she was back again because the three Rheidol engines could not cope with holiday traffic as well as meet the demands of the wartime timber suppliers. In 1921 the Cambrian hired *Palmerston* yet again because the Rheidol engines were needing overhaul just to keep them going. This time it was from July until 27th September when she got dropped and damaged while being loaded for the return journey. The last visit was from 30th July until 25th August 1922 at 50/- per day. For 1923 the Festiniog

Palmerston **piloting a down train at Cwm-yr-ogos, c.1920.**
Courtesy of W. E. Hayward

had to refuse because several of their own engines were not in very good shape either.

Palmerston was a better puller than *Rheidol* and could take three coaches and a van quite easily in dry weather, but in wet she had less grip and could lose time in slipping. It seems odd that so many stories should have been recalled about the short stays of one engine, but she was different and so seems to have stuck in everyone's memory. Perhaps it was because of the Festiniog's brick-red livery with double yellow lining with black infill and fine red picking, all beautifully polished by Old Dafydd's loving hands.

Motive Power etc which failed to arrive

Early in 1902 Kerr, Stuart & Co. Ltd. wrote offering an engine for sale. The Board resolved that no action should be taken. At the end of 1904 James Rees proposed a passenger service along the Harbour Branch for which a motor would be needed.

In 1909 he reported that the winter service might be run more economically if a petrol car could be obtained. Williams Foundry gave a preliminary quotation of £600 to £700 but did not consider that such a car would work successfully on the company's line. On 29th April 1910 the Board discussed a proposal that Williams should construct a petrol car for £300 to be paid after a six week trial period and £300 at the end of three months. This suggestion, that if it worked they would get paid, and if it didn't they wouldn't, did not appeal to Williams. One rather vague reference suggests that a steam-powered version could have been thought about.

A fourth engine was discussed for 1910 but the Engineer thought that the three engines could cope with the additional work generated by the camp at Lovesgrove.

In November 1912 the Cambrian-directed Board proposed to buy a fourth engine, with the proviso that the decision should be deferred until a report had been received about the alterations to *Prince of Wales*, whereupon *Edward VII* would also be altered.

This was the plan to convert the two engines to outside motion, and the success of hiring *Palmerston* removed the necessity for a fourth engine.

Ridley & Young Ltd. of Darlington wrote to the GWR in 1923 stating that it was known that they were short of an engine and offering them the former North Wales Narrow Gauge Railway Company's single Fairlie, the Hunslet 0-6-4 tank *Gowrie*. As the GWR were about to become not at all short of an engine the offer was refused.

In 1943 the Festiniog inexplicably offered to sell to the GWR a new boiler intended for *Prince* in case they might have a use for it.

There had been a much earlier chance of another coach. There was a decision in 1905 that 'The Car Llanvihangel be not purchased.' So the Milnes coach, built for the Plynlimon & Hafan Tramway, did not come to Aberystwyth to be run, and instead was brought to Llanbadarn to serve as a summer-house and eventually to decay within the sound of the Rheidol trains.

In 1912 the Cambrian-controlled Board was recommended to consider the purchase of three more open coaches, but no action was taken.

First-Third Composite No. 2 in Cambrian livery in 1922. Note the screw-tightened coupling.

GWR Official

CHAPTER NINE

ROLLING STOCK
The Original Carriages

Tenders were invited for 12 identical carriages from Ashbury's Railway Carriage & Iron Co. Ltd, The Midland Carriage & Wagon Co. Ltd, and from G. F. Milnes & Co. Ltd. The MC & W got the order for delivery early in 1902 but, noting progress and realising that prompt delivery would be unlikely to be matched by prompt payment, the coaches were manufactured and delivered only just in time for the real opening date. The Chairman had tried to get the firm to hasten deliveries to be in time for the hoped for approval of Major Druitt at his second inspection.

They were simple sound commonsense vehicles, $32' \times 6'$ and $8'6\frac{1}{2}''$ from rail to rooftop, which gave $6'3\frac{1}{2}''$ headroom in the centre. The frames were of oak with flitchplates along the solebars and iron buffer beams. The metallic quality of both would be equivalent to a very mild modern steel, and was thicker. The 3 ft wheelbased bogies carried the frames at 22 ft centres and had 4 spoke chilled cast iron wheels with broad webs and springs $2'3''$ long. Body framing and external and internal matchboard planking were pitch pine, said to have been specially imported from Norway. Timber varies a lot in weight and tares were between 6 t 14 cwt and 7 t 5 cwt. The seven waist-high compartments held 8 passengers each with a door at each side, 56 passengers in all. Three oil lamps provided the communal lighting. The couplings were of the centre-buffered Norwegian 'chopper' type with cumbersome screw devices to close the heads together after dropping the chopper. Braking was powered by $12''$ bore $\times 6''$ stroke slipping band vacuum cylinders of Gresham & Craven make, supplied by the Vacuum Brake Co. Ltd. Finish inside and out was plain varnish with black underframes and white roofs.

They were delivered demounted from the bogies on a variety of flat and well wagons and the Cambrian brought in two mobile hand cranes to set them onto Rheidol rails. The carpenter had made the discs bearing the company device and these were screwed on at Aberystwyth. Souvenir hunters stole most of them in the first five or six years.

By the end of 1904 the resinous pitch pine was rejecting the varnish and a local painter named P. B. Loveday quoted £5 per coach for painting over in a dark chocolate and finishing off with a coat of varnish. He got the job with 2 coats of varnish at £6 per coach. At times the window beading was picked out in pale cream and roofs became light grey.

In April 1905 authority was given for the staff to convert two carriages into 1st/3rd composites at a cost of under £10. The middle three seating sections were separated from the *hoi polloi* by matchboard partitions and the centre doors were screwed up. A row of seating was sacrificed from the middle and the whole section was interconnected with gangways cut through the middle, giving full access via only four doors, and more leg room. This left four seats across each end, two back-to-back singles, four in a back-to-back pair, an odd single and an odd pair. No other railway ever managed to have a 17 seater 1st class compartment. Covering was in that revolting woven split cane so much in vogue in trams, and which gave much scratchy discomfort to small boys in short trousers, as the author well remembers. The doors had 'First' in red on white enamel plates and most of the clientele were season-ticket users from Llanbadarn. Soon afterwards a third composite was contrived.

In May 1907 the Traffic Superintendent suggested that income could be increased by putting two open cars on the summer trains. Tenders were obtained from Pickerings, the MC & W and the Birmingham Carriage & Wagon, and the sight of the quotations ended that idea; but it was partially pursued by the conversion of two timber trucks to passenger-carrying which is dealt with later. In 1908 some unidentifiable modification was made to the couplings and the instant popularity of the converted timber trucks directed thoughts towards conversion of two of the existing closed 3rds via that ever-available and much cheaper facility, the shed staff. A slight touch of caution led to only one being converted at first and this went into service in the 1909 season at a cost of only £43 18s 0d. It was another immediate success and the company found that an extra 3d per seat could be charged.

Accordingly two more were ordered to be converted. One was made over for the 1910 season in exactly the same manner as the 1909 job, and the other, their masterpiece, is described later with all the other multi-purpose stock.

Starting in 1910, the acetylene generators were removed from the middle three stations and were mounted inside the three brake-vans and the closed coaches were converted to acetylene lighting, all being complete by 1911. The GWR carriage examiners listed each one as gas-lit putting 'incandescent mantles' against Nos 1, 3 & 4. This could suggest that the others had only fishtail burners but it might be that one individual was a bit more precise than the rest, or three oil-gas conversions.

The Cambrian, after the official acquisition of 1913, painted them in bronze green outside and inside, and the author has childhood memories of travelling inside the most depressingly-painted stock he has ever recalled to mind. The words CAMBRIAN and RAILWAYS were set on separate little boards in their standard gold shaded red transfers at Oswestry, to be screwed onto the carriage sides. The numbers were placed centrally and the Cambrian did some re-arranging. The three composites took 1, 2 and 3. The unaltered 3rds became 4 to 9. Nos. 10 and 11 were the two open-above-the-waist conversions and the fully-open toast-rack was given No. 12, whereas it is known that this was the original No. 9.

When the Cambrian put bars up the centres of the droplights they came in for much ridicule and protest. Either they never finished the job or the more activist among the passengers took some of them off. Wheel renewals were six-spoke chill-cast steel.

The first problem dealt with by the GWR was that of keeping them securely on the winding and narrow. Isaac Jenkins, in his memoirs, has left an account, of which the following is a précis. 'Well ganger, what about all these derailments?' 'Are you blaming the track sir?' 'Yes, it cannot go on like this, the Great Western Railway does not have derailments.' 'Well, sir, I suggest that you examine the bearing brasses on all the coaches.' The examiner went round all of them and stopped eight vehicles as 'Not to go'. The brasses were only thin half shells and, when they wore, the keyway could break off and the shell would then revolve till it was underneath the journal, or the entire shell could break up. Some were restored to service fairly soon but several had to wait until after drawings for new axle boxes had gone through the pattern shop and machine shop c. April 1923. Indicators were added to the train alarm systems, and the cumbersome screw-tightened couplings were replaced by eccentric pins moved away by drop latches to bring the heads together.

Repainting was put in hand after preparation of painter's drawings in February 1923. It was the full regalia, brown and cream with lining, and Garter crest with arm and wing. Horizontal safety bars were affixed midway across all droplights, and the two open cars 4149 and 4150 received tubular safety rails. The addition of steam heating was initiated for the winter of 1925/26, and eight were so fitted, with another one in 1928. The 1sts appeared to have some preferential treatment by way of a temperature gauge by the footboards and some form of adjustment.

Nos. 4 to 11 were renumbered as 3rds 4143 to 4150. Nos. 1, 2 and 3 were renumbered as compos 6335, 6336 and 6337, but went down to thirds 4995, 4996 and 4994 after the abolition of 1st class in 1928 and 1929. (1st class was withdrawn as from 11th July 1927.) Nos. 6335 and 6336 were rebuilt as brake composites in Oswestry in January 1926.

Repaints after 1928 bore the new style coat of arms with GWR above, and they remained in this livery until withdrawn. By the mid 1930s the timber frames were sagging despite the metal solebar plates, and roofs had bowed, being kept to profile by internal tubular struts; the decision at Swindon was 'Back to the drawing board'. The result was almost total renewal and the old vehicles were formally condemned on 30th April 1938.

Third no. 4145 repainted in GWR gartered crest style on the warehouse road, Aberystwyth, in 1923. *Charles Hollick*

ROLLING STOCK

The Swindon-Built Carriages

Summer car No. 4998 of Lot 1333 of 1923 before the addition of safety bars.   *GWR Official*

The result of the photographer's visit in 1922 and the ensuing report on the coaching stock was the authorisation for the building of Lot 1333, four brand-new steel-framed Summer Cars Nos. 4997 to 5000 at an estimated cost of £600 each. They had diamond-mesh safety panels above the waist, a door at each corner, and a gangway from end to end on the side which came against the rock faces. The twelve reversible-backed fixed seats took 3 persons each, with a fourth sitting on a drop-flap across the gangway, 48 in all. They were beautifully finished in brown and cream with lining, and Garter crest with arm and wing. Mr Rees, writing afterwards, averred that, magnificent as they were, they never attained the public affection bestowed on his home-brewed toast-racks. They were delivered in July and August 1923, and additional safety rods were affixed above the mesh in time for the 1924 season. It was then decided (fortunately) not to withdraw the three old open carriages, and the subsequent returns justified their retention. The four new vehicles had the same change of livery after 1928 as the others already described.

The proceedings of the GWR Committees when the time came for the replacement of the old Rheidol carriages, are fully given in the minutes and illustrates the standard GWR thinking on these matters. On 28th October 1937 the Locomotive, Carriage & Stores Committee approved the construction of ten 3rds for £5,900, two Brake 3rds for £1,240 and three Brake Vans for £855. Of the total £7,995, they approved £7,314 which was the estimated cost of replacing those to be scrapped with 15 identical vehicles, and which came out of the very adequate Repairs & Renewals Fund. To this was to be added £681 betterment, which was voted by the Traffic Committee on that same date. It was the logical application of the same procedure which could authorise the replacement of 100 Moguls by 100 'Halls', with the extra betterment coming from the Traffic Committee. Of course replacements on that scale had to be reported for final approval to the Board, but the Rheidol exchange was within the financial limits set upon the LC & S Committee, and was not reported to Mount Olympus. Anything totally new had to be reported, as was the building of Nos. 7 and 8. The cost of No. 1213 (No. 9) was cooked out of the Repairs & Renewals Fund.

The 12 carriages sent to Aberystwyth in 1938 were new vehicles to replace the 12 originals. Only some axleboxes and bits of running gear were cannibalised from the remains, together with some sound bogie frames. This was possible because delivery was spread over three months. Bodies and underframes were totally new. Panelling was galvanised steel on timber framing and the underframes were all steel fabricated from standard joist section. The first to arrive was Lot 1615, seven 3rds, Nos. 4143 to 4148 and 4994. Lot 1616 comprised the two Brake 3rds, Nos. 4995 and 4996. Last to arrive was Lot 1618, 3 Summer Cars Nos. 4149 to 4151.

The layout of the thirds is an ingenious exercise in economy; there are only six doors per coach instead of fourteen, so larger windows with better vision could be fitted. The seats are laid out as 16-seater bays at each end with one 24-seater bay in the middle. Each bay has a door on each side, and internal access is via semi-gangways closed by 2-seater drop flaps. The Brake 3rd is laid out as a Van, 16-seater bay closed off as a separate compartment, then two 16-seater bays, i.e. 48 seats in all, with less leg room than the others, but not enough to be noticeable. At 8'8" from rail table to roof, they were $1\frac{1}{2}$ inches higher than the original coaches, but on plan they were the same.

The three Summer Cars are of the same basic layout as those of 1923 but there are several visual differences. The mesh is square instead of diamond pattern and the vacuum pipes do not pass the bogies in sight below frame level, and there are quite a number of other minor details. The upper safety rods were never added to the 1923 drawing, all three arriving without them, and it took until 1956 for someone in authority to notice it.

Livery was brown and cream with horizontal black and gold lines and with the GWR 'shirt button' totem. Roofs were white and ends were black. The vacuum cylinders were still 12" bore × 6" stroke sliding seal pattern. For many years after, the only changes were to be in livery.

Third No. 4146 in post-war coat-of-arms style at Devil's Bridge c.1948.   *W. A. Camwell*

Brake third No. 4996 as new with GWR totem in 1938 or 1939.   *Courtesy D. C. Clayton*

ROLLING STOCK

Third W4145 in 'gangwayed stock' lake and cream which made the stock look very bright and cheerful. Photographed in 1955.

Close-up of the Great Western lever-latch coupling in 1955.

After the war the GWR totem was replaced by the coat of arms once again with 'G.W.R.' above. Roofs and ends remained unchanged.

Western Region painted them in mainline gangwayed stock livery of maroon and cream with black ends and light grey roofs. Numbers had the prefix W for Western Region.

For the 1956 season the old beloved 'chocolate and cream' was restored. Ends were black and roofs a darker shade of grey. Numbers now had the W suffix as well denoting construction before 1948, ie the number read W4150W.

Throughout the interiors altered but little, mostly grained mid brown, ivory, and white undersides to the roofs. Train alarm piping in the closed coaches was chocolate, but white in the opens, and door and droplight frames would be plain brown.

For the 1964 season all were painted in a drab green which was intended to be Cambrian bronze green but was far from it. Ends were black and roofs were dark grey. In the centre of each side was a large 'VR' in gold with a tiny 'of' in between. Numbering was 1 to 16 at the lower left corner of each end, obtained by listing them all in original numerical order. These numbers are still on the ends as well as the proper numbers on the sides, which has caused confusion, e.g. when the painters sent back two cars numbered 4997. With the green livery went a black and gold waist line. It was a quick and not too lasting a job and by 1967 one or two were done over again without the 'V of R' emblem.

The arrival of London Midland Region on the scene brought about another and very rapid change. All became plain Rail Blue, ends as well, with the track-and-arrow logo and numbers in plain white and 'M' before the numbers. Brake piping and gear on the ends were picked out in red except for the upper horizontal pipe. They looked very smart close to but would have been much better if a little latitude could have been given in

The chocolate and cream revival, No. W4994W newly returned from Swindon, by the exchange siding in June 1956.

painting the upper parts Rail Grey. Rail Blue goes dark and thundery on photographs unless one gives a trifle of over-exposure, say ¼ of a stop.

The closure of Oswestry Works gave rise to a new phase in carriage maintenance. A painting booth was made with tarpaulins at the end of Cambrian Bay at Shrewsbury and carriages went there for quite heavy repairs for a few years, after which they were sent to the Carriage & Wagon Shop at Chester. Timber framing does decay in time and the panelling is normally stripped off every ten years or so for a detailed examination to be made. Also LMR have been replacing the galvanised sheeting which was beginning to reject paint too soon after repainting. Etch-treated mild steel takes paint much better, it is claimed. At these two venues black and white lining was added which smartened the coaches up quite effectively. In all these subsequent repaints only the vacuum upstand pipe and the alarm tees were red.

As the 6-spoke chill-cast steel wheels wear below limits permitted, they are relaced by disc wheels as already on four of them. From about 1950 the worn-out 12″ bore slipping band vacuum cylinders were replaced by standard 15″ bore × 8½″ stroke rolling ring type. All had been so replaced by about 1980. Replacement of these is now being effected by adapting the trunnions to accept 18″ bore × 8½″ stroke rolling ring cylinders. These have been fitted to the Vista Car and to two others.

In 1972, for the 'Night Rheidol', 24 volt lightning was fitted into 4143/44/45/47 and in 4994/96 and in van 137 using two massive 12 volt batteries in series.

From May 1982 replicas of the armorial device with the three bridges were affixed, one each side, to the coaches and the van.

The 2nd April 1983 was hailed as a great day; the first six coaches to be painted once again in chocolate and cream with the GWR ran in a VIP train. Sponsored by Blundell Permoglaze Ltd., it brightened the trains up for the delighted photographers

Non-smoking third M4148 in lined BR blue with replica device in 1983.

and soon all the others were in the same livery. Ends were black, roofs were grey and the horizontal gold and black waist line reappeared. Vacuum upstand pipes and alarm tees are still red.

Then the Wales Tourist Board Ltd. and the Development Board for Rural Wales jointly sponsored the conversion of No. 4999 into a Vista Car. Seating was rearranged as two rows of upholstered seats, facing across the valley through large deep viewing windows, for which an extra charge was made. It was handed over on the 8th June 1983.

As an experiment the long compartment in Brake 3rd No. 4995 was upholstered and carpeted to become 1st class in 1983. No. 4996 was similarly treated later in the next year and the work was sponsored by the Westinghouse Brake & Signal Co. Ltd. There was a handing over ceremony on 7th May 1984.

Historical surroundings, M4998 awaiting overhaul at Shrewsbury on 10th March 1978.

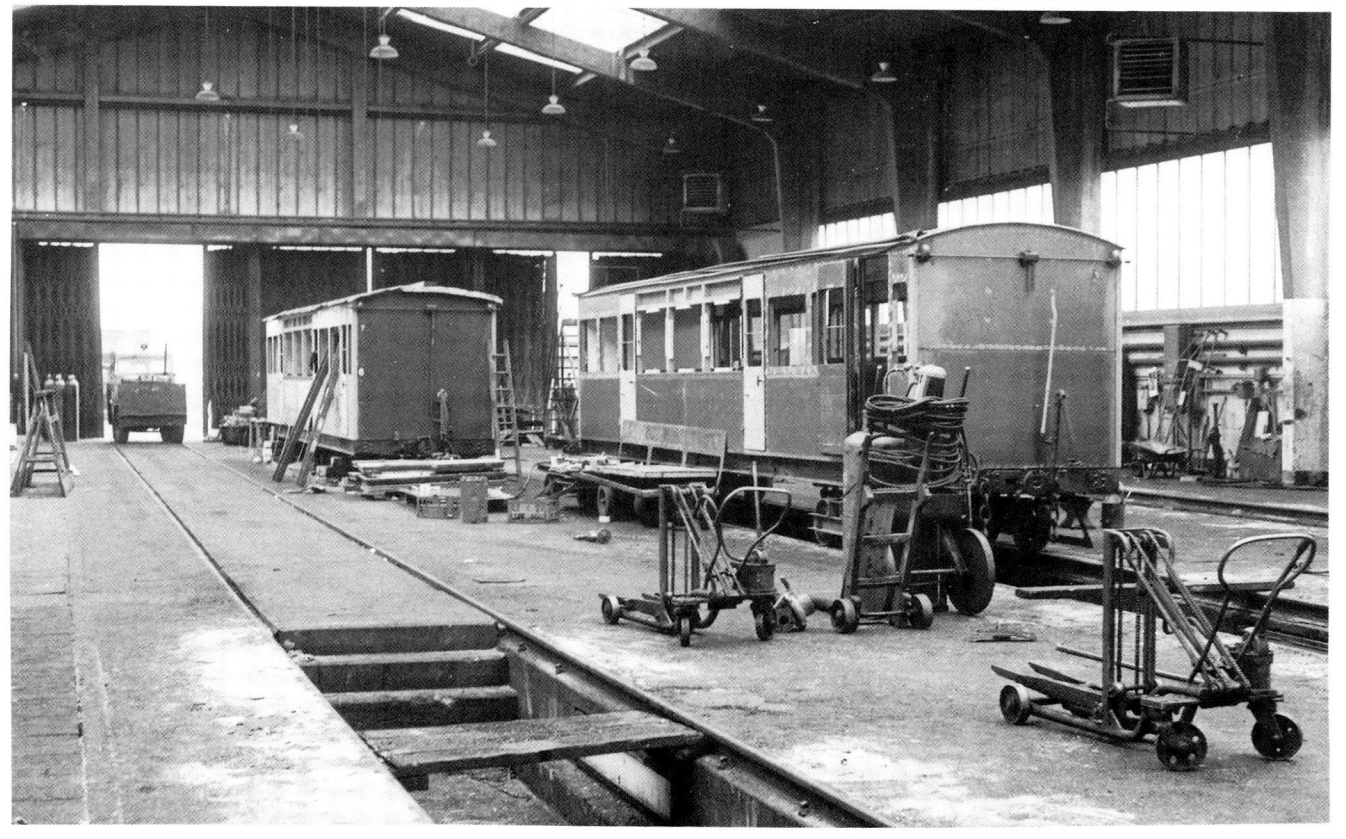

Nos. 4148 and 4145 in course of rebuilding at Chester on 17th February 1984.

Second chocolate and cream revival, third No. 4144 in 1983.

The Vista Car, No. 4999, in 1983.

Summer car No. 4997 of Lot 1333 of 1923, showing 'diamond' arrangement of mesh, 'small square' rivet patterns of shallow cross beams and no trace of vacuum pipe, in 1986.

ROLLING STOCK

Summer car No. 4150 of Lot 1618 of 1938 showing the squared arrangement of the mesh, the more complex rivet pattern securing deep bogie bearer cross members and the vacuum pipe in full view past the bogie. There are other smaller differences and official drawings show a hybrid to which nothing was ever built. Photographed in 1986.

The superficial differences between the two lots of summer car. On the left of this 1957 view is a car from Lot 1618 of 1936 and the one on the right is from Lot 1333 of 1923. The arrangement of the mesh is obvious and the doors and riveting on the frames vary also. There are other forms of difference which will be made clear in Volume 2.

Vans 137 and 136 still in chocolate and cream in 1915.
H. F. Wheeller

Van No. 157 c.1936, showing more clearly the metal sheeting covering deterioration in the original cladding, and this time repainted as 'a brown vehicle'.
G. H. W. Clifford

No. 135 of Lot 1617 of 1938 as new. *Courtesy of D. C. Clayton*

The Vans

Three neat little guard's vans came from the Midland Carriage & Wagon Co. Ltd. with the carriages in 1902. They were of the same cross section and general construction and finish and were 13 ft long on a wheelbase of 6' 6". There was a guard's brakesetter column and a screw-down handbrake working on all four wheels for operating goods trains. Initially they were numbered separately 1 to 3 but the Cambrian numbered them 13 to 15 following the coaches, and added lettering reading 'GUARD and LUGGAGE COMPT.' Loading capacity was 1 ton. As recounted already, in 1910 the unfortunate guards got evil-smelling acetylene generators to tend.

It is perfectly obvious that by 1910 the guard's vans had ceased to carry an even more worrying cargo, explosives. After offering to have one of them lettered 'GUNPOWDER VAN', the company adopted the standard Byelaws of the Explosives Act 1875. These required the company to line the van permanently or temporarily with canvas or wood to keep the containers away from iron or steel (the van floors were covered with steel sheeting) and to fix securely on the outside a notice bearing the word 'EXPLOSIVES' whenever explosives were being conveyed. Probably the quantities never exceeded 10 tons in any one year and no recollection has been offered of any one van lettered permanently.

The GWR renumbered them 134 to 137 and they followed the carriages through the various livery changes even to an artificial division of the vertical planking by painting the upper section cream. Lettering became 'GUARD' and 'LUGGAGE'. In the early 1930s 137 received steel panelling over the doors and over the ducket or look-out and was repainted brown all over and probably the other two followed suit. At the end of 1924 steam-heating was fitted with a regulating valve inside and gauges on both solebars.

In 1938 three new vans came out, and the originals are recorded as condemned on 30th April 1938. As with the carriages, parts of the undergear in fit condition were re-used. Lot 1617, as they were recorded, came out on 25th June 1968. The main structural differences were steel underframes and panelling, and two windows at one end instead of a look-out. They were painted all brown and thereafter followed the carriages in all repaints without ever reverting to lighter upper panels.

In 1968 LMR showed their total disregard for historical values and scrapped No. 135, and sold No. 136 to the Welsh Highland Railway where it recommenced running on 6th August 1980.

When the change back to chocolate and cream for the carriages had been completed, No. 137 was repainted in BR Factory Brown, the colour used on the carriage seats.

The guards seem to have been a conscientious and dutiful section of the staff and there are no stories about outstanding failure. There was one, however, showing how resourceful they could be on occasions. This time the engine had failed at Llanbadarn and there was a lengthy wait while the matter got sorted

Left: M137 in lined BR blue in 1983. Right: The survivor in the latest livery, BR Factory Brown, to match the wooden seating in the carriages, 1984.

out and the train was able to proceed. On the ledge section the train stopped. The communication cord had been pulled and the crowded train had halted. A man badly needed toilet facilities, and on one side the bank was steep and below there was clear visibility down among the tree trunks for more than fifty yards. Despite these difficulties, the guard found the importuning passenger the privacy he so badly needed – between the rails right behind the van.

In 1923 the GWR added a new variety of vehicle to the fleet, by building two Welshpool & Llanfair-style cattle trucks. This was prompted, no doubt, by stories of sheep being carried in open wagons under nets or even under wagon sheets. By mistake Lot 914 was registered under 8-wheelers and this was not corrected until 1927. All that was needed was consignments of cattle and sheep to go in them, but by then all were going by road. A note in pencil in the GWR's great stock registers reads 'Regauged to 2′6″.' Both 38088 and 38089 went to the W & L in 1937. 38088 was sold in 1960 to the Festiniog Railway where it was rebuilt into a very good-looking horse-box; or maybe, with internal dimensions of 13′10″ × 5′4″ × 6′1″ headroom, and being in Wales, it is a pony-box.

One of the cattle vans at Devil's Bridge in 1935.

H. F. Wheeller

The Box Wagons

This was the Rheidol company's term for what are usually referred to as opens, in this instance it is the more apt for they are just little boxes on wheels. Early in 1901 the Midland Carriage & Wagon Co. Ltd. offered the company 'some trucks they had on hand for the Plynlimon & Hafan Railway', probably another instance of buying back or repossession out of that firm's liquidation proceedings.

A batch of ten was bought at first and another five after Pethicks had complained that their contract was being delayed by shortage of wagons. They were bought by the company at a cost of £27 10s 0d each and were put into Rheidol livery and hired to Pethicks. They were of lifting end-door pattern with internal capacity of 9'2½" × 5'3" × 2'6", and were rated at 5 tons to be carried. The wheelbase was only 4 ft and the coil-sprung axleboxes slid between broad hornplates reinforced by a tie bar. Braking was by a single shoe per axle set cornerwise, and application was by crankhandles at the ends set on vertical shafts. The couplings were Bagnall's own with large oval heads, with two coil springs set on either side of the coupling bar. Regauging was effected by bolting spacers inside the framing, just long metal blocks one and five-eighths of an inch thick, and level with the lower flange of the frame so that the hornplates could be set inwards. It was not done very well and at the end of 1902 repairs costing £81 done by Williams & Metcalfe had to be carried out and the cost recovered from MC & W. The springing was much too stiff for part-loads, particularly if left at one end, and they frequently bounced off the track.

Cambrian days, showing lettering on both types and the vice-handle handbrake on one of the flats in 1921.

Three were made into a pair of bolsters and a match truck for carrying rails. The livery was Cambrian in style with light grey woodwork and black ironwork. Lettering was 'VR L^T R^Y' and the numbers were at the lower right corner of the body. In 1904 three were fitted at the up end with chopper couplings to fit the carriage stock, to eliminate the snatching caused by loose-coupling a rake of them behind a passenger train.

In 1905 the Board were discussing the purchase of 'box and timber wagons' to cope with the upturn in goods traffic. Timber

Wagons lettered GW at Devil's Bridge c.1928.

Courtesy J. I. C. Boyd

A 'box and timber' wagon, No. W34104, at Devil's Bridge in 1955.   *J. J. Davies*

was bought for use in converting to timber trucks so presumably, and as a stopgap, one or two more pairs of the ex-Hafans were made over. In 1906 six side-door wagons arrived from the MC & W and, from that first expression, box and timber trucks, they were dual-purpose vehicles. Certainly there is no trace anywhere of the six new timber trucks claimed to have been bought by James Rees in his letters and in an article.

The steel underframes were gauged for 2'3" if fitted with flat W-irons, and came with W-irons cranked inwards $1\frac{1}{2}$" to fit the 2 ft. Set cranked outwards, they were wagons for 2'6" gauge; narrow gauge stock was built like that. Body capacity was $10' \times 5'8" \times 2'1\frac{1}{2}"$ and load capacity was 5 tons. Braking was by one shoe on one axle only. They were numbered 18 to 23 following the 15 Hafans and 2 timber trucks.

The Cambrian-controlled Board had had the 15 ex-Hafans fitted with chopper couplings compatible with all the other stock. The Cambrian Railways lengthened the wheelbases of some of them to 4'6" but the GWR recorded finding them all to be still 4'. They renumbered them quite differently. The original rail-carriers and check wagon became Nos. 1 to 3. The unaltered 12 ex-Hafans became 10 to 21. The six MC & Ws took 4 to 9. A pair of longer timber trucks were 16 and 17. They are known to have been repainted and lettered 'CAMBRIAN' but not as far as is known 'CAM RYS'. Driver Edwin Davies has recalled that during Cambrian ownership, and possibly earlier, some of the side-door MC & W wagons were adapted for carrying cattle by raising the sides. The wagon-sheets were yellow but the odd Cambrian replacement was black. Numbers appeared on the ends.

The GWR renumbered them all using gaps in the numbers of standard gauge wagons, and chose yet a third order of marshalling. Nos. 10–21 became 34117/19/20/21/22/24/25/27/34/36/38 and 41. Nos. 4–9 became 34104/05/06/08/10 and 11. (See next section for the timber trucks.) All braking systems were improved, the MC & W wagons had their vacuum pipes removed (see later) and the ex-Hafans had their wheelbase increased to 5'6". This was done after an incident when concrete posts for new fencing were partly unloaded, and, on restarting the train, the lot went off the rails, as remembered by Isaac

The simple Cambrian drop-latch couplings in 1955.

ROLLING STOCK

Jenkins. This alteration included new axleboxes similar to the MC & W pattern, leaf springing and an entirely new braking system. Paintwork was dark grey above the solebars and black below with 'GW' painted on freestyle in 10 inch characters. After 1928 some of the ex-Hafans were lettered 'LOCO' in 7 inch characters, probably four of them.

When the new carriages were built in 1938, the wagon situation was reviewed also. Of the ex-Hafans, only the four loco coal survived lettered in four levels 'LOCO', small 'GW', '4t' and the number. Of the MC & Ws one was scrapped, No. 34106 was cut down as a bolster truck and reclassified as a timber wagon, and 34104, 34108, 34110 and 34111 were reclassified as Engineer's Ballast and left unlettered. The four Loco Coals were 34124, 3413, 34136 and 34141. The separate designations were always a waste of effort, for the crews just took the nearest wagon handy and used it for coal or anything else that was needing to be moved.

The eight little wagons lay around outside during the war and the paint peeled down to bare wood until Western Region caught up with them after 1948. The Loco wagons were painted almost as before as to placing, without the 'GW' and with the 'W' prefix added to the numbers. The MC & Ws bore '4T' above the number which was prefixed 'W'. This repaint was a rough do and all were soon back to bare wood again, only the tiny incised numbers showing which wagon one was photographing. After this, various liveries came and went so fast that it was almost like waiting for traffic lights to change.

From 1964 the Hafans went light grey with black letter panels still with 'Loco' and a 'W'. The MC & Ws went black with a DW number.

From 1964 they started to go grey again and all got 'ED' over an 'M' prefix number in small gold characters, but before this could get round all of them, white numbers crept back again on grey panels.

Ex Hafan end-door wagon No. 34136 in 1955.

From 1968 they were to conform with LMR rationalised standard practice. The Hafans went bauxite brown with a large 'AD' over M-prefixed numbers on black panels and the MC & Ws went bright blue with a small 'DW' in front of the number.

From 1981 the technicolor dreamcoat phase passed away and much better things came about. One by one all wagons went to the Carriage & Wagon Shop at Chester for a thorough structural overhaul. The Hafans all received new underframes made from standard gantry channel, and, because of the shapes of some of the upper ironwork, it was simpler to copy the originals and fit regauging blocks. Much corroded strapping was renewed as were 100% of the timbers. They returned as good as new in smart grey with black ironwork and lettered with the ADM designation because their general usage is in ballast trains. A few were done at Wolverhampton. One of the Hafans was beyond repair, No. 34134 was scrapped.

Renewal of ex-Hafan end-door wagons at Chester. This picture shows Nos. 34124 and 34136 completed, and a new frame for No. 34141 being made from signal gantry RSJ by Roger Goss and Ken Weatherley.
Lynton Bowen

Timber Trucks, Toast-Racks and Trolleys

These were, quite literally, the line's mixed up kids and for them V o R meant Very often Reshaped.

The Permanently-Converted ex-Hafan Timber Trucks

The first of them were the three ex-Hafans cut down to make two bolsters – and a match truck so that Pethicks could transport the rails from the Stone Quay, along the Harbour Branch and up the valley. They may have been any three but the Cambrian renumbered them 1 bolster, 2 match, 3 bolster. Tom Savage altered the brake system to pull on by screwing a sort of vice-handle out from the headstocks. Under the Cambrian they bore numbers only. When used for carrying 51 ft larch poles the two bolsters were coupled by a 22 ft chain which frequently struck sparks from the rails on curves. Wheelbases were lengthened to 4′6″. The flat match truck ran under the overhang. The GWR allotted 8510, 8512 and 8513 with a note that 8512 was a low flat. They were lettered 'GW'. With the other ex-Hafans the wheelbase was lengthened to 5′6″ with all other necessary alterations.

Then came the sort-out of 1938. One of the MC & W side-door wagons No. 34106 was given the bolster off No. 8513 and was registered as part of a twin timber set. That seemed a bit odd with two timber trucks which did not match, so they swapped Hafan 8512 and MC & W 34106 over in both number and role. This left two matching ex-Hafan bolsters numbered 8510 and 34106 and two odd flats 8512 (ex-MC & W) and 8513 (ex-Hafan). Of course it could have been a mix-up in the paint shop but that is how the Statistical Office at Swindon explained it away. In livery thereafter they followed the MC & W side-door wagons. All four are still in service. The two bolster wagons missed the blue repaint and went rusty instead.

The MC & W long Timber Trucks

In 1902 two new timber bolster trucks were bought from MC & W for £59 each. They were on the same underframe as the brake vans with the same 6′6″ wheelbase. Their numbers were 16 and 17, and they worked quite normally until 1908.

The ex-Hafan wagon cut down to flat track which is now No. 8513 with vice-handle braking and as lengthened to 4 ft 6 in wheelbase by the Cambrian. Photographed in 1923.

Charles Hollick

The conversion of a timber truck into a toast-rack. Seated on the back bench: Dulcie Thomas, S. B. Rees, J. G. Rees, J. A. (Don) Rees, Mr. James Rees. Standing, with straw hat, Mr. Sheraton (W. H. Smith's agent), stationmaster Edwin Davies. Note original double-breasted uniform jackets. *A. J. Lewis*

Vacuum braking was fitted because the Board of Trade, when asked, refused to pass them as passenger carriers while unbraked. Five ornately-scrolled bench seats which could be reversed were fitted with mesh sides and gates and a footboard along the side away from the rockfaces. At first they were painted pale cream with grey below floor level. Later they had a green band below floor level. In fact they had become narrow gauge railway versions of that ever-popular form of seaside tram, the 'Toast-Rack'. And popular they were too, with passengers scrambling for the privilege of the novelty, the fresh air and the views. Henceforth the summer months were spent in carrying passengers and the rest of the year in carrying timber. The Cambrian retained the original numbers 16 and 17 and, during the war, used them for carrying long timber such as telegraph poles. When used for this purpose the two facing choppers were taken out and they were linked by a 16′2″ long forged bar. After 1918 they remained as purely passenger carriers, and in Oswestry Works matchboard ends and a roof were fitted. The GWR put them into passenger stock with the numbers 4152 and 4153 and they ran, probably, for the next two years in the Cambrian all-over bronze green. In December 1923 they were put into timber truck stock with the numbers 17375 and 17376. They were withdrawn on 2nd April 1938.

The Temporarily-Converted ex-Hafan Timber Trucks

As an expedient while the new vehicles were on order, at least two of the ex-Hafan end-door wagons were dismantled and fitted with bolsters. Afterwards they were fully-restored as box trucks. They would have been so converted between 1905 and 1906 only.

ROLLING STOCK

225

Everybody enjoying themselves immensely, which shows how much tougher our great-grandparents really were. Open No. 11 in cream and black, followed by No. 9 in all-green followed by three of the grey troop carriers made from box and timber trucks, c.1913.

A. J. Lewis

No. 9, the all-open car and No. 16, both in the cream and green style of painting. Behind are the two ex-Hafan flats as bolster wagons (under the load of larch poles), the third (match-truck) flat and a loose bolster off one of the others, also ex-Hafan wagon No. 9, in 1910.

A. J. Lewis

The Six Box and Timber Trucks

These are the same six trucks with side doors which have been mentioned as coming from MC & W in 1906 in the chapter about the box trucks. Now James Rees is quite clear in his statements in an article, in a letter to the late Selwyn Higgins, and when giving Lewis Cozens information for his book in 1950, that six trucks and six timber wagons were supplied by MC & W. Only six dual-purpose vehicles fit all the known facts, and it seems likely that the six wagons arrived with bolster and the necessary mountings.

The third role, as cattle carriers with temporarily-raised sides, has already been mentioned, and from 1910 they played a fourth role. After reference to the Board of Trade, they were connected in two rakes of three each and fitted with continuous vacuum piping so that if they did break loose the train would at least come to a halt. They could only be marshalled safely at the Devil's Bridge end of the train and never at the back of an up train. The fencing was much cruder than that on the two long timber trucks (they were only intended for the army after all) and the seating was even worse. There were no less than five fixed bench seats so that 30 soldiers in all could be carried on each one. And if a set was travelling empty, the ordinary passengers crowded on to enjoy(?) the uncomfortable novelty. This usage ceased after 1914 and during the war they were used to carry pit-props stacked at slopes in the box bodies.

The Lusitania

The great success of the first two small toast-racks led to the conversion of the last of the three bogie cars to be opened out into a similar form, and this was completed in time to run during the summer of 1910. The coach selected was V of R No. 9 and she was fitted out very much the same as the two smaller cars, her roof was resupported on stanchions and the ends were left open. Twelve reversible seats provided room for 48 passengers. The mesh sides were continuous on the rock-face side and gated on the other and a continuous footboard was fitted. As before, it was an instant success. The colours were pale cream for the seating and mesh, and green along the solebars.

The wartime need for transport for pit-props led to Lewis Hamer having the top removed entirely and two tee stanchions fitted at each end. In this form 7 ft pit-props were stacked transversely at the ends and 6 ft ones in the middle. The frame was rather inadequate for this harsh treatment and she sagged in the middle with bits banging on rails over points. It was averred that it looked as if she was likely to sink and so got nicknamed 'Lusitania' after the torpedoed Cunard liner.

Open No. 11 as it ran in Cambrian days, with lettering in relief, unlike the others. *Courtesy E. R. Mountford*

ROLLING STOCK

The photograph taken to justify scrapping the lot. No. 2 as 1213 parades at Troed-rhiw-felen with Nos. 16 and 17, then old No. 9, old No. 11 and van, in 1922.
Great Western Official

Old No. 9 in GWR days as 4151, with safety rails and metal panels installed originally to carry wing, gartered crest and arm. Also she has got turned back to front so that the end panelling is at the Aberystwyth end, but the gates are in the right position for joining at the GWR terminus. The vehicle is standing on the siding made by truncating the down side of the original loop.
H. F. Wheeller

The other three cut-downs in Great Western days. No. 8512 ex side door, which should have been 34106, No. 8510, ex end door, and mis-numbered end door 34106, on the warehouse road, c.1939.
Frank Hemming

In the summer she was restored as a passenger carrier, and it was a right old game finding all the bits and pieces and some were bound to have got appropriated for another job. After 1918 she stayed as a passenger car and the Cambrian fitted a matchboard end at the Devil's Bridge end only. She had been renumbered 12 under the Cambrian régime.

The GWR renumbered her 4151 and turned the structure inside out so that the gates were still on the view side but the end that was panelled faced Aberystwyth. Three narrow steel panels were added on the view side and one large one on the rock-face side to carry the Garter crest and the wing & arm.

Despite the construction of an official replacement, she was, like the two above-the-waist-only opens, not scrapped, and followed all the livery changes already given until withdrawal on 30th April 1938.

The Proposed Bogie Timber Truck

This was drafted at Oswestry on 16th November 1917, a bit late to be of any use, and was never built. It was designed 32 ft long like the carriages and would have had 6 bolsters, being much less useful than a pair of independent bolster trucks.

W8512 carrying in 1955 the weed-killer trolley which ruined all those luscious strawberries.

ROLLING STOCK

The Wickham as running in 1983 with the tiny Moto Lombardini engine. The train consists of an improvised trolley and a hand-braked man-rider made from a platform trolley.

The Platelayers' Trolleys

At first there were at least half a dozen left from the days of construction. They were approximately 6′ × 4′ on plan and had 12″ diameter wheels set 3′6″ apart on very crude solid iron half-bearings. All had coupling eyes or hooks for attaching to the rear of any convenient train. At the upper section there was always one with a handbrake for returning by gravity.

As these wore or rotted away they were replaced by a variety of one-offs concocted as directed by expediency. One of the rider trolleys was a very effective affair on 20 inch wheels and the last seen looked as if one of its ancestors had been a porter's platform trolley.

Unbraked ones, when descending, used a pickshaft as the braking mechanism.

In 1963 Wickham Trolley TR26 was cut down to 1′11½″ gauge in Wolverhampton Works and arrived in lake and cream livery. It had the usual massive air-cooled twin-cylinder J.A.P. engine which was normally gravity or push-started. It measured 9′6″ by 6′ on plan on a 3′8″ wheelbase. As delivered there was only one glazed windshielding end, but later both ends were protected. The sides could be screened by unrolling canvases. It worked very well indeed until the J.A.P. engine wore out for lack of spares and a single cylinder cord-start Moto Lombardini was fitted. It was not nearly so good after that. The final livery was yellow after about 1974. It last ran effectively in 1984 and then the gang had to do without.

On 29th October 1985 DX 68804, a gleaming new narrow gauge version of a Permaquip Personnel Carrier, ventured up to Devil's Bridge. All-enclosed and fitted with all mod cons, it should improve working conditions a great deal.

Once, folk who like spreading such tales, put it about that the top section was haunted. Strange lights there were, and singing. After midnight a man and his wife were walking home along the track from Devil's Bridge intending to descend into the valley at Rhiwfron. Suddenly there was a rumble and light behind them and they jumped down the bank for dear life. A trolley hurtled past with two men crouched on it with their torches boring into the dark and singing. The cadences of that beautiful hymn tune 'Aberystwyth' faded into the distance. After attending a local Eisteddfod at Capel Trisant, Isaac Jenkins and Jim Dolgamlyn were going home too.

The improvised trolley, 1984.

The remains of two old Pethick trolleys at Nantyronen in 1957. Note the crude pedestal bearings.

VALE OF RHEIDOL LIGHT RAILWAY.

TIME TABLE OF TRAINS

FOR THE MONTH OF OCTOBER, 1905.

UP TRAINS.

STATIONS	WEEK DAYS						SUNDAYS
	Mondays only Passr.	Passr.	Passr.	Wednesdays and Saturdays only Passr.	Mondays only Passr.	Passr.	Passr.
	A.M.	A.M.	P.M.	P.M.	P.M.	P.M.	P.M.
ABERYSTWYTH, dep	7 0	10 30	2 0	3 0	3 30	6 0	2 15
Llanbadarn "	7 5	10 35	2 5	3 5	3 35	6 5	2 20
Glanrafon "	7 10	10 40	2 10	3 10	3 40	6 10	2 25
CAPEL BANGOR "	7 20	10 50	2 20	3 20	3 50	6 20	2 35
Nantyronen "	7 32	11 0	2 32	3 32	4 2	6 32	2 45
Aberffrwd "	7 38	11 6	2 38	3 38	4 8	6 38	2 53
Rheidol Falls "	...	11 a18	2 a49	3 a49	A	6 49	A
Rhiwfron "	...	11 a30	3 a0	...	A	...	A
DEVIL'S BRIDGE, arr	8 5	11 35	3 5	4 5	4 35	7 5	3 20

A—Calls when required to pick up or set down Passengers.

DOWN TRAINS.

STATIONS	WEEK DAYS					SUNDAYS
	Passr.	Passr.	Passr.	Wednesdays and other days only Passr.	Saturdays only Passr.	Passr.
	A.M.	A.M.	P.M.	P.M.	P.M.	P.M.
DEVIL'S BRIDGE, dep	8 30	11 50	4 45	6 15	7 20	5 15
Rhiwfron "	8 a35	11 a55	4 a50	...	...	A
Rheidol Falls "	8 a45	12 a5	5 0	6 30	7 35	5 30
Aberffrwd "	8 55	12 17	5 12	6 40	7 45	5 40
Nantyronen "	9 3	12 25	5 18	6 48	7 53	5 48
CAPEL BANGOR "	9 14	12 35	5 29	6 58	8 3	5 59
Glanrafon "	9 24	12 45	5 40	7 8	8 13	6 a10
Llanbadarn "	9 30	12 50	5 45	7 15	8 20	6 15
ABERYSTWYTH, arr	9 35	12 55	5 50	7 20	8 25	6 20

A—Calls when required to pick up or set down Passengers.

The published Time Table of the Vale of Rheidol Light Railway Company are only intended to fix the time before which the trains will not start and the Company do not undertake that the trains shall start or arrive at the time specified in the Time Tables, nor do they guarantee the connections with the M & M or Cambrian Trains at Aberystwyth. And the Company give Notice that they will not be answerable for any loss, inconvenience, or expense which may arise from delay or detention, or from the non-correspondence of Trains at Aberystwyth.

Traffic Superintendent's Office,
Aberystwyth.

J. REES.

The 2 ft 9 in long public notice — see text for the small print.

Courtesy Colin Evans

CHAPTER TEN
A SAMPLING OF TIMETABLES

The timetabled service began quietly enough with three trains down and three trains up as given out by the *Aberystwyth Observer*. It was an awkward arrangement requiring an empty train going up for the start and an empty returning at the end of the day. It commenced from 5th December 1902 onwards, with one train each way on Sundays.

A Service Timetable for June 1903 gave five full-distance trains each day and one on Sundays. Also there was an 8.15 a.m. from Aberystwyth to Capel Bangor except on Mondays. A 6.15 a.m. up goods on Mondays only came back as a passenger train as far as Capel Bangor and both trains filled in for a 9 o'clock morning train from Capel Bangor to Aberystwyth, which thus ran every day. The whistle codes given under Regulations and Practices appear with the older spelling Breaks for Brakes. There is an oddly misspelt 'Insruction' [sic] that 'The approaches to the arrival platform at Devil's Bridge must be closed at least ten minutes before incoming trains are due and the public must not be granted admittance to platforms to await arrival of trains.'

The Service Timetable for July, August & September 1903 shows the fuller summer service.

The *Aberystwyth Observer* gave services from 11th February 1904 as three trains each way daily plus a 7 a.m. on Mondays and a 2.15 p.m. on Tuesdays with no mention, not unnaturally, of a service on Sundays.

The Service Timetable for July, August & September 1904 really shows how things passenger are getting going. There were nine up trains daily, with two being hooked on at Devil's Bridge to others to make seven down trains. There were four crossings at Aberffrwd and two at Capel Bangor. Rhiwfron is back again with limited stops and stop if signalled. Four trains ignored it, and Glanrafon fared as badly. One of the up trains was 27th July to 10th September only and was the first indication of short-term timetabling.

Winter Services for 1904 began on 1st October as published by the *Aberystwyth Observer* and reverted to three up and three down with empty train working to start and finish the days 'at the wrong ends'. Extra afternoon trains ran on Wednesdays and Saturdays and the first Sunday Winter Term trains left at 2.30 p.m.

This, with slight variations, became the settled pattern for a few years. For July, August & September 1905 the *Aberystwyth Observer* gave six trains daily each way but only one on Sundays, with the note that extra trains would be run from 10th July to 11th September. A public display board 2′ 9″ long gave for October 1905 the usual winter three, the Sunday afternoon, with extra afternoon trains on Wednesdays and Saturdays, and a 7 a.m. up on Mondays only used that otherwise empty journey. The small print below read 'The published Time Tables of the Vale of Rheidol Light Railway are only intended to fix the time before which the trains will not start and the Company do not undertake that the trains shall start or arrive at the time specified in the Time Tables, nor do they guarantee the connections with the M & M or the Cambrian Trains at Aberystwyth. And the Company give Notice that they will not be responsible for any loss, inconvenience, or expense which may arise from delay or detention or from non-correspondence of Trains at Aberystwyth.'

By June 1909, as extracted from Bradshaw by J. I. C. Boyd, there were still basically six trains each way, with five down on some days and the one afternoon train on Sundays. Glanrafon got a much better service, with all trains booked to stop, all down trains stopped at Rheidol Falls and Rhiwfron, all up trains might be stopped at Rheidol Falls and all but two at Rhiwfron. Throughout all these examples journey times could be a bit quirky, there being little or no reason apparent as to why one train should be booked to go from one end of the line to the other in 65 minutes whereas the next had to get a better move on to do the run in one hour.

The Cambrian-controlled Board tried hard initially to keep up the standard, and a very nice pictorial publicity card showed six trains each way daily from 24th March to 30th June but none on Sundays. However a neat little pink card measuring 3″ × 4½″ for July, August & September 1913 in the true Cambrian period showed eight trains each way, no less, with an extra late evening trip to Capel Bangor and back on Mondays, Wednesdays and Saturdays in August. Two afternoon trains were run on Sundays. Their first winter service for 1913 was the usual three trains each way but retimed to dodge those additional empty journeys. This was the first indication of that trait about which James Rees was to complain so bitterly some years later when he was writing about his experiences. 'The Cambrian ran the line for their own convenience and not for that of the passengers.'

Still, during the summer, they were continuing to run six trains each way, with one additional train leaving at the less usual time of 12.30 between 2nd August and 28th August. This pattern appeared in the timetable for 12th July to 30th September 1915. There was one train making the Sunday afternoon excursion, giving nearly two hours for sightseeing and refreshment at Devil's Bridge. The winter service for 1915 was three trains as before but they hardly fitted the needs of folk going down to Aberystwyth to work. There is a note at the foot of the table to the effect that the service would be augmented from Easter 1916. The 7 a.m. up had come back briefly, so folk living in Aberystwyth and going to work at the hotel could have used it; but there cannot have been more than one or two. Working Timetables for this wartime period reveal that two, and sometimes three, of the trains could run as Mixed during the summer and special goods would run as needed during the winter.

After the end of the war the summer service, as given in the Working Timetable for 12th July to 20th September 1920, was four passenger trains, of which two ceased after 11th September, the 7 a.m. Mixed, and a 6.20 p.m. Mixed during August, but Mondays and Saturdays only during July and September. On other days this could be run as a goods train. The winter service was again three each way with a Monday only 6.30 p.m. up, with only ten minutes at Devil's Bridge before starting the return journey. By this time the condition of the engines was beginning to tell and after about 1918 the time allowed for up journeys had been increased to 70 minutes with 60 still for the return. On 4th May 1921 the Cambrian produced a special timetable which suspended all existing timetables as from 5th May. It was their swan-song and the Vale of Rheidol bore only two trains daily, with one addition on Mondays only for the evening viewing of

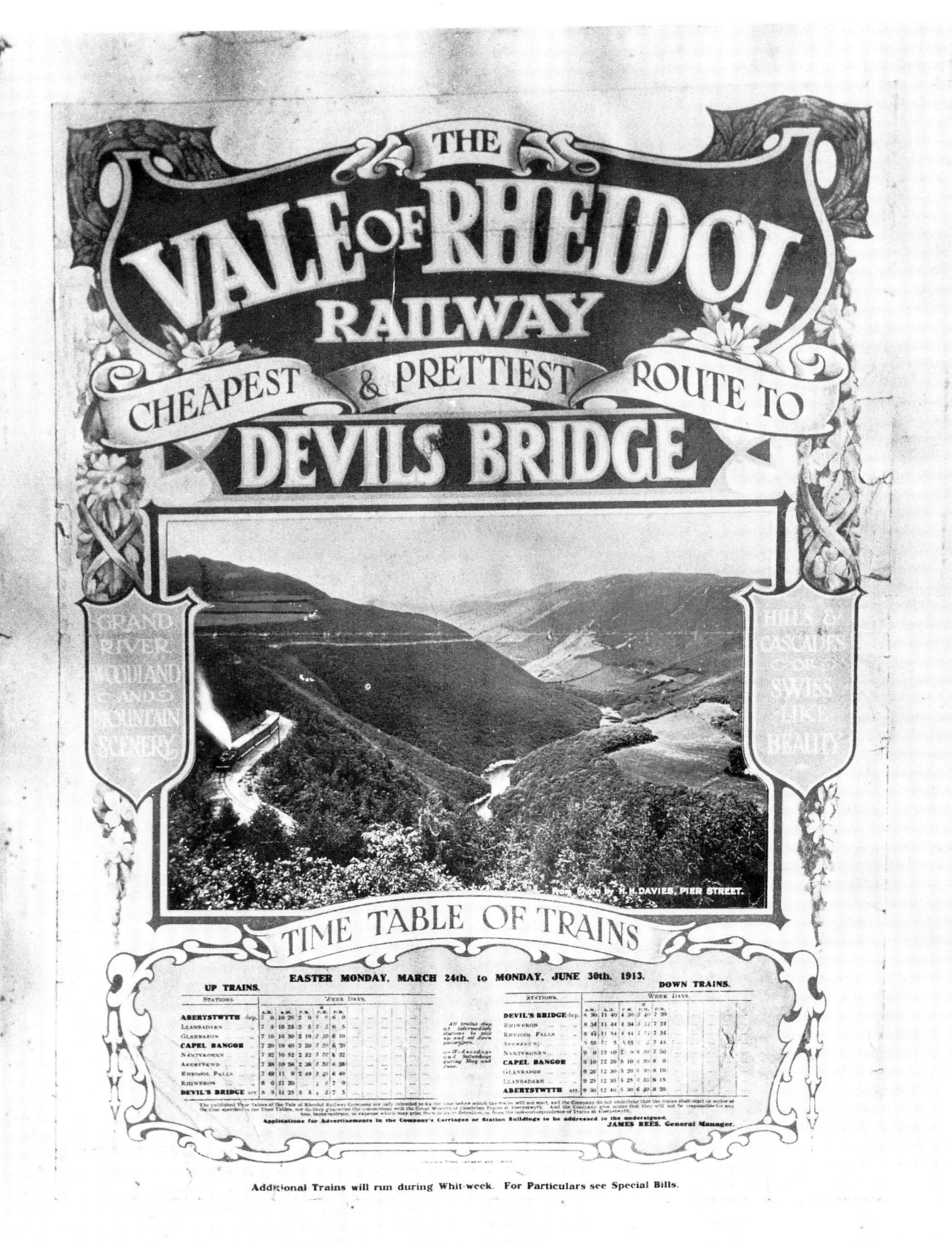

The last pictorial public timetable issued by the Cambrian-controlled Board.

Courtesy E. Savage

A SAMPLING OF TIMETABLES

the scenery, with only ten minutes for taking water at Devil's Bridge. The heading included the words 'No Sunday Trains'. The Cambrian timed and stopped most trains at all the halts.

While they were feeling their way into the running of the Rheidol, the GWR reverted to three trains each way daily, plus the extra on Monday evenings, and continued with 70 minutes for the up journey and 60 minutes back. After the new engines had made their power evident, the time for the up journey was reduced to 65 minutes and that for down was increased to 62 minutes. This pattern held until the summer of 1927 with extra trains at Bank Holidays and at the height of the season. The privilege of First Class ceased after 19th September 1926.

For the summer of 1927 the service timetable reveals six regular trains, of which one was Mixed, and a Monday Mixed. Only two trains ran on Saturdays, a 10 a.m. to take folk up and a 6.15 (Mixed) which brought the energetic back again. There was once again a train on Sunday afternoon. The winter service was down to two trains each way, plus a Mondays only and the evening Mondays and Saturdays only, and ceased as from 1st January 1931.

The great slump of the early 1930s manifested itself all too clearly in the tables for 1932. Basic trains were down to four each way, with two on Saturdays and one on Sundays. Only Aberffrwd and Capel Bangor appear as intermediate stations.

VALE OF RHEIDOL BRANCH.
(NARROW GAUGE.)

Up Trains.   **Week Days Only.**

Miles from Aberystwyth	STATIONS.		1 B Mixed	2	3 B Pass.	4 B Pass.	5 B Pass.	6	7 B Mixed MSO	8	9	10	11
M.C.			A.M.		A.M.	P.M.	P.M.		P.M.				
....	c Aberystwyth	dep.	7 0	....	10 0	2 0	2 30	....	6 15	..	..	...	....
1 2	Llanbadarn	,,	7 4	....	10 4	2 4	2 34	....	6 20	..	..	..	..
2 13	Glanrafon	,,	7 8	....	10 8	2 8	2 38	....	6 25	..	..	...	..
4 40	c Capel Bangor { arr. dep.		7 18 / 7 20	....	10 18 / 10 20	2 18 / 2 20	2 48 / 2 50	....	6 X35 / 6 40	..	..	...	..
6 40	Nantyronen	,,	7 32	....	10 32	2 32	3 2	....	6 52	....	....	....	..
7 40	c Aberffrwd { arr. dep.		7 38 / 7 43	....	10 38 / 10 43	2 38 / 2 43	3 8 / 3 13	....	6 58 / 7 3	..	....	....	..
9 15	Rheidol Falls	,,	7 54	....	10 54	2 54	3 24	....	7 14	....	....	....	....
10 65	Rhiwfron	,,	8 5	..	11 5	3 5	3 35	..	7 25	..	..	..	..
11 60	c Devil's Bridge	arr.	8 10	....	11 10	3 10	3 40	....	7 30	..	....	....	....

Down Trains.   **Week Days Only.**

Miles from Dl's Bridge	STATIONS.		1 B Mixed	2	3 B Pass	4	5 B Pass	6	7 B	8	9 B Mixed MSO	10	11
M.C.			A.M.		A.M.		P.M.		P.M.		P.M.		
....	c Devil's Bridge	dep.	8 25	....	11 20	....	4 45	....	5 50	....	7 40	....	....
75	Rhiwfron	,,	8 30	..	11 25	..	4 50	..	5 55	..	7 45	..	..
2 45	Rheidol Falls	,,	8 40	....	11 35	....	5 0	....	6 5	....	7 55	..	..
4 20	c Aberffrwd	,,	8 50	....	11 45	..	5 10	....	6 15	....	8 5	....	..
5 20	Nantyronen	,,	8 55	....	11 50	....	5 15	....	6 20	....	8 10	....	....
7 20	c Capel Bangor	,,	9 5	..	12 0	..	5 25	....	6 A 35	..	8 20	....	..
9 47	Glanrafon	,,	9 15	..	12 10	..	5 35	....	6 § 45	..	8 30	....	..
10 58	Llanbadarn	,,	9 20	..	12 15	..	5 40	....	6 § 50	..	8 35	..	..
11 60	c Aberystwyth	arr.	9 25	....	12 20	....	5 45	....	6 55	....	8 40	....	

A Arrives Capel Bangor 6X30 p.m.

§ Advertised to leave 5 minutes earlier from Capel Bangor, Glanrafon and Aberffrwd.

In the foregoing pages 89 to 128, the following general notes apply:—

    Z Stops when required to set down passengers on notice to Guard, and to pick up passengers when signalled to do so.

    W Stops to pick up or put off Cattle, Perishable and important traffic only.

The letters *a*, *b* and *c* placed before the names of certain Stations have the following signification:—
    a. Staff Station.
    b. Block Station.
    c. Tablet Crossing Station.

The GWR working timetable for the summer of 1923.   *Courtesy P. Webber*

From 12th to 26th September there was one morning and one afternoon train. The Rheidol line had moved finally into the role of a tourist line in lieu of its old casting as a general public service, a transition which had been spread over at least twenty-five years.

Llanbadarn was put back into the tables probably in 1934, and for 1938 the season ran from June to 25th September with two basic trains all the week and two additional from 18th July to 2nd September, but not on Saturdays. The one Sunday train ceased after 11th September. The pattern for 1939 was almost identical and the trains were run to the end of the advertised season, all the stock being laid away after 24th September. The GWR did the same as the Cambrian throughout the foregoing period on Bank Holidays, by putting on extra trains whenever it seemed propitious to do so. The journey time had been brought down to one hour at some time between or during 1930 and 1931.

After the 1939/45 war the 1945 season started on 23rd July with a train which was accorded a considerable ovation. The 1946 season commenced on Sunday 9th June and a familiar pattern had come into being. There was one train up in the morning which returned in time for lunch and two in the afternoon, and one in the afternoon on Sunday. The heading had changed from 'One Class Only' to 'Third Class Only.' On Saturdays only one of the afternoon trains went up.

The main difficulty in interpreting GWR timetables and in arriving at the services they proclaimed is caused by the publication of Easter and early summer trains in the winter timetables of which few have survived to be studied.

ABERYSTWYTH and DEVIL'S BRIDGE
(VALE OF RHEIDOL)

Single Line worked by Electric Token Block System.   Crossing Stations · Capel Bangor, Aberffrwd.

NARROW GAUGE.) **SERVICE SUSPENDED** Third Class only.

Up Trains. — Week Days. — Sundays.

Miles from Aberystwyth and M.P. Mileage	STATIONS		B Pass. a.m.		B Pass. SX p.m.		B Pass. p.m.				B Pass. p.m.		
M. C.													
— —	ABERYSTWYTH	dep.	9 45	..	2 0	..	2 30	..	..	..	2 30	..	..
1 14	Llanbadarn	,,	9 52	..	2 7	..	2 37	..	..	..	2 37	..	..
4 49	Capel Bangor	{ arr. dep.	10 5	..	2 20	..	2 50	..	..	..	2 50	..	..
7 53	Aberffrwd	{ arr. dep.	10 17 / 10 20	..	2 32 / 2 35	..	3 2 / 3 5	..	..	..	3 2 / 3 5	..	..
11 70	DEVIL'S BRIDGE	arr.	10 45	..	3 0	..	3 30	..	..	..	3 30	..	..

Miles from Devil's Bridge	DOWN TRAINS. STATIONS		B Pass. a.m.		B Pass. SX p.m.		B Pass. p.m.				B Pass. p.m.		
M. C.													
— —	DEVIL'S BRIDGE	dep.	11 30	..	4 45	..	5 45	..	..	..	4 45	..	..
4 17	Aberffrwd	{ arr. dep.	11 54 / 11 57	..	5 9 / 5 12	..	6 9 / 6 12	..	..	..	5 9 / 5 12	..	..
7 21	Capel Bangor	,,	12 11	..	5 26	..	6 26	..	..	..	5 26	..	..
10 56	Llanbadarn	,,	12 24	..	5 39	..	6 39	..	..	..	5 39	..	..
11 70	ABERYSTWYTH	arr.	12 30	..	5 45	..	6 45	..	..	..	5 45	..	..

Maximum Loads of Trains for Engines Nos. 7, 8 and 1213
PASSENGER TRAINS.

Aberystwyth to Devil's Bridge, 51 tons—6 Coaches and 1 Van.
Devil's Bridge to Aberystwyth, 75 tons—10 Coaches and 1 Van.

Two Passenger Trains formed of more than Engine and 5 Coaches and Van, and Freight or Mixed Trains formed of Engine, Van, and 15 Wagons must not cross at Capel Bangor, nor at Aberffrwd if formed of more than Engine and 7 Coaches and Van, or Freight or Mixed Trains formed of more than Engine, Van, and 21 Wagons.

MIXED TRAINS.

The maximum loads for Mixed Trains when worked by engines Nos. 7, 8, and 1213 should be:—

	Class 1 Traffic	Class 2 Traffic	Class 3 Traffic	Empties.	
Aberystwyth to Devil's Bridge	6	7	9	12	When working with one Coach and Passenger Brake Van.
Devil's Bridge to Aberystwyth	9	11	14	18	

Note—When additional coaches are worked on a Mixed Train the load should be reduced by 2 loaded wagons of Class 1 Traffic (or its equivalent) in respect of each additional coach.

The first summer tourist service after the end of the 1939/45 war from a suspended service (working) timetable starting on 7th October 1946. Note the anachronism of regulations concerning make-up of goods trains.
Courtesy Roger Wilson

CHAPTER ELEVEN

SPECIAL EVENTS AND OCCASIONS

This is another subject which will have to be covered by sampling because no other railway has been called upon to run or arrange so many. Their scope is so varied and the ingenuity with which some of them have been stage-managed is a most fascinating study in itself. Those involving combinations of ordinary services with outside attractions have already had some attention.

The first on any large scale were the Bluejacket Specials. Admiral Sir 'Jackie' Fisher believed in letting the nation see what a splendid navy they had, and cruisers and battleships were to be seen at anchor off all the popular resorts in turn, and the new Dreadnoughts of 1906 onwards were surrounded by the circlings of the 'Trip Round the Bay' motorboats. The matelots themselves were given trips up the Rheidol. The manager of that well-known large store, Jack Hughes Peacocks, was a guard on the trains at the age of 13. He has recalled how the sailors, in defiance of byelaws, would climb out of those originally unbarred windows to sit up on the carriage roofs, until the train reached the places where the telegraph wires crossed the line. Of course they all had to jump for it at precisely the same place. Picture if you can a large heap of bruised and swearing humanity all attired in spotless Number Ones.

In 1910 it was the turn of the army to sample the delights of narrow-gauge travel. Sir Francis Lloyd, General Officer Commanding the Welsh Territorial Division, thought that there was no place like Aberystwyth for his summer camps, and they went for several years to Lovesgrove where the special halt was built for them. The Division included the Cheshires and the Shropshires so they literally came from all over. Mr Thomas Craven, one of the Cambrian directors, had the ear of someone in the War Office and soon regular troops were encamped both at Lovesgrove and at Devil's Bridge. In 1912 there was a contingent from the North Midland Brigade based at Lichfield and Mr Rees had dealings with the West Riding Division, the South Wales Field Artillery and the Welsh Howitzer Brigade. At one time there were over 1,000 from St John's Ambulance Brigade. Lewis the Mart produced souvenir cards of the camps and of the train, e.g. the one inscribed 'Souvenir of the 18th Infantry Brigade Camp'. The last troops there, the ones who had to march over the roads to Llanidloes because the little line could not have moved them out quickly enough, were a battalion each from the East Yorkshire Regiment, the Northumberland Fusiliers and the South Staffordshire Regiment. They left the Vale of Rheidol to become a part of what the Kaiser was to call 'a contemptible little army'.

Mr Emlyn Morgan has written of his recollections of annual Sunday School outings. This one took place around 1920, and

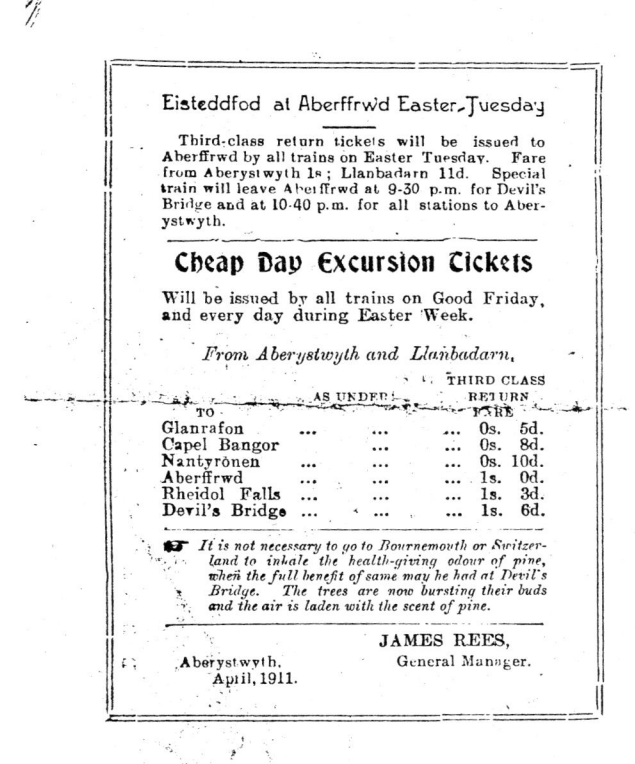

An effusive Easter special event leaflet.

Author's collection

235

Outing of wives and families of privilege ticket holders at Devil's Bridge c.1927. *Courtesy Glyn Griffiths*

it combined the children and families of the congregations of the two chapels of Llanbadarn. The heavy train struggled as far as Rhiwfron and the crew had to give up, divide the train, and take only half on to Devil's Bridge. The occupants of the stranded portion walked up in the wake of the train and thoroughly enjoyed the novelty. He put the trouble down to the train being too heavy but in fact it was the appalling state of the engine that was the real cause.

The formation of railway and engineering societies in the 1920s brought some charter business via trips along the standard gauge which terminated with the trip to Devil's Bridge, but these never amounted to much until after the 1939/45 war when people began to realise that steam railways as they had known them were fast becoming things of the past. Typical of those first post-war tours was that of the Birmingham Society of Model Engineers organised by Jack Adams on 10th July 1954.

There was a less usual kind of event in 1956, during which the Locomotive Inspector Frank Roberts and the train crew were having kittens all the way to the top. It was a visitation from the Western Region Board with the Chairman, Mr Hanks, and the General Manager Mr. K. W. C. Grand, and a host of lesser top brass. After a good repast the party piled onto the train and the Motive Power Superintendent H. E. A. White insisted on going up on the front platform of No. 7 along with the Chief Mechanical Engineer Mr Smeddle. They avowed that it had been the finest train journey of their lives and more 'repast' was absorbed at the Hafod Arms. On the way down, one of the merry party crowned it all by pulling the communication cord on Mr Hanks who had taken the regulator on the up journey after Aberffrwd. The anxious driver hovering behind Mr Hanks, was Les Morgan who had to make sure that the train stopped at a safe spot.

The National Association of Local Government Officers ran highly successful NALGO Expresses in 1956 and 1958, but the 1959 attempt never left Aberystwyth because No. 7 derailed on the shed crossover before going on to the train, so they had to seek consolation in local places of refreshment. Of course all the evening specials pivoted around a good meal at the Hafod Arms Hotel and a return in a contented frame of mind through the gathering dusk.

Special push-pull train going to Royal Welsh Agricultural Show at Llanbadarn approaching the M & M bridge in April 1956. *Pat Dalton*

CHAPTER TWELVE
UNDER LONDON MIDLAND REGION

15th July 1963 onwards

It is not easy to write of events one has watched without overstatement to the point of unfairness. It is easy to resort to the Book of Common Prayer and write of 'things done which should not have been done' and 'things left undone which should have been done'. Sir Richard, later Lord Marsh, talking long afterwards of his time as Chairman of the British Railways Board, has summed up the position at that time better than anyone else. 'Had I been instructed to offer shares in British Rail run under the conditions imposed on that organisation, and had any member of the public bought any, I would have tried to sell him the pigeons in Trafalgar Square'.

Before going on further with the history of this period it is worth taking a moment to look at all the bodies with whom BR have to deal, and who can exert influence, beneficial or otherwise, on the running of the Rheidol line.

ASLEF and NUR are the two railwaymen's unions and most concerned in matters of pay and conditions of service.

Bwrdd Twrist Cymru, The Wales Tourist Board Ltd, promotes tourism and has shown the Rheidol line in its brochures.

Bwrdd Datblygu Cymru Wledig, The Development Board for Rural Wales, exists to aid any worthwhile occupational or tourist activity likely to be of benefit to Rural Wales and has paid for the cost of converting the Vista Car.

Central Electricity Generating board, North Western Region has opened an attractive nature trail along the south side of the reservoir below the railway and allows visitors to the power station and to a well-laid out exhibition further down the valley. It would like to encourage walkers to do the circuit from the train using Rheidol Falls Halt. It owns tall woodland between the line and the reservoir.

Coleg Prifysgol Cymru, The University College of Wales, has an active Railway and Transport Society and students have presented a delightful painting of the train with a Welsh theme, and the mosaic on the wall alongside the terminus.

Comiswn Coedwigaeth Gwarchodfa Gogledd Cymru, the North Wales Conservancy of the Forestry Commission, has well-grown stands of conifers planted very close to the formation of the line.

Cyngor Dosbarth Ceredigion, Ceredigion District Council, operates a lively Tourism & Amenities Department in Aberystwyth which never fails to mention the railway whenever possible, e.g. in a lovely little leaflet *Rheidol River Country*.

Cyngor Gwarchod Natur Rhanbarth Dyfed-Powys, The Dyfed-Powys Region of the Nature Conservancy Council, owns and cares for mature woodlands bordering the railway and has designated parts of the valley as Sites of Special Scientific Interest.

Cyngor Sir Dyfed, Dyfed County Council, is the principal local authority caring for roads abutting the crossings and for remedial work and flood measures all along the River Rheidol.

Grŵp Gweithredu Rheilffordd y Cambrian, The Cambrian Coast Line Action Group, devotes itself entirely to keeping open the railway connection to and along the coast of Cardigan Bay, thereby bringing potential trippers to the lein fach.

The Narrow Gauge Railways of Wales Joint Marketing Panel is the association of all the little lines which produces annually the comprehensive leaflets giving services and times under the title 'The Great Little Trains of Wales'.

The line traverses the areas of three Parish Councils. Leaving Aberystwyth, it crosses Lower Llanbadarn y Creuddyn, entering Upper Llanbadarn y Creuddyn by the 3 mile post. The final change into Upper Llanfihangel y Creuddyn takes place at the stream on the Horseshoe Bend in Cwmyrogo, the site of the Erwtomau Mine.

The Vale of Rheidol Railway Supporters' Association, which in Welsh is Cymdeithas Cefnogwyr Rheilffordd Dyffryn Rheidol, would like to do much more for the line than it has already done but this can only be achieved by constant increase in membership in terms of subscribers who wish to join and contribute purely for the sake of the Rheidol line itself. It cannot offer members the opportunity of using a shovel or a polishing rag. Mr. James Knapp, the General Secretary of the NUR, made his views on this point quite clear in a letter to the *Cambrian News* on 29th March 1985. 'The Vale of Rheidol line is part of the British Rail network and it is entirely unacceptable that it should be downgraded and use made of non-professional railwaymen and women.' While this seems a pity, it is not difficult to understand his attitude; his concern is to retain or make jobs for his members in difficult times.

Having set the scene, let us now return to our history.

In 1963 the expected Beeching Report was published and Chester division, under its Divisional Manager Mr. A. B. Arundale and with Oliver Veltom as Assistant Divisional Manager, were obliged to comply with its recommendations. In particular there were instructions about redundant assets which were anything which could conceivably be dispensed with, and recoverable assets which were anything which could conceivably be sold.

So, in 1963, Capel Bangor and Aberffrwd had to lose their loops despite the fact that the gang time expended on rip-it-out-and-flog-it would never be covered by the sale of those two short bits of useful rail. Of course the notional cost of working the loops was also removed, being believably on the same basis as the working of the same number of levers at Clapham Junction; BR costing is such a mystery.

After the Beeching Report had appeared there was a question mark still hanging over the Rheidol line but management was still doing its best to keep it popular with the public. Coaches were repainted in a semblance of Cambrian livery but, in common with those on the main line, all intermediate halts had been closed and were represented only by nameboards and by tickets which were still available at Aberystwyth and Devil's Bridge. Aberystwyth standard gauge shed closed in 1965 and from then on the Rheidol engines were attached for rostering and maintenance to Machynlleth. By then another new image for the organisation was being fostered and British Rail and BR had become the proper references.

With this change came another; Chester Division ceased to be a separate entity and, with the whole of the BR system in North

The day the last Pease Economic Facing Point Lock failed, 29th May 1967, at Devil's Bridge. *N. T. Field*

Wales, the Rheidol line came under Stoke Division on 12th September 1966. The Divisional Manager was Mr. George Dow, an experienced and professional railwayman with the ability to get things done and the knowledge of how to go about it if it was possible to do.

The Rheidol was one of the first lines he inspected and he planned several improvements to be ready in time for the 1967 season. The station building at Devil's Bridge was renovated, new nameboards embodying the heights above sea level were put up at the stopping places, and the locomotives and carriages were repainted in Rail Blue. This looked very smart at close quarters, but the little trains did tend to get lost visually at any distance when up the valley. They would have looked better if rules could have been bent a little to permit a lightening of the upper parts of the carriages by using Rail Grey, but this would have increased cost at a time when cost considerations were paramount.

At the same time George Dow was pressing for the authority to expend some £5,000 on a scheme which would be most advantageous to the running, maintenance and protection of the Rheidol line and its rolling stock. That vexatious level crossing at Aberystwyth was to be eliminated by making a new terminus in the Manchester and Milford bay at Platforms 4 and 5, and, by using the old standard gauge engine shed, the locomotives and most of the carriages would be housed in much better circumstances. The other advantage which would have appealed more to unemotional higher authority was that a good slice of relatively under-used land would become free for disposal for what one has to admit would be a good use. Nowadays the majority of Rheidol trippers arrive by car and need somewhere reasonably close by to park them.

Euston turned the scheme down flat and ordered the line to be sold because Mr. Dow's appraisal had revealed that it was actually running at an annual loss of about £1,200, although this could have been wiped out within twelve months by further economies which he had recommended. Quite literally, and to keep higher management content with the idea of continuing to run it, the Western Region returns had been 'cooked' for years. Mr. Dow still refused to give in and gave his reply to his superiors that before actually offering the line for sale, a proper valuation of the fixed and mobile assets would be needed, and that would take some time as it should be done most carefully. (And it *was* due to have taken quite a long time). It was a very courageous line of action to have taken at a time when everything was subservient to the great gods Diesel and Electricity, and to be seen, however covertly, to be trying to promote and preserve steam was not the way to popularity among BR's higher echelons.

Despite the fear that if the plan to sell the line failed then it might be allowed to run down until it could be closed on the grounds of passenger safety, George Dow was still watching events most carefully. He heard that the Minister of Transport,

A great occasion at Devil's Bridge. From left to right: Mr. Glyn Pickering, Mayor of Aberystwyth; The Right Honourable Mrs. Barbara Castle MP, Minister of Transport; The Right Honourable John Morris MP, Secretary of State for Wales; Mr. George Dow, Divisional Manager, Stoke Division; Mr. Harry Rees, Area Manager. 1st July 1967.
A. R. G. Dow

Mrs. Barbara Castle, was going to visit Aberystwyth on 1st July 1967 to address a rally of the Labour Party. Gentle words in the right ears introduced a trip down from Devil's Bridge into her itinerary. With the Right Honourable John Morris, Secretary of State for Wales, he accompanied Mrs. Castle, who was readily receptive to the suggestion that the Rheidol line was a splendid asset to BR and to the tourist trade of Wales and that it should be neither sold off nor closed. The withdrawal of the plan to sell was formally confirmed at Parliamentary Question Time on 6th November 1967 and the go-ahead was given for the £5,000 improvement scheme.

All the external arrangements were completed in time for the start of the 1968 season on 20th May when the first public train left Aberystwyth station over the deviated line. The rusting old corrugated iron sheds with pits half full of water, oil and muck when the river level was too high, were abandoned and all the old track was lifted to make way for that much needed car park. It would take a year or two more to complete the task of settling in at the new quarters, but in future repairs and overhauls would be accomplished to a degree hitherto impossible with the old 'facilities'.

Spurred on by Harry Rees, the able local Area Manager, the railwaymen took direct action to improve interest in the line and to help to preserve their jobs. Men off duty drove round in their own cars with packs of posters which were displayed by all the shops, boarding houses, pubs and places of entertainment, and if any place had a spot where a poster might be usefully displayed then one was put up. It was a very good effort and it helped the situation a great deal. Now that it was seen that BR would continue to find the running costs at no cost locally, all became much more helpful and the officials more directly responsible for the day-to-day affairs of the line took heart once more and gave of their best.

However, behind the scenes, the Euston management had not yet turned entirely away from the prospect of selling the line, and their initial bid had aroused interest in several different quarters. Some of these were easily discouraged by the first failure and lost interest, but there was still a consortium for

Laying the new course of the Rheidol line through the engine shed yards, looking towards Aberystwyth, in April 1968.
J. I. C. Boyd

In canopied splendour, the first summer of use of the old M & M bay, on 2nd September 1968. *J. J. Davis*

Chaos in new quarters — engines, carriages, coal wagons and ragged concrete as the fitters' pit is being broken out of the old shed floor in 1968.

Shed neck and main line, looking towards Devil's Bridge, in 1969.

whom John Snell, now Managing Director of the Romney, Hythe and Dymchurch Railway, was the principal activist and front man. He had a meeting with Mr. Dow on 26th October 1967, at which future possibilities were discussed, but these were overtaken by the Parliamentary announcement of 6th November 1967. On 29th June 1968 Mr. Dow retired and at the same time went Mr. Harry Rees, the last of the outstanding 'Mr. Rheidols' of the old school of railwaymen. Departing too was Mrs. Barbara Castle, and her place as Minister of Transport was taken by Sir Richard, now Lord Marsh. With all the opposition removed, the field was once again clear for Euston to revive the plans for selling the line.

Early in 1969 Mr. Robert Lawrence, Chairman and General Manager of London Midland Region, asked Pat Whitehouse, the well-known railway enthusiast and author, to lunch. 'Would it be possible', he asked, 'for a large enough group of private individuals to band together and raise sufficient capital to purchase the line from British Rail and so decently get them out of the problems and costs which must arise if BR have to continue to run an isolated short length of steam railway?'

Pat Whitehouse and John Snell called together a most impressive group of names and expertise, which included those of one of Britain's foremost civil engineering contractors, McAlpine's, who had recently completed the great Nant-y-Moch reservoir. On 12th August 1969 The Vale of Rheidol Railway Ltd was incorporated but objections to the name were lodged and it was changed to The Vale of Rheidol Railway Equipment Company Ltd. Two 0-8-0 tender locomotives from East Germany were purchased; the first arrived in England in December 1970 and the second in July 1972. They had come originally from the Mecklenburg–Pommersche Spurbahn. No. 9, later 99.3461 on the Stadt Bahn, had been built by Stettiner Maschinenbau-Aktiengesellschaft Vulcan in 1925. No. 12, later 99.3462, was similar but slightly larger and had been built in 1934 by Orenstein & Koppel Aktiengesellschaft of Dortmund.

Meanwhile, according to an article in *The Cambrian News*, the correspondence concerning this second bid to privatise the

Aberystwyth ground frame and diagram in 1969. Note proposed line to run outside shed wall to sidings at rear. The access to the stock sidings is actually through the shed. The internal shed loop is not shown at this time.

No. 7 on the 14.15, passing the shed and rolling stock siding, on 8th April 1969.

Rheidol had been leaked to ASLEF who would naturally not be in favour of such a sale. ASLEF, it was reported, enlisted the support of Mr. John Morris and Mr. Elystan Morgan (now Lord Elystan Morgan) one-time MP for Cardiganshire, with the result that by the time the second engine had arrived the line was once more no longer to be sold. Later BR did contemplate buying 99.3462 and inspected her at Boston Lodge but decided against the idea.

So both engines were sold back across the channel, and both are now on permanent holidays compared with what would have been required of them had they been brought to Aberystwyth.

99.3461 runs now on the Chemin de Fer Froissy-Dompierre near Amiens, along the beautiful canal and lakes of the Somme and up through the Bois à Cailloux, using a reversing stage taking 40 minutes for the journey of 6.8 kilometres. The steepest gradient is over the reversing stage but it is 1 in 30.

99.3462 is at Die Dampf-Kleinbahn Mühlenstroth near Gütersloh which is West Germany's finest narrow-gauge museum. Twelve immaculately-restored 600 mm gauge locomotives are on display or taking visitors round a circuit of one kilometre through pleasant farming country. By the station and shed is a restaurant, a picnic area and a children's playground.

Before John Snell actually got the two engines from East Germany, many other fascinating possibilities had been carefully considered and rejected. Some of them would have lacked the flexibility needed for making the best timing along the flat before settling down to the final continuous slog, and so might not have been able to maintain schedule. They were:—

0–8–0 Tank, Tramme Pithivilliers à Toury.
0–4–4–0 Articulated Tank, Natal Railway. (Not favoured)
4–6–2 Baldwin Tank, Eastern Province Cement Co.
2–8–2 South African Railways.
2–6–2 + 2–6–2 South African Railways. (Not really likely)
0–6–0 tanks from Spanish railways.

The two engines were sold and went back to the continent in 1978 and Vale of Rheidol Railway Equipment Co Ltd was struck off the register of companies on 7th February 1984. In retrospect several members of the group are heartily thankful that they did not succeed in the acquisition. It may have looked to have been a snip at £27,000, but, in the light of a 90% re-sleepering programme, it could have become a grievous burden.

Which would have been the better policy will always remain a matter of opinion. Would the consortium have fostered a railway entity second to none as a tourist attraction for Wales? Was Aberystwyth being offered a golden chance at no cost to the ratepayers? Would, as was thought, all the Rheidol men have been needed and employed by 'the London syndicate'? Would there have been even more jobs for railwaymen at Aberystwyth? Only one thing is certain; each individual did, at the time, what he sincerely believed was right.

Reverting from politics to practicalities, Mr. Dow's place had been taken by a new Divisional Manager, Mr. F. W. Young. On the permanent way side, the Rheidol allocation had to be worked out of the main line allocation, which was already inadequate, just as the £359,000 allocated under the Transport Act 1968 to aid the running and maintenance costs of the standard gauge from Shrewsbury to Aberstwyth was inadequate. This was intended as a support grant towards the cost of unremunerative trunk services, so the Rheidol saw not one penny of it. Hence, not unnaturally, the Rheidol was much out of favour in higher

Leaving the river for the last time beyond Lovers Lane Crossing, 31st March 1970.

Along the river bank into Capel Bangor, 12th April 1971.

permanent way circles and there was much difficulty for the Rheidol permanent way men now needing sleepers and time as never before, when these could only be had at the expense of the main line.

In 1969 there was once more a shop at Devil's Bridge, to be followed by proper refreshment facilities, and in 1970 a letter service was introduced with its own special V of R stamps. In 1970, too, The Vale of Rheidol Railway Supporters' Association, known in short as VORRSA, was formed to promote public interest in the fortunes of the line and to try and give it some of the benefits of a preservation society, towards which it has done good service ever since. By 1975 the number of passenger journeys had nearly doubled since those of 1969. Two external stimuli started to help when in 1971 the joint marketing panel 'The Great Little Trains of Wales' came into being and the Tourist Board for Wales lent a hand with publicity.

During the abnormally dry summer of 1976, firing with the coal provided by LMR, which did not really suit the fireboxes made for Welsh steam coal, caused a number of fires in the woodlands which had grown up close to the track since the 1940s. The Forestry Commission were running patrols carrying binoculars along the valley floor to watch the progress of each train and to summon help by radio. BR were asked to pay for the cost of these patrols and so an enquiry into the possibility of conversion to oil-firing was initiated. An immediate solution would have been to have got some of the correct coal up from South Wales.

On November 1976 the *Liverpool Daily Post* announced that soon the Rheidol line would have diesel locomotives which was 'likely to horrify railway enthusiasts'. This was their version of the proposal to convert the locos to oil firing. Later two members of VORRSA, suggested that instead of providing the line with two new coaches, the Association should provide a diesel locomotive. Even more recently there have been thoughts as to the possible acquisition of a diesel-powered locomotive from the continent as a standby.

The first engine was converted to oil-firing during the winter of 1977/78 and oil has proved easier to handle, but never seems to give that old plume of clean white steam which was the highly-photographic product of coal firing, and the smell too has never been the same since.

In 1980 Mr. Young left Stoke and Mr. Hugh Jenkins took his place as Divisional Manager and he, too, was to prove a good friend to the little line away at Aberystwyth. In October was

Preparing for the run. Driver Owen Jenkins and fireman Bill Eden going over No. 7 in 1978.

Arrival at Devil's Bridge. No. 8 brings in the first 'Welsh Dragon' on 4th May 1981, a Gala Day.

held the first Open Day and on 4th May 1981 there was the first Gala Day when all three engines worked trains in succession to Devil's Bridge and were to be seen there all at the same time. This day, too, saw the inaugural run of 'The Welsh Dragon' carrying the headboard which was in future to be carried each day by the 14.30 Up. The locomotive, No. 8, *Llywelyn*, on the suggestion of VORRSA, had been repainted in GWR Brunswick green with the circular totem, the first of the new policy of renewal of historical liveries.

On 8th March 1982 Mr. E. A. Gibbins succeeded Hugh Jenkins at Stoke and, following the suggestion by VORRSA, pursued the idea of getting commercial firms to contribute towards the cost of additional work with much enthusiasm and success. The first enhancement arising from his policy was the sponsoring by Mr. Richard Metcalfe of the repainting of No. 9, *Prince of Wales*, in the original livery of *Prince of Wales* as built by his grandfather. By 1984 all the engines and coaches had been repainted in one or another of former authentic styles. One at a time the two brake thirds were refitted as brake composites and one of the open cars was rebuilt as the Vista Car.

For a short time there was another enthusiastic 'Mr. Rheidol' in the person of Mr. Andy Hancock, a graduate of the University College of Wales, who stayed on at Aberystwyth to make railways his career. As Traffic Manager he played the part well but was soon away elsewhere on promotion, but there is now a fresh and popular nominee for the title, the present Mr. Tony Donovan.

On 7th May 1984 VORRSA launched a new project, a permanent Vale of Rheidol publicity exhibition in the waiting room at Aberystwyth station, which was opened by Mr. Gibbins. At the end of May 1984 a complete layer was removed from the management pyramid of BR by the abolition of the divisions. Under the new arrangements the Rheidol became the responsibility of the Provincial Manager (Midlands and Mid Wales Services) at Birmingham.

In 1984 VORRSA mooted the idea that the coaches should be named as Pullman cars were. The author offered a list of sixteen of the charming names given by the Welsh to their ladies. On the afternoon of Sunday, 24th August 1986 No. 4146 was named Myfanwy for Myfanwy Talog, Wales' favourite TV announcer, and No. 4994 was named Lowri for Laura Ashley, the celebrated designer of ladies' fashionwear whose workrooms are close to the old Cambrian main line at Carno. Plates recording the event are to be fixed later. Others, it is hoped, will follow.

While all these events were in cycle, from 1982 onwards, the unpublicised work of restoring the permanent way had been put in hand with fine broad Jarrah sleepers, modern track bolts and fabric pads, all of a quality likely to last well into the 21st century.

As already related the newest management have provided the line with its third terminus.

Aberystwyth London Midland Region Terminus

On 20th May 1968 the first train left from the terminal loop situated between bay platforms 4 and 5. At last the Rheidol Branch was properly integrated within the configuration of the main station and this was to prove the best circumstance so far. The separate ticket office was retained, and access to the trains was still along Platform 3 and turn right, and then turn left down a ramp leading to ground level between the bay platforms.

ABERYSTWYTH BR — TERMINUS & NECK

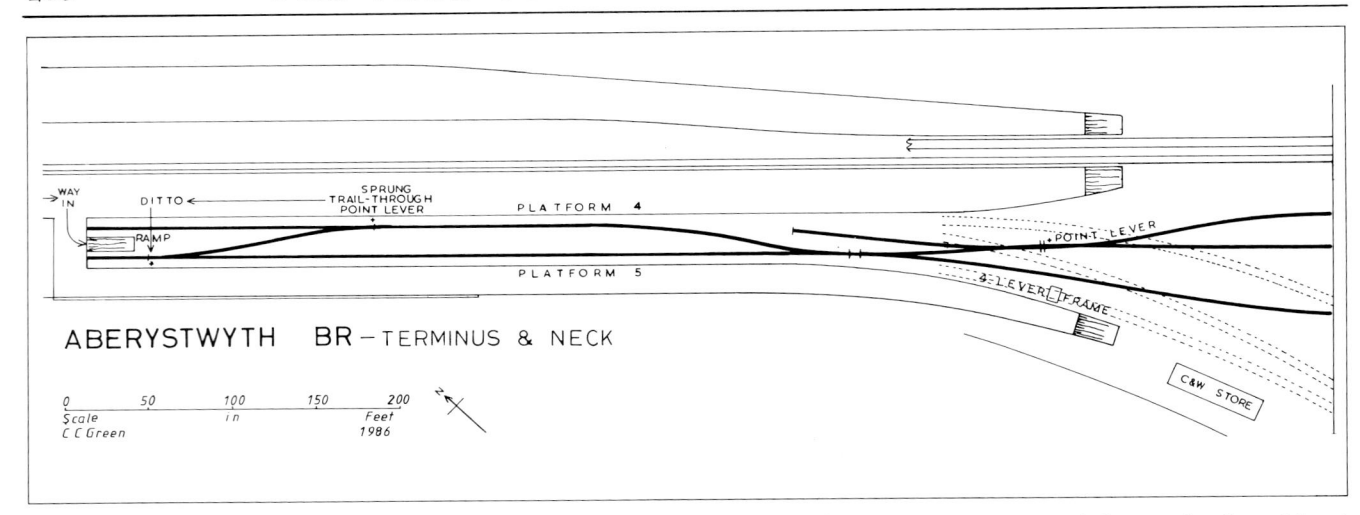

Scale 0 50 100 150 200 Feet
C C Green 1986

At first the small carriages were dwarfed and shaded by the commodious canopies which dripped right past the windows in heavy rain; these were removed after the following season.

Back in the concourse there was room to site the double-sided showcase with publicity photographs by the BR photographers. This case is a splendid example of Edwardian craftsmanship and was made in Oswestry Works for the White City Exhibition of 1908. It then crossed the Atlantic Ocean to an exhibition in Chicago. It was restored in 1977 with the aid of contributions from VORRSA. On festive and gala days it stands surrounded by models and stalls, and the wide spaces of the platforms are used for exhibitions, ceremonies, and the town's talented band and Morris dancers are to be heard and watched. In the waiting room VORRSA have provided a display of photographs and maps, also publicising the Rheidol line which was opened in 1984. Facilities are completed by Lewis's bookstall and buffet in which is hung the delightful fantasy picture of a Vale of Rheidol train painted by students from the University College of Wales. UCW students also designed and applied to the back wall of Platform 5 an extensive mosaic with a Rheidol railway theme which added a welcome touch of brightness to a rather dilapidated relic of the M & MR.

Leaving the new terminus. No. 8 taking the inaugural run of the return to 'chocolate & cream' on 2nd April 1983.

ABERYSTWYTH BR SHED & SIDINGS

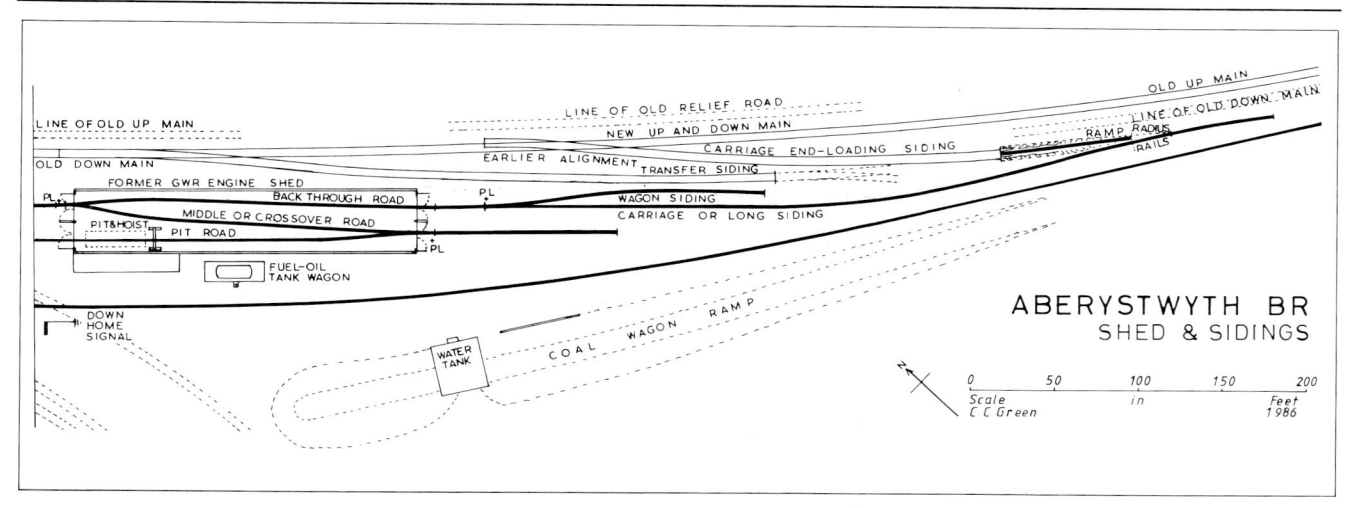

The move into new quarters was made with much haste and it was a few years before all the passenger area received a dressing of level tarmac. To have completed all arrangements inside the shed before the move in the time allotted was even more impossible and the priority was trackwork first so that the rolling stock could be moved away from the old shed and sidings; then the old layout could be lifted and the land sold. Before this could be done, the standard gauge track had to be lifted out of the loco yard and the ashpits and shed pits filled in. Inside the shed the rails and sleepers were dropped on top of the concrete floor with ash ballast, and sidings for the stock were hastily devised, with a transfer siding from the standard gauge for coal.

Thereafter there was much finishing and adjustment to be done and the priority job was the loco maintenance pit. Pit Road, next to the workshop and stores, is almost entirely given over to stock undergoing repair, and Crossover Road is used partly for stock and for parking two of the locomotives; the watering point is between this road and the pit. After 1977 fuel-oil filling pipes to reach across were installed, fed from 13,000 litre oil tank wagon ADB 999011 sited outside in a concrete retaining dam large enough to retain the entire contents of the tank in case of a leak. A main compressor and a standby, working at 100 lbs per square inch, for starting up the oil-firing systems are in an old store, and again the air lines reach across to locomotives standing on Crossover Road. A power failure could hold things up but it would be possible to adapt a line from a portable compressor. The source of the water supply is the GWR 45,000 gallon tank left after demolition of the yard to supply also the station. The water comes from the railway's own well and pumphouse by the 1 mile post. After the unexpected snowstorm of January 1982, the shed was thoroughly overhauled and made weathertight. Now repairs and overhauls that would have been thought quite impossible a few years ago are carried out inside the shed.

Regular staffing arrangements consist of a water chargehand traction fitter, a traction fitter and an assistant who is particularly responsible for preparation and firing up. Carriages and wagons are attended to by a C & W chargehand technician and a C & W technician. All have standard gauge responsibilities and duties as required. When major overhauls are in hand, additional craftsmen are drafted in from Machynlleth, Crewe and Tyseley. The whole operations are under the supervision of the traction engineer, Birmingham, the area maintenance engineer and the area maintenance supervisor at Shrewsbury.

The Back Road of the shed is used partly as a running line through to the sidings and partly for storage of carriages when no more through movements are expected. For several years when carriages were being sent to Shrewsbury and Chester for major overhauls, there was an ash ramp end-on to a spur from the standard gauge. The two siding rails were unbolted and slewed across to unite with the foot of the ramp. From the top of the ramp a bridging of old point-rod channel carried the coach onto a bogie flat, along which point-rodding was laid as a track. If there was no winch handy, the coaches were shoved up the ramp on the run by seven or more men. The spirit of ingenuity has not left the Rheidol yet and after the standard gauge spur was disconnected carriages were got away by mobile crane working between Platforms 3 and 4.

Movement control is effected very simply from a ground frame made of four LNW pattern levers, standing opposite the short neck which acts as a headshunt to the engine shed sidings. Lever No. 1 in the frame works the Down Home signal, Lever No. 2 works both ends of the crossover from the engine shed to the running line, lever No. 3 works the points for the two platform lines, and No. 4 operates the facing-point locks on points 2 and 3. The Down Home signal can only be lowered when the shed crossover points are set for the running line and headshunt, both being connected to No. 2 lever. Lever No. 3 works the points at the entrance to the loop and can only be locked by FPL 4 for down trains to go into the left-hand side of the loop so that down trains usually follow the old rule of entering a loop via the road on the left. The loco crossover points are worked by single ground levers whch hold the blades in place with powerful springs, so that when set for crossover, the loco drives through without the crew having to stop and change points. These and the various levers around shed and sidings are a museum in their own right. They were mainly made by Henry Williams Ltd of Darlington and there is one early J. Wynn-Williams and an Anderston bob-weight lever.

If the train is not wanted again either that day or next morning, the carriages are propelled through the shed, via the back road, and into the sidings. When only one train is running, it leaves and returns on the platform 5 side and only the locomotive returns to shed by running round as described. The

The modern mobile Presco, in the wrong place at 8½ miles, after having been blown away downhill, in 1983. It and the sign belong at Rheidol Falls.

signalman is domiciled in the former Inspector's office on Platform 3, which contains the main line token instrument and is where the Rheidol staff and tickets are kept when not in use. Train departures are usually supervised by a member of the station staff who gives the driver the 'Right away' by whistle.

Other LMR Modifications

Changes are to be seen along the valley as well. At Rhiwarthen there is now a modern blue BR style of hut and there is another at Nantyronen. Two Prescos were placed at Rheidol Falls and Rhiwfron and, being light and handy, they tend to get about a bit in wintertime. When, in 1983, the new nameboards were sent up, the instruction was given for Rheidol Falls 'Look for the Presco'. As it happened it was down at $8\frac{1}{2}$ miles on an exposed little bluff. And so the line got two Rheidol Falls halts, for the old board was still up in the right place. When the mistake was discovered, the gang was asked to take it down so they stashed it away in the Presco. Two nights later a heavy storm whipped the lot away 70 ft down the hillside.

There have been three generations of nameboards commemorating the sites of closed halts and of stations. The first set, with large white letters on lake backgrounds, were erected in June 1957. A smaller set, with black lettering on white, were put up in or soon after 1963. A more imposing set was put up in 1983 with raised white lettering on black grounds. Unfortunately the heights given were inaccurate and gave rise to facetious comments about undetected earthquakes. Also they give the name of the line incorrectly in Welsh as Rheilffordd Cwmrheidol. Cwmrheidol is only the steep-sided upper part of the valley and the correct name in good old-fashioned Welsh, according to Mr. Rees, was Rheilffordd Dyffryn Rheidol, with Ysgafn after Rheilffordd to include the world Light – Rheilffordd Ysgafn Dyffryn Rheidol.

Most of the V of R wooden gradient posts have rotted away and have not been replaced. Two survived above and below

Contradictions – in fact neither is correct. 1984.

Devil's Bridge, London Midland Region style, 1983.

The latest addition, the Tea Bar. Revision of the general layout to include better parking facilities and a picnic area are in hand. 1986.

Sleeper train leaving Aberystwyth in October 1984.

Ballast train on Gwaith-coch, February 1984.

P.W. train No. 7 'coming home' in 1984.

Top left: A new way of loading an old wagon, Devil's Bridge, 1984. Top right: The Permaquip Personnel Carrier No. DX68804 at Aberystwyth in 1986. Above left: Box and timber truck ADM 34111 loaded with pre-chaired sleepers. Note that the truck on the left has the original ⌒ end stanchion while that on the right has the replacement using two lengths of straight angle iron. The new signal gantry framing is deeper than the original. 1985. Above right: Old sleepers being offloaded by Richard Holland in 1983.

Nantyronen as permanent way depot, water point and reporting centre, looking towards Devil's Bridge in 1983.

No. 8 on the SLOA Pullman Special on 16th October 1982. The headboard is missing because BR boards don't fit GWR lamp brackets.

The upper flood plain towards Capel Bangor. Being the first train of the year, the main part of the flock of sheep has taken fright and is scampering away, leaving the one inquisitive ewe eying the camera with her lamb protectively screened behind her. 28th March 1983.

Aberffrwd into the 1960s and there was one misplacement at the $2\frac{1}{2}$ milepost at the foot of the 1 in 132, stating 1 in 264.

The ultimate statements in logical application of rulebooks have been provided by the Central Electricity Generating Board. Wherever power lines cross railway lines there must be a warning notice. One directs the ringing of a telephone number in Bristol if it is desired to proceed with the jib of a crane extended to a height exceeding 39 feet.

Not all the lifted sleepers from the 1920s have gone for firewood. At Ynyslas, OS Map Reference 607943, there is a walkway through the sand dunes of old Rheidol sleepers.

Running the Line

The weather can have a considerable effect on both engine handling and on driving conditions; nothing can be worse than a damp day, a film of rust on the rails and the sand clogged in the pipes. Such conditions faced Gwilym Davies and Bill Eden with a six coach VORRSA Special on 4th December 1982.

A notice has to be placed by regulation but this one aspires to the height of improbability, above 6½ miles, 1983.

Carrying nearly all adults and most of those beefy men, the train was much heavier than the average holiday train would have been and there was not a single vacant seat. Two months had passed since the last train of the season and the rails were for all practical intents and purposes coated with a light lubricant. *Owain Glyndwr* slipped and spun and slipped and spun; being keen to give their passengers what they had come for, the two men persevered. They managed to get up to Devil's Bridge in the record time for a continuous run of only a minute under the two hours. It says much for the adequacy of the water supply in the tanks, for *Owain* was in full steam for more than double the reckoned time for the final four miles.

Today (1986) there are around a dozen men passed for steam and two or three guards passed as knowing the ways of the narrow gauge, and Rheidol men can be seen on DMUs at Pwllheli, Shrewsbury, Crewe and Stafford.

Now that the engines are oil-fired there is a fitters' assistant with the special duty of lighting up and getting all ready for when the crew books on. The shed staff attend to topping up the lubricators etc, and the driver looks all round as before. Firing up still commences at 05.30 and the first thing is to switch on the compressor-blower. The oil is lit and the flow and air flow have to be finely adjusted and left to begin the warming-up process while other matters are attended to. As soon as there is sufficient pressure to enable the engine to be walked about, it is disconnected from the life-support machine without risk of premature demise. The fuel tanks can be topped up from one of two long hoses while firing is in progress, but the engine may have to be moved to reach the inside water valve. The outside water crane is used when refilling after a trip.

Emerging from the cutting across the floor of the quarry on 2nd May 1983.

The 'Night Rheidol' on the Gwaith-coch, 5th May 1986.

The Passenger Services

The new management really did try to improve matters, starting in 1964 with Easter trains, and a car sticker in white on blue for employees and devotees. The look of the timetables was on the upgrade as well, particularly that for 1968 which was in full colour. Actually there were two which could be misleading to historians. The leaflet advertised the Easter and full season and the larger hang-up version came out six weeks later without the Easter service. During the whole of this period Llanbadarn appeared as the only intermediate booked stop, but tickets were available for all the closed halts and the 1970 leaflet mentioned them.

1970 saw the start of the Letter Service and, even more beneficial, the formation of the Vale of Rheidol Railway Supporters' Association, VORRSA for short, which would in future assist in publicity matters, organise many special events, and do many other things for the good of the line as operated by British Rail. Llanbadarn was dropped from leaflets as a booked stop. The first attempt was made to attract incoming visitors from 'over the border' by erecting a large and prominent signboard by the main road just before the Bow Street turn-off, but the Ministry of Transport ordered its removal. Subsequent attempts were destroyed by local agency because the whole thing was not duplicated in Welsh. The evening train, run during the main part of the season and now known as the 'Night Rheidol', ran first in 1973. Also passengers holding a return ticket who had missed the last down train were permitted to return without additional payment on the 17.35 Crosville bus, a facility which lasted for only a few years. 1975 proved to be the record year with 179,200 passenger journeys. 1976 was less productive because during the drought many morning trains were not run. Since then there has been a most regrettable fall in the number of passengers carried because there is less money about, and the railwaymen's strike in 1982 caused a sharp dip for that year. Looking at the services at present (1986) the pattern developed by London Midland Region appears all set to continue, with better quality leaflets, the longer season opening at Easter, with a lighter service up to the main holiday period, and again during September and well into October.

There was one unhappy note struck in 1986. Just as the Tourism Department of Ceredigion District Council have produced a most excellent set of walking routes on cards devised by Doctor Denis Bates, BR have stopped issuing the lower-priced tickets to and from all the halts, a matter which can be put right in the future.

Special Events and Occasions

This period includes many popular success stories. Harry Rees had to make the arrangements for a very large Rover camp at Devil's Bridge. This involved some heavy trains going up with

Arrival at Devil's Bridge with the 'Night Rheidol' on 14th September 1986.

Aberystwyth to Devil's Bridge by Vale of Rheidol railway

Some of the finest scenery in Wales including the Rheidol Falls and Devil's Punchbowl

DAY FARES FROM ABERYSTWYTH

	Adult	Child
By morning or evening services	55p	30p
By afternoon service in April, May, June, September and October	65p	30p
By afternoon service July and August	70p	30p

Fares include souvenir ticket

the only steam on **British Rail**

ONE OF THE GREAT LITTLE TRAINS OF WALES

SPRING AND EASTER (SATS & SUNS 7, 8, 14, 15 APRIL WEEKDAYS AND SUNDAYS 20 APRIL TO 20 MAY)

Aberystwyth	dep	13 30A	14 15	Devil's Bridge dep 15 45A 16 30
Devil's Bridge	arr	14 30A	15 15	Aberystwyth arr 16 40A 17 25

A — 21 to 25 April only

EARLY SUMMER (MONS TO SATS 21 MAY TO 30 JUNE)

Aberystwyth	dep	10 00	13 30B	14 15
Devil's Bridge	arr	11 00	14 30B	15 15
Devil's Bridge	dep	11 45	15 45B	16 30
Aberystwyth	arr	12 40	16 40B	17 25

B — 25 May to 1 June only

SUMMER (MONS TO SATS 2 JULY TO 8 SEPTEMBER)

Aberystwyth	dep	10 00	10 40E	13 30E	14 15	17 30C
Devil's Bridge	arr	11 00	11 40E	14 30E	15 15	18 30C
Devil's Bridge	dep	11 45	12 25E	15 45E	16 30	19 30C
Aberystwyth	arr	12 40	13 20E	16 40E	17 25	20 25C

E — Sats excepted   C — Mons, Tues, Weds, Thurs only 23 July to 30 August

AUTUMN (MONS TO SATS 10 SEPTEMBER TO 6 OCTOBER)

Aberystwyth	dep 10 00	14 15	Devil's Bridge dep 11 45 16 30
Devil's Bridge	arr 11 00	15 15	Aberystwyth arr 12 40 17 25

SUNDAYS (27 MAY TO 7 OCTOBER)

Aberystwyth	dep	10 15D	13 00F	14 15
Devil's Bridge	arr	11 15D	14 00F	15 15
Devil's Bridge	dep	12 00D	15 25F	16 30
Aberystwyth	arr	12 55D	16 20F	17 25

D — 29 July to 2 September   F — 27 May and 17 June to 2 September

---

Trains start from the British Rail station at Aberystwyth and call as required at Llanbadarn, Glanrafon, Capel Bangor, Nantyronen, Aberffrwd, Rheidol Falls and Rhiwfron.

Note: Bookings commence at Aberystwyth 30 minutes before departure times (No advance booking except for parties).

Inter-availability: Train/Bus — Passengers holding British Rail return tickets from Devil's Bridge to Aberystwyth may return by the 17 35 Crosville Motor Services bus from Aberystwyth to Devil's Bridge without extra charge.

For fares from Devil's Bridge and intermediate stations — enquire at Aberystwyth or Devil's Bridge stations or on the trains. Reductions for parties by prior arrangement.

All fares and facilities shown are subject to alteration or cancellation.

TRAIN TIMES 1973

Vale of Rheidol railway letter stamps and covers on sale at Aberystwyth and Devil's Bridge stations

Presents and souvenirs are available at Devil's Bridge station shop

Published by British Rail (LM) & printed by James Cond, Birmingham.

A specimen of the more modern London Midland Region series of attractive hand-out timetables.

Unusual working. The SLOA special needed six coaches above normal working so the 16.35 down is a very short train. 16th October 1982.

two locomotives, and by working up empties the day before, a down train of ten coaches and a van were run. The precise dates have not been found but 'The Friendly Midland Red' ran some coach tours to Devil's Bridge for a rail trip down to Aberystwyth for lunch and the day ended with a high tea at the Hafod Hotel before returning to Birmingham and intermediate pickup points *en route*.

A delightful evening was spent in the autumn of 1968 in connection with the investiture of the Prince of Wales, with a viewing of the floodlighting of the reservoir and falls at Aberffrwd. The train halted at Aberffrwd for the unloading of supper which went to the venue by road, and the halt for the passengers was at the same spot where the drivers used to stop unofficially for the small pupils at Miss Trotter's School, Meithrinfa Halt. The way down through the woods was lit by a string of electric lamps powered by a portable generator erected by the P.W. Department. Hugh King recalls the last nostalgic moment when, as the party wended their way back to the train, the Aberystwyth Silver Band played them away with 'Good Night Ladies'. Alas, the magistrates have refused the licence required for another similar occasion.

Two more highly noteworthy events followed in 1969. In the middle of March, in celebration of National Libraries Week, the Cardiganshire Librarian Mr. Alun Edwards arranged a Trên O Gân – A Train of Song. The train was greeted at halts by school choirs and there was a massed concert at Devil's Bridge. All was recorded by Harlech Television who paid for the train and screened a very attractive programme on 24th March. Scarcely a week later the Aberystwyth Chamber of Trade organised a well-attended and extremely well-dressed Costume Train. Over 350 people travelled and more than 100 of them were wearing clothes worn by their grandparents, one lady turning up in a dress which had been worn by her great-grandmother. Besides the traditional Welsh garb there was a charming outfit from Bulgaria.

Then there were the Father Christmas Specials such as that run for the Wirral Railway Circle on 3rd December 1977, with Ossie Davies from Cemmes Road in the lead part, and there were the Cowboy Specials. These, mainly for children (they said), have been the best of all and have been arranged by VORRSA and latterly by the Aberystwyth Round Table. On the way up the trains get attacked by Indians, recruited as often as not by the Young Farmers' Association, but anyone can join in the fun. The Territorial Army Volunteer Reserve have

Indian attack being repelled with water pistols, a scene on one of the ever-popular Cowboy Specials. *Courtesy Norman Greenwood*

provided both Indians and the equivalent of the U.S. Cavalry. Attacks are repelled by water pistols, squeezy bottles and garden sprayers, and even larger water containers. One mother brought a 5 gallon drum of water to keep her sons from running out of ammunition.

British Rail have put on many specials in connection with the history of the line and its locomotives, starting with a 70th Anniversary in 1972, a 75th in 1977, and there were several great occasions in 1982 celebrating the 80th Anniversary. The first of these on 24th April commemorated the birthday of the original engine *Prince of Wales*; Mr. Richard Metcalfe unveiled a plaque affixed to No. 9 *Prince of Wales* and he and a party of his associates journeyed up the line afterwards. On the 3rd of May, which was a bank holiday, six trains were worked up and back, and these included a works outing from Davies & Metcalfe, which returned with one of the others as yet another of those fascinating ten-coach-plus-van trains. No. 9 *Prince of Wales*, which had taken the Davies & Metcalfe Special up, returned light engine at dusk when the brilliance of the new livery was attractively lit by a saffron-coloured afterglow. Unfortunately VORRSA's projected Pullman Scenic Land Cruise was lost through the strike by the railwaymen but they managed a Father Christmas Special on 4th December instead. SLOA Marketing ran the Pullman train as 'The Cambrian Limited' on 16th October. 1982 closed with an immaculate *Prince of Wales* on display at the National Railway Museum at York, so it was quite a vintage year.

In 1983 there was another of the ever-popular Gala Days when all three engines were to be seen together at Devil's Bridge and, being 3rd May, it coincided with the Gwyl Festival down in Aberystwyth. To suit this occasion VORRSA arranged 'The Rheidol Express from Manchester which one of the newspapers managed to report as a through train to Devil's Bridge. Another well-arranged event was the Mid Wales Festival of Transport over 18th and 19th of June with vintage buses as well. Nos 7 & 8 carried headboards commemorating their Diamond Jubilees. Three celebrations connected with rolling stock were the VIP train on 2nd April for the revival of chocolate and cream livery, on 18th June the first run of the Vista Coach, and on the 19th the restoration of First Class was commemorated.

Then things went a bit quieter and BR did score an 'own goal' with a publicity map of rail travel facilities for pensioners including attractions like the steam centres. The Rheidol line was shown as if it was standard gauge and had no steam centre.

However matters looked up again on 13th and 14th of September 1986 with the visit of the Festiniog Railway's Alco 2–6–2T *Mountaineer*. She ran very well and was much photographed, and it is hoped that more such events will be arranged in the future.

Considerations for the Future

The old besetting problems of cost and of robbing the main line of gang time to do the necessary on the Rheidol, have not yet been resolved. On 26th May 1986, a down train burst the curve at $6\frac{1}{4}$ miles, fortunately with comparatively little harm to the passengers. While the immediate cause was the poor condition of the sleepers and fastenings, the underlying cause was probably the accumulation of pressure caused by the downhill creep of the upslope rails, as was made more clear in the chapter on permanent way.

This incident prompted Dr. John Marek, the Honourable Member for Wrexham, to ask a question in Parliament about British Rail's management of the line. This raised a storm from the Tory benches where the contention was that British Rail should be running key transport railways and not minor tourist lines. So privatisation is being mentioned once more and two bodies are rumoured to be taking interest.

Meanwhile Mr. David McIntosh, the new Provincial Manager (who arranged for the visit of *Mountaineer*), is advocating

The Festiniog Railway's American Alco 2–6–2T *Mountaineer* with her British Vale of Rheidol cousin, GWR 2–6–2T No. 9 *Prince of Wales*. Provincial Manager Mr. David McIntosh, who spent the weekend at Aberystwyth to make sure that all went well, is seen dusting off *Mountaineer's* polished nameplate. *Mountaineer's* train crew are driver Evan Davies, the Locomotive Foreman of the Festiniog Railway talking to Vale of Rheidol fireman Murray Dodds (in cab).

Passing one of the cut-away ribs of track below Rheidol Falls is the 10.30 a.m. ex Aberystwyth on 14th September 1986. Driver Mike Thomas of the Rheidol line is acting as Vale of Rheidol pilotman.

fresh measures to improve operation and viability and discussions at both administrative and staffing levels have produced the following ideas.

1. Assembly of a full-time permanent specialist Rheidol staff who would operate the trains during the season and overhaul stock and permanent way for the remainder of the year. This would restore the old expertise in mountain railway track lost when the old Rheidol gangs were merged with the main line rotas. The Festiniog Railway could be called on to act in a consulting capacity.
2. Provision of a 7-car loop at Nantyronen worked by hydro-pneumatic (gasbag) points. This site is favoured by the staff in preference to Aberffrwd. Thus more trains could be run which would balance out the effect of the next item.
3. Fitting of all stock with sound seats removed from condemned DMUs, and the reduction in total seating could be offset by running more trains.
4. Enclosure of all the Summer Cars, but with adequate drop-windows.
5. Replacement by conventional transverse seating of the unpopular longitudinal seating from the Vista Car.
6. Provision of an additional diesel-powered locomotive to eliminate the 05.30 start for lighting up in time to get steam up to take out the 10.30. The Ravenglass & Eskdale Railway have done this successfully for several years and their first down train brings people from Eskdale to Ravenglass in good time for the start of the working day.

There is further good news of proposals for the allocation of larger sums of money for track renovation.

The journey which all should make.

Taith a ddylai pawb ei gwneud.

POSTSCRIPT

The future of this, the finest of all the little lines, is still uncertain, lying as it does, in the hands of politicians. As a National Asset of Wales it deserves a preservation order in its own right, yet lacks any form of protective covenant.

All we can do to help is to provide funds by buying tickets for that wonderful journey which all should make.

OL-NODYN

Ansicr, o hyd, yw dyfodol hon, un o leiniau gorau y trenau bach, gan mai yn nwylo gwleidyddion y gorwedd yr awenau. Nid oes unrhyw warchodaeth gyfreithiol iddi ar hyn o bryd a gellid dadlau y dylid bod, o ystyried ei phwysigrwydd atyniadol i Gymru.

Y ffordd orau i gyfrannu at sicrhau ei dyfodol yw trwy brynu tocyn ar gyfer y siwrne fendigedig i fyny Cwm Rheidol.

Yet another way of helping would be to join VORRSA. Send your name and address to: Ceredigion District Council, Aberystwyth, Dyfed, SY23 2EB, who will kindly forward your enquiry.

Ffordd arall i helpu fyddai i chi ymuno â VORRSA. Gallwch gysylltu â'r gymdeithas gan anfon eich ymholiad, gyda'ch enw a chyfeiriad, i Gyngor Dosbarth Ceredigion, Aberystwyth, Dyfed, SY23 2EB.

APPENDIX
A SAMPLING OF TICKETS

Tickets are nostalgic reminders of journeys. Who made them? Why are some tickets clean and undamaged? Who sat in the train fumbling with the Cambrian 'Parliamentary' Third? What kind of dog was taken to Devil's Bridge for 6d? Obviously it was not given the ticket to carry. That threepenny bicycle ticket — was it just for a bicycle or was the passenger wealthy enough to be towing an infant around in a Child's Mail Cart? Note the expression 'Forward' used by the independent company for the outward journey. Which 'Certain Trains' could have been used for that combined Borth to Devil's Bridge return? And the Great Western Railway Rail Motor Car ticket makes strange reading for no such vehicle has yet been seen on the Rheidol line.

In general the British Rail ordinary tickets are much less colourful though the Bell Punch trio are interesting variations. That halved Aberffrwd ticket was the passport for two small sisters. The rarer halt·tickets were saved by a gentleman most fond of walking in the valley. The vivid orange Dinner ticket was given to Mr. and Mrs. J. E. Davies; at that time 'Jack Bach' was the oldest living Rheidol driver. That unusual First Class ticket was issued to the author when fixing up the first photographic publicity display at the suggestion of Harry Rees. The joke was played out to the end with the loan of a cushion from the Inspector's office.

Assembled from the collections of Wingate Bett, C. C. Green, W. E. Hayward, Selwyn Higgins and Richard Mester.

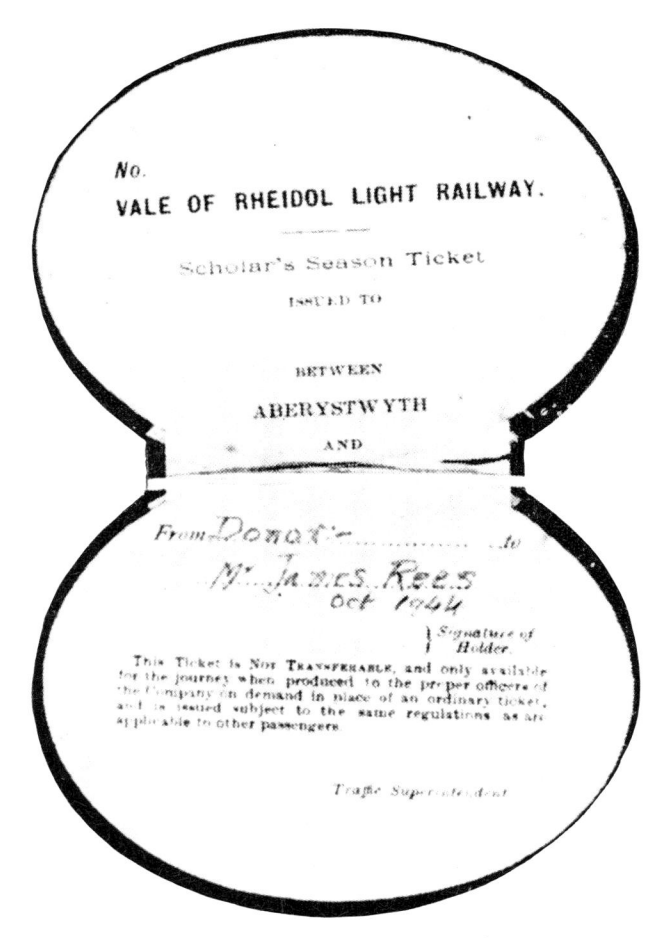

A Scholar's Season Ticket, roughly 3 1/8 x 2 7/16 inches when closed.
Courtesy W. E. Hayward

THE INDEPENDENT BOARDS

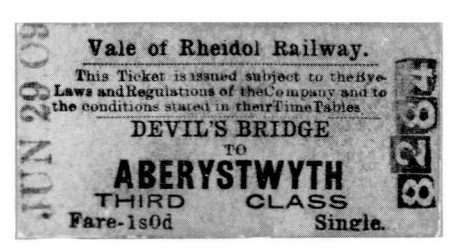

Deep orange-red    *White   Brown-red* 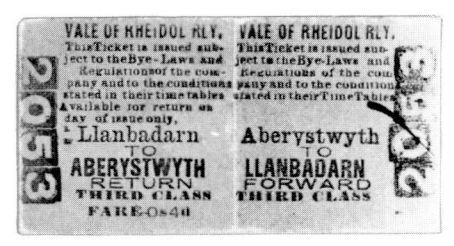   *Orange-red   Mid-blue*

Pale green    *Green — faded*

THE CAMBRIAN BOARD

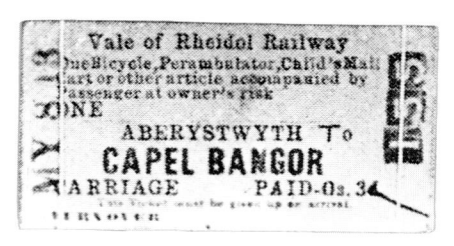

Fawn 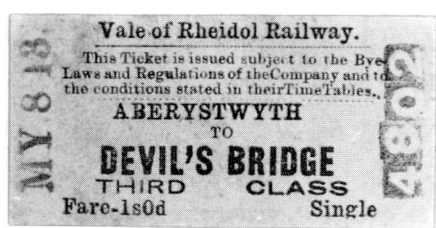 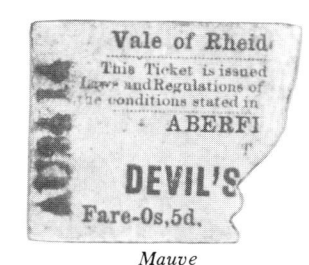   *Mauve*

THE CAMBRIAN RAILWAYS

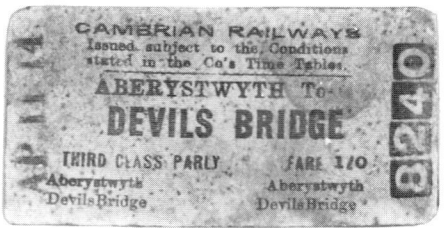

Bright green 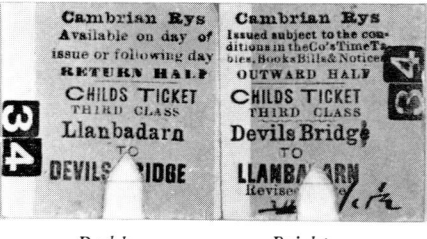   *Red-brown   Bright green* 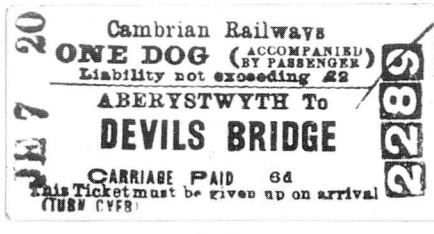   *Buff*

THE GREAT WESTERN RAILWAY

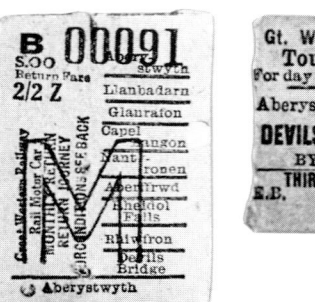

Pale green    *Green*   *Cream-yellow*    *Deep plum*

WESTERN & LONDON MIDLAND REGIONS

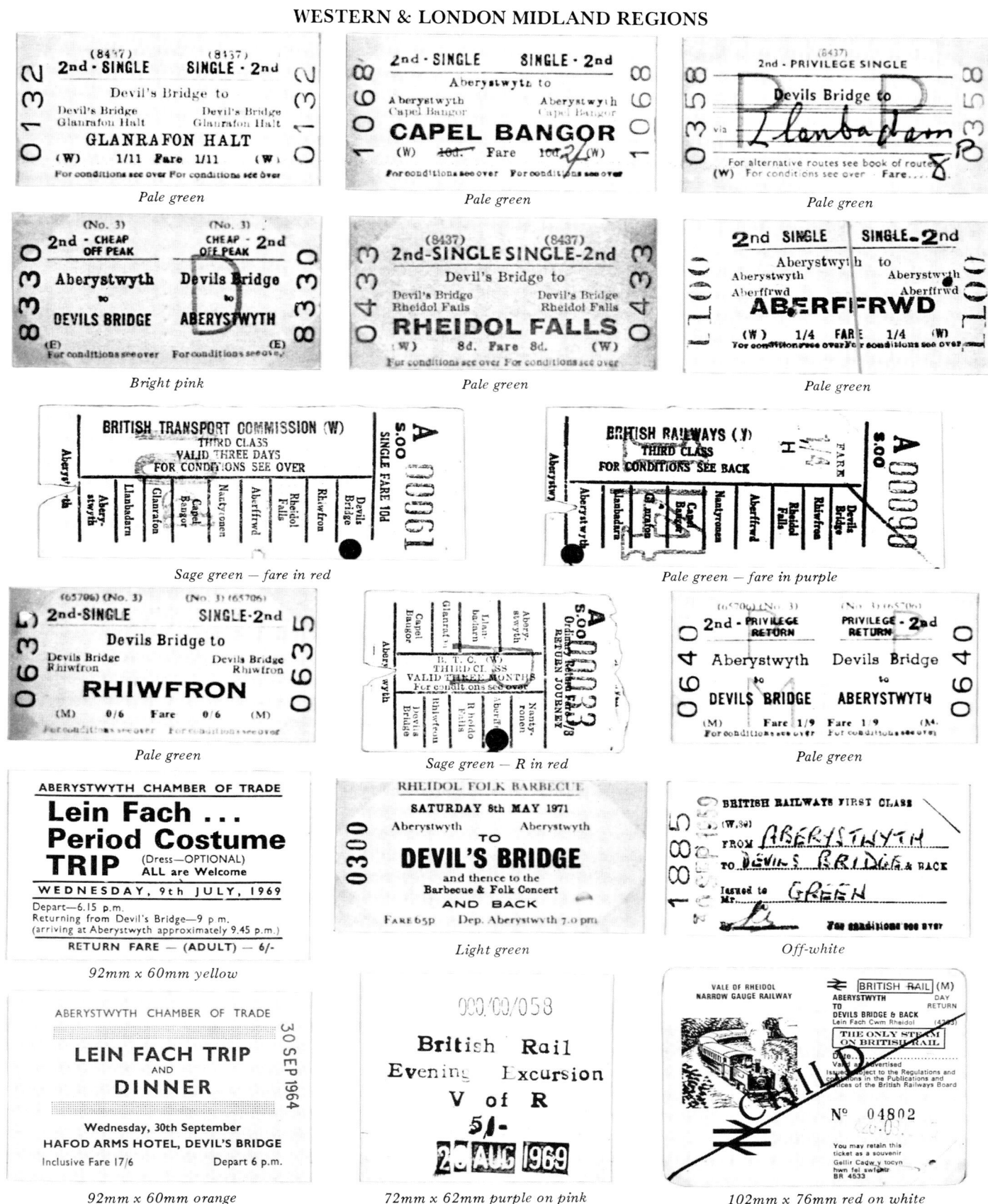

Pale green — Devil's Bridge to GLANRAFON HALT (2nd Single, 1/11)

Pale green — Aberystwyth to CAPEL BANGOR (2nd Single)

Pale green — Devils Bridge to Llanbadarn (2nd Privilege Single)

Bright pink — Aberystwyth to DEVILS BRIDGE (2nd Cheap Off Peak)

Pale green — Devil's Bridge to RHEIDOL FALLS (2nd Single, 8d)

Pale green — Aberystwyth to ABERFFRWD (2nd Single, 1/4)

Sage green — fare in red — British Transport Commission (W), Third Class, Valid Three Days, Single Fare 10d

Pale green — fare in purple — British Railways (W), Third Class

Pale green — Devils Bridge to RHIWFRON (2nd Single, 0/6)

Sage green — R in red — B.T.C. (W) Third Class, Valid Three Months, Return Journey

Pale green — Aberystwyth / Devils Bridge PRIVILEGE RETURN (Fare 1/9)

92mm x 60mm yellow — ABERYSTWYTH CHAMBER OF TRADE, Lein Fach... Period Costume TRIP (Dress—OPTIONAL) ALL are Welcome, WEDNESDAY, 9th JULY, 1969. Depart—6.15 p.m. Returning from Devil's Bridge—9 p.m. (arriving at Aberystwyth approximately 9.45 p.m.) RETURN FARE — (ADULT) — 6/-

Light green — RHEIDOL FOLK BARBECUE, SATURDAY 8th MAY 1971, Aberystwyth to DEVIL'S BRIDGE and thence to the Barbecue & Folk Concert AND BACK. FARE 65p. Dep. Aberystwyth 7.0 pm

Off-white — BRITISH RAILWAYS FIRST CLASS, FROM ABERYSTWYTH TO DEVILS BRIDGE & BACK, Issued to Mr GREEN

92mm x 60mm orange — ABERYSTWYTH CHAMBER OF TRADE, LEIN FACH TRIP AND DINNER, Wednesday, 30th September, HAFOD ARMS HOTEL, DEVIL'S BRIDGE. Inclusive Fare 17/6. Depart 6 p.m. 30 SEP 1964

72mm x 62mm purple on pink — 000/00/058, British Rail Evening Excursion V of R, 5/-, 28 AUG 1969

102mm x 76mm red on white — VALE OF RHEIDOL NARROW GAUGE RAILWAY, BRITISH RAIL (M), ABERYSTWYTH TO DEVILS BRIDGE & BACK, Lein Fach Cwm Rheidol, THE ONLY STEAM ON BRITISH RAIL, CHILD, N° 04802, BR 4533

15th January 1982 when winter showed its hand inside the shed. *Stephen Clements*

ACKNOWLEDGEMENTS

A story from the past, the sight of old papers, permission to cross land, hospitality by a fireside, the writing of letters in reply — help towards the writing of a book comes in so very many ways, and the author is deeply grateful to: A. S. Askam; Allan Baker; Adrian Banfield; Cliff Barratt; The British Ornithologists' Union; Denis Bates; Mr. & Mrs. Dennis Benjamin; J. S. Berry; David Bick; J. I. C. Boyd; V. J. Bradley; W. A. Camwell; R. S. Carpenter; M. Christensen; G. H. W. Clifford; C. M. Colclough; A. W. Croughton; Pat Dalton; Mervyn Dandrick; Frank Daniel; Mr. & Mrs. Emrys Davies; Edwin Davies; Evan Davies; Jack Davies; Mr. & Mrs. J. E. Davies; J. H. Denton; George Dow; Dyfed County Council; John Edgington; A. E. S. Fluck; Forestry Commission, North Wales Conservancy; Norman Greenwood; Glyn Griffiths; Lewis Hamer; Eric Hannan; W. E. Hayward; Frank Hemming; Selwyn Higgins; Ifor Higgon; Phillip Hindley; Brian Hollingsworth; John Hughes; Mr. & Mrs. Arthur Jenkins; Mr. & Mrs. Isaac Jenkins; Mr. & Mrs. Owen Jenkins; Jack Jones; The Brothers Jones, Troed-rhiw-sebon; Miss Margaret Kay; Stan Kidsley; Dewi Lewis; Idwal Lewis; Mr. & Mrs. John Lewis; Mr. Lewis, Tyllwyd; Phil Lewis; Peter Lord; Lord Richard Marsh; J. M. Maskylene; David Mason; Mr. & Mrs. John Mason; Mr. & Mrs. Richard Mester; Richard Metcalfe; Mid Wales Development; R. W. Miller; Haulfryn Morgan; Les Morgan; Nature Conservancy Council, Dyfed Powys Region; G. H. Platt; Monsieur Jacques Pradayrol; Don Rees; Harry Rees; John Rees; Regional Met. Officer for Wales; J. P. Richards; Joseph Rowe; Herr Walter Seidensticker; Richard Shaw; John Snell; John Stratton; Tourism & Amenities Dept., Ceredigion Council; Mr. & Mrs. B. Vaughan; Oliver Veltom; Mr. & Mrs. S. Walker; Simon Watts; Patrick Whitehouse; Phillip Wragg.

Also much courteous help was obtained from Archivists, Curators and Librarians and their staffs, and notably at the City of Birmingham Library, Dyfed County Library, The House of Lords Record Office, The National Library of Wales, The National Railway Museum at York, The Public Record Office at Kew.

A great deal of help, too, came from the staff of British Rail at all levels, but only those no longer serving have been named.

Thanks are also due to the Lewis family for permission to use the photographs taken by Mr. A. J. Lewis — Lewis the Mart.

Many items came from old and valued friends and acquaintances who are no longer with us. Their collections, or parts thereof, have since become generally accessible as follows: Wingate Bett (Birmingham Central Library); W. E. Hayward (The Public Record Office, Kew); Selwyn Higgins (The National Railway Museum, York); H. L. Hopwood (The Locomotive Club of Great Britain); K. A. C. R. Nunn (The Locomotive Club of Great Britain); and Roger Wilson (Birmingham Central Library).

c016.95.